Sunset

THE COMPLETE
Wok
COOK BOOK

By the Editors of

Sunset Books

and Sunset Magazine

Sunset Publishing Corporation ■ *Menlo Park, California*

Steamed in your wok just until tender-crisp, bright green broccoli joins other vegetables in fresh-tasting Marinated Broccoli & Mushrooms. The recipe is on page 150.

Coordinating Editor
Linda J. Selden

Contributing Editors
Ginger Smith Bate
Sue Brownlee
Rebecca LaBrum
Susan Warton

Design
Joe di Chiarro
Cynthia Hanson

Illustrations
Susan Jaekel

Photo Stylist
JoAnn Masaoka Van Atta

Food Stylist
Judith A. Gaulke

The Versatile Wok

Little changed over centuries of use, the Chinese wok has won the respect of chefs everywhere. And its versatility is as impressive today as throughout its long history.

One wok does the work of at least three ordinary pans. The wok stir-fries, deep-fries, and steams with mouth-watering effect. If made of stainless steel or with a nonstick finish, it can also braise and stew.

Beyond the Oriental stir-fry that made it famous, the wok also adapts deliciously to Mexican, Italian, and other cuisines. Today's wok turns out such surprises as a wilted greens salad, Southwestern fajitas, and even a steamed carrot pudding. You'll discover these and many other examples of your wok's versatility throughout this book.

For our recipes, we provide a nutritional analysis prepared by Hill Nutrition Associates, Inc., of New York, stating calorie count; grams of protein, carbohydrates, and total fat; and milligrams of cholesterol and sodium. Generally, the nutritional information applies to a single serving, based on the largest number of servings given for each recipe.

The nutritional analysis does not include optional ingredients or those for which no specific amount is stated. If an ingredient is listed with an option, the information was calculated using the first choice. Likewise, if a range is given for the amount of an ingredient, values were figured based on the first, lower amount.

For their valuable editorial assistance, we extend special thanks to Tori Bunting and Mary Jane Swanson. We also thank The Abacus and Crate & Barrel for their generosity in sharing props for use in our photographs.

About the Recipes

All of the recipes in this book were tested and developed in the *Sunset* test kitchens.

Home Economics Editor, Sunset Magazine
Jerry Anne Di Vecchio

Photographers: Victor Budnik, 50, 82; Norman A. Plate, 151; Darrow M. Watt, 7, 10, 66, 106, 119, 146; Tom Wyatt, 42, 47, 58, 63, 114; Nikolay Zurek, 2, 15, 18, 23, 26, 31, 34, 39, 55, 71, 74, 79, 87, 90, 95, 98, 103, 111, 122, 127, 130, 135, 138, 143, 154, 159.

Cover: The wok translates Italian cuisine into exuberant Shrimp Pesto Stir-fry (recipe on page 67). Design by Williams & Ziller. Photography by Nikolay Zurek. Photo styling by JoAnn Masaoka Van Atta. Food styling by Judith A. Gaulke.

Editor, Sunset Books: Elizabeth L. Hogan

Fourth printing June 1991

Contents

Special Features

Wok Cooking

When you think of wok cooking, you probably think first of stir-frying—of quickly tossing and stirring bite-size pieces of meat and vegetables in a little hot oil, letting them barely touch the sides of the steel bowl. You think of Asian dishes, of foods with crisp textures and fresh flavors.

But Oriental stir-fries are by no means the only recipes a wok can handle. Though it may not be the universal utensil with as many uses as a Swiss army knife, this simple pan is undeniably versatile. It doubles as a deep-fryer; it's a perfect steamer for seafood, dumplings, delicate pâtés, even puddings. And stainless steel woks and those with a nonstick finish are ideal for stewing and braising.

Thanks to its unique shape, the wok is also a model of efficiency: the sloping sides and rounded bottom heat up quickly and evenly, and provide the greatest possible surface for cooking. Whether you use an electric or a gas range, you'll find that wok cookery saves you time and energy.

Choosing & caring for your wok

Woks are available in two basic shapes and a variety of sizes. The traditional wok has a rounded bottom, reflecting its original use—it was designed to be suspended in a brazier over a hot fire. The curved shape is as efficient as ever today, but the brazier has been replaced by a perforated ring stand that holds the wok steady on the range top.

A fairly recent introduction is the flat-bottomed wok, intended to sit directly atop burner or element. You'll need to purchase this style if you can't get a round-bottomed wok close enough to the heat source (see "Using a wok on your range," facing page).

Woks typically have two handles, one on each side. Some models are equipped with wooden handle covers; if yours lacks this feature, you'll need to

protect your hands with potholders when you cook. Woks with a single long wooden handle are also available. They're easy to maneuver when you stir-fry—but when you want to lift a one-handled wok full of food or oil, be sure to lift it from *both* sides.

Woks range from 9 to 30 inches in diameter, but the 14-inch size is usually the best choice for home cooks: it's ample in capacity, yet simple to manage. Obviously, a wok of this size is also easier to store than a really big one would be—but all woks take up a fair amount of shelf space, and round-bottomed types tend to wobble instead of sitting flat. Many cooks find it more convenient to hang woks from pot hooks than to keep them in a cupboard.

In addition to selecting the wok shape and size, you'll need to choose the best material for your needs. Woks were originally made of cast iron, but today the most commonly used metal is heavy-gauge rolled *carbon steel*. Carbon steel woks conduct heat well, making them great for stir-frying, but they do require seasoning and proper care to keep the surface in good condition and prevent rusting.

Seasoning a carbon steel wok is a simple procedure. Before the first use, wash the wok with mild soapy water, then dry it directly over medium heat on your range until no moisture remains. Next, rub the inside with a paper towel dampened with about 2 teaspoons of salad oil; wipe off any excess oil with a clean paper towel. After each use, wash the wok with sudsy water, using a dishwashing or bamboo brush to scrub out any sticking food; then rinse well and dry again on the range. If not kept completely dry between uses, carbon steel woks will rust.

Aluminum and *stainless steel* woks—often with copper bottoms and sides to improve heat conduction—are also available. They need no seasoning; they won't rust, so you can simply clean them as you would any other aluminum or stainless pan. These woks are particularly good for steaming and stewing; they're fine for stir-frying, too, though they don't distribute heat as evenly as carbon steel woks do.

Top choice for tabletop cooking are *electric* woks. You'll find them especially suitable for poaching foods in hot broth, such as in Mizutaki (page 24). They also work well for steaming and deep-frying, but because they tend to recover heat rather slowly after food is added, they aren't always successful for stir-frying.

Clean and care for your electric wok according to the manufacturer's directions, always removing the heat element before washing. And if you've chosen a nonstick model, be sure not to use sharp utensils for stirring.

Wok accessories

Purchasing a wok doesn't mean re-outfitting your kitchen with dozens of new accessories. Though you can certainly buy specially designed wok tools if you wish, you'll be just as successful using basic utensils you already own.

The most useful wok accessory is a *long-handled spatula* with a wide, curved edge (a regular spatula will do). The handle is often tipped with wood to prevent it from getting too hot to touch during cooking.

A dome-shaped *wok lid* is helpful in stir-frying and braising, and necessary for steaming unless you use lidded *stacking bamboo* baskets. Also required for steaming is a metal or bamboo *rack* to hold food above boiling water (use a round cake rack, if you like).

When steaming or deep-frying, you'll find a *ring stand* with slanting sides helpful for balancing the wok over the range burner or element. Other accessories for deep-frying include a *wire skimmer* or slotted spoon for removing bits of food from the oil, a semicircular wire *draining rack* that attaches to the top of the wok, and a *deep-frying thermometer*.

Using a wok on your range

Woks can be used on either gas or electric ranges. Flat-bottomed woks are designed to rest directly on the cooking element of either kind of range, but round-bottomed types may need to be set in a ring stand. Before you start to cook in a round-bottomed wok, experiment with an empty wok to find the arrangement that works best for the sort of cooking you want to do.

To cook on a gas range. If you're planning to stir-fry, you can simply place the wok directly on the metal burner support above the flame; it should rest fairly steadily. For deep-frying or steaming, you'll probably need to stabilize the wok on a ring stand (see photograph on page 7): place the ring stand on the range, then set the wok on top. The bottom of the wok should be within 1 inch of the flame. If it's too far away, turn the ring stand over to bring the wok

closer to the burner; or remove the burner support and place the ring stand directly on the range top.

To cook on an electric range. For stir-frying, set the wok directly on the element. A more stable arrangement is necessary when deep-frying or steaming; though: invert the ring stand over the electric element, then suspend the wok in the stand so that it rests directly on the element or no more than 1 inch above it.

Cooking in a wok

Once you have the wok set up on your range, you're ready to cook. Stir-frying, deep-frying, and steaming are the three techniques for which the wok is best suited; we've focused on these methods in the following pages, but you'll also find a few braised dishes. Each chapter concentrates on one technique and offers menu selections from appetizers to desserts. Although particular attention is paid to the foods of Asia, recipes from other cuisines are presented.

Stir-frying in a wok. The one cooking method that is uniquely Asian, but adaptable to many different foods, is stir-frying, the technique basic to the recipes in the first chapter of this book.

As the name implies, stir-frying is an active method that involves plenty of stirring. Foods aren't really fried, though: they're flash-cooked in a little hot oil, constantly tossed and lifted to bring every side of each piece in contact with the hot wok and to seal in juices and flavors.

Stir-frying isn't difficult to master, though you will have to learn to work with higher-than-usual heat. It's easiest to use one hand to hold the wok, the other hand to stir; this lets you move the wok on and off the heat as needed to control the temperature. The one utensil you'll need is a long-handled spatula.

The stir-frying technique is outlined step by step on page 11, but a few general pointers are worth repeating here. The first unbreakable rule is to have everything ready to go before you begin, since there's no time to assemble ingredients once you start cooking. Cut up meat and vegetables as the recipe directs (see also "Slicing & chopping tips," page 6); mix up any cooking sauces.

With all ingredients ready at hand, set your clean, dry wok over high heat (or as the recipe directs). When the wok is hot, add the oil—always salad oil, since it can withstand high temperatures without burning. When the oil is hot enough to ripple when the wok is tilted from side to side (but not smoking hot), begin cooking, adding ingredients as directed. If you need to add more oil at any point, bring it to rippling hot before adding more food. *Note:* If a recipe specifies butter, heat should be reduced to, at the most, medium-high. If your stir-fry contains firm vegetables such as carrots or asparagus, you may need to add water and cover the wok for a few minutes to let the vegetables steam tender. Let the recipe be your guide, and use the chart on page 12 for additional information on stir-frying vegetables.

Braising & stewing in a wok. The wok shape is fine for braising and stewing, and we've included a few simmered dishes. It's important, though, to make your soups and stews in a stainless steel wok or one with a nonstick finish. Foods simmered for any length of time in a carbon steel wok often take on a metallic taste.

To braise in a wok, follow the same initial steps for stir-frying: brown the meat in oil and cook any vegetables briefly; then add liquid and simmer, covered, until the meat is tender. If you're using a round-bottomed wok and a large amount of liquid, you'll need to set the wok in a ring stand.

Deep-frying in a wok. If you have a wok, you can easily make fried onions, crispy chicken, fritters—or anything else you'd make in a deep-fryer. The two basic utensils you'll need are a wire skimmer or large slotted spoon and a deep-frying thermometer; if you're using a regular round-bottomed wok, you'll also need a ring stand to hold the wok steady when it's filled with oil.

The details of deep-frying in a wok are covered on page 107. At least two rules apply to deep-frying in any pan, though. First, remember that successful results depend on keeping the oil at the right temperature. To prevent the oil from cooling too much when food is added, keep the wok over high heat (unless otherwise instructed) and add food just a few pieces at a time. Second, always be careful when you deep-fry: slide or lower foods into oil to minimize

spattering, lift a wok full of oil with *both* hands, and let the oil cool before pouring it out of the wok.

Steaming in a wok. Steaming foods in a wok is so easy and gives such good results that you may want to use this technique for some of your regular cooking tasks. For example, steaming fish or chicken breasts for a salad takes no longer than cooking these foods in simmering water, and there's less flavor loss. And you can easily enhance the flavors of foods while they steam: sprinkle them with salt, pepper, or herbs; surround with slices of onion, lemon, or ginger; or drizzle with soy.

As far as equipment is concerned, you'll need only a ring stand, a lid, and a metal rack—one made especially for the wok, or just a round cake rack—to turn your wok into a steamer. Also available are stacking bamboo baskets (see photo on page 7) that let you steam several different foods (on different tiers) at once. Basket lids are sold separately; if you buy one, you'll be able to steam in your wok even if you don't have a wok lid. The main advantage of a bamboo lid, though, is that it minimizes condensation by absorbing moisture. If you use a metal wok lid, drops of water will form on it, then drip into the food; you may want to protect some foods (such as custards) with wax paper.

For the how-to's of steaming in a wok, see page 131. Additional information on steaming fresh vegetables is on page 132.

Slicing & chopping tips

Uniform cutting means uniform cooking. That's true no matter what method you use. But cutting pieces of equal size is particularly important for stir-frying; because this technique is so fast, there's no time for differences in size and shape to even out. If you don't cut ingredients evenly, the finished dish may

To diagonally slice fibrous vegetables, such as celery, cut crosswise on the diagonal into ⅛- to ¼-inch-thick slanting slices.

To slice meat, such as flank steak, cut while partially frozen, across the grain, at a 45° angle.

To thinly slice food, such as mushrooms, cut straight down at a right angle.

To cut food, such as zucchini, into julienne strips, first cut vegetable into 2- to 3-inch lengths. Then cut into ⅛-inch-thick slices, stack 2 or 3 slices at a time, and cut slices into ⅛-inch-thick strips.

To dice food, such as potatoes, cut as directed for julienne strips, then cut crosswise into small squares. For larger dice, start with thicker strips.

Wok options and accessories include (clockwise from lower right):
electric wok with lid; round-bottomed wok with skimmer and steamer rack;
stainless steel wok with copper lid and bottom, set in a ring stand; spatula
and cleaver; bamboo steaming baskets; wok lid; flat-bottomed wok with
long wooden handle; semicircular wire draining rack; and chopsticks.

well end up as a blend of undercooked, overdone, and just right.

Cutting into slanting or diagonal slices is a very effective way to cut through fibrous vegetables (such as celery) and meat (such as flank steak) to tenderize them and to expose the greatest possible area to the heated wok sides. Our recipes usually call for ⅛- to ¼-inch-thick slanting slices (see illustration on page 6). Use a very sharp knife or cleaver, and cut meat across the grain at a 45° angle; you'll find that meat is easier to slice if it's partially frozen.

If a recipe simply calls for foods to be thinly sliced, it usually means cutting straight down, not at a slant (see illustration on page 6). Julienne strips should be about the size of a wooden matchstick; diced foods should be cut into small cubes. Such consistent chopping and slicing contribute to both the preparation and presentation of any dish—one that tastes good and looks good, too.

Planning meals for wok cooking

Though the wok is an Asian invention, you don't have to use it exclusively for Oriental-style recipes. In fact, you may find yourself reaching for your wok to fry chicken or boil pasta! Keep in mind, though, that a wok can't do everything at once. If you want to steam one dish, braise another, and stir-fry a third, you'll need to use more than one wok or choose alternate pans. And no matter how many woks you have, preparing several stir-fries at once is difficult—unless you have extra range tops and kitchen help!

Wok cookery & sodium

If you frequently use your wok for Oriental-style cooking, you should think about the amount of sodium you may be consuming. Soy sauce is a basic seasoning in many of these recipes, and that can mean high levels of sodium.

It's not too difficult to reduce the sodium content of most dishes, though. First, you can use low-sodium soy sauce and substitute homemade low-salt chicken broth (see page 93) for the canned or reconstituted variety; you can also season foods to taste with salt rather than automatically adding the amount specified. You can simply cut down on serving sizes and round out the meal with plenty of plain rice or noodles. In China, rice is actually the bulk of the meal; some 250 pounds per person are consumed annually, compared to 10 pounds per person in the United States. A generous helping of steamed rice or boiled noodles serves another purpose, too—to soothe the palate when the main course is extra spicy.

Stir-frying

W hat could be
simpler? A wok, a spatula, and a few minutes of
your time—these, plus fresh ingredients, are the
elements of stir-frying. Understandably, it's a
popular technique with time-conscious cooks.
But beyond its efficiency, stir-frying also brings
out the best of good food. It seals in juices and
flavors, along with vitamins and minerals; it
intensifies colors. Vegetables become crisp,
meats silken and tender. Measure, chop, and
organize all ingredients before you start,
because stir-frying goes very quickly.

Stir-frying Chinese Chicken & Zucchini (Recipe on facing page)

1 Soak dried mushrooms in warm water for 30 minutes. Cut off and discard hard stems; cut caps into ¼-inch-thick slices.

2 Cut boned chicken breasts into bite-size pieces. Then add chicken to soy marinade flavored with garlic, ginger, and fermented black beans; stir to coat and let marinate for 15 minutes.

3 Roll-cut zucchini by making a diagonal slice straight down through squash, giving it a quarter turn, and slicing again. Cut pepper into 1-inch squares; cut bamboo shoot into small pieces.

4 When vegetables are tender-crisp, return cooked chicken to pan and toss to heat through.

5 Add cooking sauce, pouring it in around edges of pan so it will heat quickly. Cook, stirring constantly, until sauce thickens (about 30 seconds).

6 Stir-fried vegetables have bright color, crisp texture; chicken morsels are tender and juicy. To serve the meal Chinese style, provide each diner with an individual bowl of rice.

How to stir-fry in a wok

When you stir-fry, you don't really fry; you cook foods quickly by stirring and tossing them in a small amount of hot fat. This kind of flash-cooking seals in juices and keeps flavors fresh; it's a technique you can use to make dishes of every kind, from appetizers to desserts. All stir-fry recipes follow the same basic steps; once you've mastered the method, you can easily create recipes of your own.

In addition to your wok, the only tool you need for successful stir-frying is a long-handled spatula with a wide, curved edge. You'll also need to keep these pointers in mind:

- Do all your cutting in advance. Foods should be cut into small, uniform pieces or thin slices.

- Prepare any seasonings and sauce mixtures in advance. Once you start to cook, you won't have time to stop and create a sauce.

- Assemble the cut-up meat and/or vegetables, seasonings, sauce mixture, and salad oil or other fat near the range.

- Place a clean, dry wok over the heat specified in the recipe—typically high heat, sometimes medium or medium-high. When the wok is hot, add the fat as directed. Heat oil until it's hot enough to ripple when the wok is tilted from side to side; heat butter until it's foamy.

- Add any seasonings (garlic or ginger, for example). Holding the wok handle in one hand and a wide spatula in the other, stir and toss the seasonings until lightly browned.

    Now add meat, if used. (Never add more than about 1 pound at a time; if you have more, cook it in batches.) Spread the pieces evenly over the wok's surface; stir and toss until lightly browned all over. Turn meat out of wok.

- Add 1 to 2 tablespoons more oil (or other fat). When oil is hot, add vegetables, one variety at a time. Start with the type that has the longest cooking time (see page 12); stir-fry just until tender-crisp to bite, lifting and tossing vegetables to coat them with oil. Turn out of wok; repeat to cook remaining vegetables. (Or simply add all vegetables in sequence, timing your additions so all will be done at the same time.) For dense or fibrous vegetables such as broccoli or asparagus, you may need to add a little water, then cover the wok and steam the vegetable slightly, stirring often.

- Return meat and vegetables to wok. Stir cooking sauce to reblend cornstarch; pour into wok. Stir until sauce boils and thickens. Serve.

NOTE: Use the cooking times given in our recipes as guides, not absolutes. Actual cooking time will vary, depending upon the kind of wok you use and the intensity of the heat source.

(Pictured on facing page)

Chinese Chicken & Zucchini

Preparation time: About 20 minutes, plus 30 minutes to soak mushrooms

Marinating time: 15 minutes

Cooking time: About 10 minutes

Follow the step-by-step photos on the facing page to make this classic stir-fry of crisp vegetable chunks and spicy chicken.

>   5   dried Oriental mushrooms
>   2   teaspoons *each* soy sauce, cornstarch, dry sherry, and water
>   Dash of white pepper
>   1   clove garlic, minced
>   ½   teaspoon minced fresh ginger
>   2   teaspoons fermented salted black beans, rinsed, drained, and finely chopped
>   1½   pounds chicken breasts, skinned and boned
>   3½   tablespoons salad oil
>   Cooking Sauce (recipe at left, page 43)
>   ½   pound zucchini
>   1   whole bamboo shoot, cut into small pieces, or ½ cup sliced bamboo shoots
>   1   red or green bell pepper, seeded and cut into 1-inch squares

Soak mushrooms in warm water to cover for 30 minutes, then drain. Cut off and discard stems; squeeze caps dry, thinly slice, and set aside.

In a bowl, mix soy, cornstarch, sherry, water, pepper, garlic, ginger, and beans. Cut chicken into bite-size pieces; add to marinade and stir to coat, then stir in 1½ teaspoons of the oil. Let marinate for 15 minutes. Meanwhile, prepare Cooking Sauce; set aside. Roll-cut zucchini as shown on facing page.

Place a wok over high heat. When wok is hot, add 2 tablespoons of the oil. When oil is hot, add chicken mixture and stir-fry until meat is no longer pink in center; cut to test (about 3 minutes). Remove from wok and set aside.

Pour remaining 1 tablespoon oil into wok. When oil is hot, add mushrooms, bamboo shoots, zucchini, and bell pepper. Stir-fry for 1 minute, then add 2 tablespoons water, cover, and cook until zucchini and bell pepper are tender-crisp to bite (about 3 more minutes). Return chicken to wok. Stir Cooking Sauce, pour into wok, and stir until sauce boils and thickens. Makes 3 or 4 servings.

Per serving: 296 calories, 29 g protein, 12 g carbohydrates, 15 g total fat, 65 mg cholesterol, 836 mg sodium

Stir-frying Fresh Vegetables

Perfect stir-fried vegetables are bright, colorful, and naturally sweet in flavor, with a texture that's crisp yet tender to the bite. They're quick to fix, too—most types cook in 5 minutes or less.

To stir-fry:

1) Cut vegetables into slices or small pieces, as directed in chart below.

2) Place wok over high heat. When wok is hot, add specified amount of oil; when oil is hot, add vegetables all at once and stir-fry, uncovered, for time noted in chart.

3) Add designated amount of liquid (regular-strength chicken or beef broth or water); cover and cook for remaining time. As vegetables cook, all or most of liquid will evaporate; because there's no cooking liquid to drain off and discard, vitamins and minerals are retained.

Remember that the times noted below should be used as guides. Actual times will vary, depend-ing on the freshness and maturity of the vegeta-bles and on individual preference. Taste after the minimum cooking time; if you prefer a softer texture, continue cooking, tasting often, until vegetables are done to your liking.

If you'd like to cook a medley of several vege-tables, add the firmest kind to the wok first; cook for the time indicated, adding the more tender vegetables near the end of the cooking time. Or cook each vegetable separately, then combine them all for reheating and blending of flavors.

A final pointer for success: never crowd the wok. Cook no more than 5 cups of cut-up vegeta-bles in a 12- to 14-inch wok. To prepare more serv-ings than you can cook at once, just cut up the total quantity of vegetables you'll need, then cook them in two or more batches. Stir-frying is so fast that you can keep the first portions warm, without flavor loss, while the others cook.

Vegetable *4 to 5 cups cut-up vegetable*	Tablespoons salad oil	Minutes to stir-fry uncovered	Tablespoons broth or water	Minutes to cook covered
Asparagus. Cut into ½-inch slanting slices	1	1	1–2	2–3
Beans, green, Italian, wax. Cut into 1-inch pieces	1	1	4	4–7
Bok choy. See Swiss chard				
Broccoli. Cut into ¼-inch slices	1	1	3–5	3–5
Cabbage, green, red, Savoy. Shredded	1	1	2	3–4
Cabbage, napa. Cut white part into 1-inch slices; shred leaves and add during last 2–3 minutes of cooking time	1	1–2	2	4–5
Carrots. Cut into ¼-inch slices	1	1	2–3	3–5
Cauliflower. Flowerets, cut into ¼-inch slices	1	1	3–4	4–5
Celery. Cut into ¼-inch slices	1	1	1–2	1–3
Fennel. Cut into ¼-inch slices	1	2–3	No liquid necessary	Not necessary
Leeks, white part only. Cut into ¼-inch slices	1	1	3–4	3
Mushrooms. Cut into ¼-inch slices	1	3–4	No liquid necessary	Not necessary
Onions, dry. Cut into ¼-inch slices	1	1	No liquid necessary	3–4
Parsnips. Cut into ¼-inch slices	2	1	6–8	4–6
Pea pods, Chinese.	1	3	1	½
Peas, green. Shelled	1	1	3–4	2–3
Peppers, green or red bell. Cut into 1-inch pieces	1	1	2–3	3–5
Rutabagas. Cut into ¼-inch slices	1	1	4–5	5–6
Spinach. Leaves, whole or coarsely chopped	1	½	No liquid necessary	2–3
Sprouts, bean.	1	1	1	½–1½
Squash, summer (crookneck, pattypan, zucchini). Cut into ¼-inch slices	1	1	2–4	3–4
Swiss chard. Cut stems into ¼-inch slices; shred leaves and add during last 2–3 minutes of cooking time	1	1	1	3½–4½
Turnips. Cut into ¼-inch slices	1	1	4–5	4–5

Appetizers

Meatballs with Ginger Glaze

Preparation time: About 25 minutes

Cooking time: About 45 minutes (about 10 minutes/batch)

A sweet and sour sauce that's nippy with fresh ginger coats these small meatballs. If you prepare the dish in an electric wok, you can serve it right in the cooking pan.

     Ginger Glaze (recipe follows)
 1 can (about 8 oz.) water chestnuts, drained and finely chopped
 1 cup chopped green onions (including tops)
 2 pounds lean ground pork
 2 tablespoons soy sauce
 2 eggs
 ¾ cup fine dry bread crumbs
    About 1 tablespoon salad oil

Prepare Ginger Glaze; set aside.

In a bowl, combine water chestnuts, onions, pork, soy, eggs, and bread crumbs. Mix thoroughly with a fork or your hands, then shape mixture into ¾-inch balls (you should have about 72).

Place a wok over medium-high heat; when wok is hot, add 1 tablespoon of the oil. When oil is hot, add 24 meatballs and stir-fry until well browned (about 10 minutes). Remove from wok and set aside. Repeat to brown remaining meatballs, adding more oil as needed. Clean wok.

Place wok over high heat; when wok is hot, pour in Ginger Glaze and stir until glaze boils vigorously. Add meatballs and simmer for about 10 minutes. If using an electric wok, serve in wok; otherwise, transfer to a chafing dish. Provide wooden picks for spearing meatballs. Makes about 6 dozen meatballs (10 to 12 servings).

Ginger Glaze. In a large bowl, smoothly blend ½ cup **water** and ¼ cup **cornstarch.** Add 1 cup *each* **unsweetened pineapple juice** and **regular-strength beef broth,** ½ cup **cider vinegar,** ⅓ cup **sugar,** 1 tablespoon **soy sauce,** and 2 tablespoons minced **fresh ginger.**

Per serving: 233 calories, 17 g protein, 19 g carbohydrates, 9 g total fat, 97 mg cholesterol, 447 mg sodium

Quick Pot Stickers

Preparation time: About 1 hour

Cooking time: About 1 hour (about 15 minutes/batch)

Traditional pot stickers (page 14) are delicious, but they do take time to make. It isn't hard to speed up the preparation, though—instead of using home-made wrappers, just start with the purchased ones (*gyoza*) sold in some grocery stores and Asian markets.

 2 small whole chicken breasts (about ¾ lb. *each*), skinned, boned, and split
 ¼ cup sesame oil
 1 cup finely chopped celery
 ½ cup chopped green onions (including tops)
 3 tablespoons dry sherry
 2 tablespoons cornstarch
 1 teaspoon sugar
 ½ teaspoon salt
 1 package (14 oz.) pot sticker wrappers (*gyoza*) or won ton skins
 ¼ cup salad oil
 1 cup water
    Rice wine vinegar, soy sauce, and chili oil

Rinse chicken and pat dry, then chop finely. Place in a bowl and stir in sesame oil, celery, onions, sherry, cornstarch, sugar, and salt.

Set out 6 to 8 wrappers at a time; keep remaining wrappers tightly covered. Mound 2 teaspoons of the filling on each wrapper. To shape each pot sticker, fold dough in half over filling. Pinch about ½ inch of curved edge closed; continue to pinch closed, forming 3 tucks along dough edge, until entire curve is sealed. Set pot sticker down firmly, seam side up, so it will sit flat. Cover lightly until all pot stickers are shaped. (At this point, you may freeze pot stickers as directed on page 14. Cook without thawing as directed below.)

Place a wok over medium heat; when wok is hot, add 1 tablespoon of the salad oil. When oil is hot, add 12 pot stickers, seam side up. Cook until bottoms are golden brown (5 to 7 minutes). Pour in ¼ cup of the water; reduce heat to low, cover, and cook until liquid is absorbed (6 to 10 more minutes). Remove from wok and keep warm. Repeat to cook remaining pot stickers, using remaining salad oil and water.

Offer pot stickers with vinegar, soy, and chili oil on the side for dipping. Makes about 4 dozen pot stickers (about 10 servings).

Per serving: 273 calories, 14 g protein, 24 g carbohydrates, 13 g total fat, 54 mg cholesterol, 151 mg sodium

(Pictured on facing page)

Pot Stickers

Preparation time: About 1½ hours, plus 30 minutes to let dough rest

Cooking time: About 1¾ hours (about 25 minutes/batch)

These savory filled dumplings—called *guotie* in Chinese—make a tasty and substantial first course for parties or everyday meals. They freeze well, so you can make them well in advance.

> **Shrimp Filling (recipe follows)**
> 3 **cups all-purpose flour**
> ¼ **teaspoon salt**
> 1 **cup boiling water**
> ¼ **cup salad oil**
> **About 1⅓ cups regular-strength chicken broth**
> **Soy sauce, rice wine vinegar, and chili oil**

Prepare filling; cover and refrigerate.

In a bowl, combine flour and salt; mix in water until dough is evenly moistened and begins to hold together. On a lightly floured board, knead dough until very smooth and satiny (about 5 minutes). Cover and let rest at room temperature for 30 minutes.

Divide dough into 2 equal portions. Keep 1 portion covered; roll out other portion about ⅛ inch thick (or thinner). Cut dough into 3½- to 4-inch circles with a round cookie cutter or a clean, empty can with both ends removed. Repeat with scraps and remaining dough.

Mound 2 teaspoons of the filling on each circle. To shape each pot sticker, fold dough in half over filling. Pinch about ½ inch of curved edge closed; continue to pinch closed, forming 3 tucks along dough edge, until entire curve is sealed. Set pot sticker down firmly, seam side up, so it will sit flat. Cover lightly until all pot stickers are shaped. (At this point, you may place pot stickers in a single layer on a baking sheet and freeze until hard, then transfer to a heavy plastic bag, seal, and return to freezer for up to 1 month. Cook without thawing as directed below.)

Place a wok over medium heat; when wok is hot, add 1 tablespoon of the salad oil. When oil is hot, add 12 pot stickers, seam side up. Cook until bottoms are golden brown (8 to 10 minutes). Pour in ⅓ cup of the broth and immediately cover wok tightly. Reduce heat to low and cook for 10 minutes (15 minutes if frozen). Uncover and continue to cook until all liquid is absorbed. Remove from wok and keep warm. Repeat to cook remaining pot stickers, using remaining salad oil and broth.

Offer pot stickers with soy, vinegar, and chili oil on the side for dipping. Makes about 4 dozen pot stickers (about 10 servings).

Shrimp Filling. Shell, devein, and finely chop ½ pound **medium-size raw shrimp.** Combine shrimp with ½ pound **lean ground pork,** 1 cup finely shredded **cabbage,** ¼ cup minced **green onions** (including tops), ¼ cup chopped **mushrooms,** 1 clove **garlic** (minced or pressed), ½ teaspoon **salt,** and 2 tablespoons **oyster sauce** or soy sauce. Mix well.

Per serving: 253 calories, 13 g protein, 30 g carbohydrates, 9 g total fat, 42 mg cholesterol, 497 mg sodium

Beef Chiang Mai

Preparation time: About 10 minutes

Cooking time: About 15 minutes

Warm, spicy beef wrapped in cool lettuce leaves makes a tempting appetizer; the dish is traditional in northern Thailand. If you like, you can wash and crisp the lettuce leaves a day ahead.

> ¼ **cup short-grain rice (such as pearl) or long-grain rice**
> 1 **pound lean ground beef**
> 1 **teaspoon *each* sugar and crushed red pepper**
> ½ **cup *each* thinly sliced green onions (including tops) and chopped fresh mint**
> 2 **tablespoons chopped fresh cilantro (coriander)**
> ¼ **cup lemon juice**
> 1½ **tablespoons soy sauce**
> **Small inner leaves from 2 large or 3 small heads butter lettuce**
> **About 36 fresh mint sprigs**

Place a wok over medium heat. When wok is hot, add rice and stir-fry until golden (about 5 minutes). Remove from heat and transfer to a blender or food processor; whirl until finely ground. Set aside.

Return wok to medium heat; when wok is hot, crumble in beef and cook, stirring, just until meat begins to lose its pinkness (about 3 minutes). Add ground rice, sugar, red pepper, onions, chopped mint, cilantro, lemon juice, and soy; stir until well combined. Pour into a serving dish and surround with lettuce leaves and mint sprigs.

To eat, spoon beef mixture onto lettuce leaves, top with a mint sprig, roll up, and eat out of hand. Makes about 12 servings.

Per serving: 123 calories, 7 g protein, 5 g carbohydrates, 8 g total fat, 28 mg cholesterol, 157 mg sodium

Golden brown Pot Stickers (recipe on facing page) are an
ever-popular appetizer, first course, or light entrée. Let guests dip these
dumplings into soy, vinegar, and chili oil, combined or served in
individual bowls.

Ginger Chicken Wings

Preparation time: About 15 minutes

Cooking time: About 25 minutes

Like the ginger-glazed meatballs on page 13, these hearty chicken wings feature a snappy fresh-ginger sauce. Serve them hot or at room temperature.

> Cooking Sauce (recipe follows)
> 12 chicken wings (about 2¼ lbs. *total*)
> 5 tablespoons salad oil
> 2 tablespoons *each* soy sauce and minced fresh ginger
> 2 teaspoons *each* cornstarch and sugar
> ¼ cup regular-strength chicken broth
> ⅓ cup sliced green onions (including tops), optional

Prepare Cooking Sauce; set aside.

Cut off and discard tips of chicken wings, then cut wing sections apart at the joint. Rinse and pat dry.

In a bowl, stir together 2 tablespoons of the oil, soy, ginger, cornstarch, and sugar. Add chicken pieces; stir to coat.

Place a wok over high heat; when wok is hot, add remaining 3 tablespoons oil. When oil is hot, add chicken mixture and cook, uncovered, stirring occasionally, until chicken is browned (about 5 minutes). Stir in broth. Reduce heat to medium, cover, and cook until chicken pulls easily from bone (15 to 20 minutes).

Stir Cooking Sauce, then add to chicken wings. Cook, stirring, until sauce boils and thickens. If made ahead, let cool, then cover and refrigerate for up to 3 days.

Serve chicken wings hot or at room temperature. To serve, arrange wings on a dish; sprinkle with onions, if desired. Makes 4 to 6 servings.

Cooking Sauce. Stir together ¼ cup **regular-strength chicken broth**, 2 teaspoons **cornstarch**, and 2 tablespoons *each* **oyster sauce** and **dry sherry.**

Per serving: 335 calories, 18 g protein, 6 g carbohydrates, 26 g total fat, 71 mg cholesterol, 733 mg sodium

Tequila-Lime Ice with Shrimp

Preparation time: About 45 minutes

Freezing time: 4 to 6 hours

Cooking time: About 5 minutes

A refreshingly tart, super-simple ice perfectly sets off the sweetness of stir-fried shrimp. Make the ice early in the day (or up to a month ahead); cook the shrimp just 30 minutes in advance.

> 1½ teaspoons grated lime peel
> 1 cup sugar
> 2 cups lime juice (about 14 fresh limes; or use bottled juice)
> ½ cup tequila
> 1 cup water
> Stir-fried Shrimp (recipe follows)
> Lime peel strips (optional)

In a 9- by 13-inch pan, stir together grated lime peel, sugar, lime juice, tequila, and water until sugar is dissolved; cover. Freeze until firm (4 to 6 hours) or for up to 1 month.

About 30 minutes before serving, prepare shrimp and set aside; also place 5 to 8 small bowls in the freezer.

With a heavy spoon, break lime ice into chunks. Whirl in a food processor or beat with an electric mixer until a thick, icy slush forms. Immediately spoon into chilled bowls; garnish with strips of lime peel, if desired. Accompany with shrimp. Makes 4 cups ice (5 to 8 first-course servings).

Stir-fried Shrimp. Shell and devein 1 pound **large raw shrimp.** Place a wok over high heat; when wok is hot, add 2 tablespoons **salad oil.** When oil is hot, add shrimp and stir-fry until pink (about 3 minutes). Stir in 2 tablespoons **tequila;** carefully ignite with a match (not beneath an exhaust fan or near flammable items) and shake wok until flames die down. Add 2 tablespoons **lime juice.** Serve at room temperature.

Per serving: 226 calories, 10 g protein, 31 g carbohydrates, 4 g total fat, 65 mg cholesterol, 97 mg sodium

Crunchy Indian Snack

Preparation time: About 10 minutes

Cooking time: About 30 minutes

Spicy Bombay *chiura*, a crunchy Indian snack, is a mixture of legumes, nuts, sesame seeds, and sweet raisins. Serve it in a bowl, as finger food.

¼ cup *each* uncooked lentils, long-grain rice, and dried split peas

3 cups water

2 tablespoons salad oil

1 tablespoon sesame seeds

1 teaspoon *each* ground coriander and ground cumin

½ teaspoon ground turmeric

½ cup *each* salted roasted peanuts and cashews

¼ cup raisins

⅛ to ¼ teaspoon ground red pepper (cayenne)

¼ teaspoon ground cloves

1 teaspoon salt

Rinse lentils, rice, and peas; drain well. Place in a 2- to 3-quart pan and add 3 cups water; bring to a boil over high heat. Boil for 1 minute; then remove from heat, cover, and set aside for 10 minutes. Drain, rinse under cold water, and drain again; spread on paper towels and pat dry.

Place a wok over medium-high heat; when wok is hot, add oil. When oil is hot, add lentils, rice, peas, sesame seeds, coriander, cumin, and turmeric. Cook, stirring, until mixture is toasted (5 to 10 minutes). Remove from heat and stir in peanuts, cashews, raisins, red pepper, cloves, and salt. Let cool. If made ahead, store airtight for up to 1 week. Makes 2 cups.

Per ¼ cup: 215 calories, 7 g protein, 20 g carbohydrates, 13 g total fat, 0 mg cholesterol, 371 mg sodium

Cold Spiced Cabbage

Preparation time: About 10 minutes

Cooking time: 3 minutes

Chilling time: About 4 hours

Garlic, sesame, and crushed red pepper season this simple cold relish. It's a fine addition to an appetizer tray as well as a good complement for a richly seasoned main course.

1 small head napa cabbage (about 1½ lbs.)

2 tablespoons salad oil

2 cloves garlic, minced

⅓ cup water

3 tablespoons *each* sugar and white wine vinegar

½ teaspoon salt

1½ teaspoons sesame oil

¼ to ½ teaspoon crushed red pepper

Cut cabbage into 2-inch pieces. Place a wok over high heat. When wok is hot, add salad oil. When oil begins to heat, add garlic and stir once. Then add cabbage and stir-fry for 30 seconds. Add water, cover, and cook, stirring occasionally, until cabbage is just barely wilted (about 1½ minutes). Remove from heat and pour off any excess liquid. Stir sugar, vinegar, salt, sesame oil, and red pepper into cabbage. Let cool, then cover and refrigerate until cold (about 4 hours) or for up to 1 week. Serve cold. Makes about 2½ cups.

Per ¼ cup: 57 calories, .85 g protein, 6 g carbohydrates, 4 g total fat, 0 mg cholesterol, 116 mg sodium

Spiced Pecans

Preparation time: About 5 minutes

Cooking time: About 3 minutes

Pecans, a favorite in the South, are sautéed in a pungent spice mixture in this Creole-style snack. Your guests will find them hard to resist!

½ teaspoon *each* salt, paprika, and ground red pepper (cayenne)

1 teaspoon white pepper

1 tablespoon fresh or dry rosemary

2 tablespoons butter or margarine

1 tablespoon olive oil

10 ounces (about 2½ cups) pecan halves

1 tablespoon Worcestershire

½ teaspoon liquid hot pepper seasoning

Combine salt, paprika, red pepper, white pepper, and rosemary. Set aside.

Place a wok over high heat; when wok is hot, add butter and oil. When butter is melted, add pecans and stir-fry until nuts are well coated with butter and oil and slightly darker in color (about 1 minute). Add Worcestershire, hot pepper seasoning, and spice mixture; continue to stir-fry until pecans are deep brown (about 1½ more minutes; be careful not to scorch nuts). Let cool. If made ahead, store airtight for up to 2 days. Makes 2½ cups.

Per ¼ cup: 225 calories, 2 g protein, 6 g carbohydrates, 23 g total fat, 6 mg cholesterol, 156 mg sodium

Hot chiles, characteristic of Szechwan province, boldly accent
lean, tender strips of sirloin in Szechwan Beef (recipe on facing page).
Slender carrot ribbons and sliced bamboo shoots contribute
color and crispness.

Beef, Pork, Veal & Lamb

(Pictured on facing page)

Szechwan Beef

Preparation time: *About 10 minutes*

Cooking time: *About 10 minutes*

Tender beef, crisp carrots, and a handful of hot chiles go into this stir-fry. Use small dried chiles or larger ones, as you prefer.

- Cooking Sauce (recipe follows)
- 1 pound lean boneless beef steak (such as top round, flank, or sirloin)
- 2 tablespoons salad oil
- 16 dried hot red chiles
- 2 large carrots, cut into about 3-inch-long julienne strips
- 1 can (about 8 oz.) sliced bamboo shoots, drained (and thinly sliced, if desired)
- Fresh cilantro (coriander) leaves (optional)

Prepare Cooking Sauce and set aside.

Cut beef with the grain into 1½-inch-wide strips; then cut each strip across the grain into ⅛-inch-thick slanting slices. Set aside.

Place a wok over high heat; when wok is hot, add oil. When oil is hot, add chiles and cook, stirring, until chiles just begin to char. Remove chiles from wok; set aside.

Add beef to wok and stir-fry until browned (1½ to 2 minutes); remove from wok and set aside. Add carrots to wok and stir-fry until tender-crisp to bite (about 3 minutes). Add bamboo shoots and stir-fry for 1 more minute.

Return meat and chiles to wok; stir Cooking Sauce and add. Stir until sauce boils and thickens. Garnish with cilantro, if desired. Makes 4 servings.

Cooking Sauce. Stir together 2 tablespoons **soy sauce**, 1 tablespoon **dry sherry**, 2 teaspoons **sugar**, and ½ teaspoon **cornstarch.**

Per serving: 349 calories, 31 g protein, 26 g carbohydrates, 17 g total fat, 65 mg cholesterol, 602 mg sodium

Beef with Napa Cabbage

Preparation time: *About 15 minutes*

Marinating time: *10 minutes*

Cooking time: *About 8 minutes*

Red bell pepper and green napa cabbage give this entrée its bright, fresh look and flavor. Napa cabbage is sold in most supermarkets; sometimes called Chinese or celery cabbage, it has a sweeter taste and a more tender texture than the familiar head cabbage.

- ½ to ¾ pound lean boneless beef steak (such as top round, flank, or sirloin)
- 1 teaspoon cornstarch
- 1 tablespoon soy sauce
- ½ teaspoon minced fresh ginger
- Cooking Sauce (recipe follows)
- About ¾ pound napa cabbage (about ½ small head)
- ¼ cup salad oil
- 1 clove garlic, minced or pressed
- 1 red bell pepper, seeded and cut into 1-inch squares
- 2 green onions (including tops), thinly sliced

Cut beef with the grain into 1½-inch-wide strips; then cut each strip across the grain into ⅛-inch-thick slanting slices. In a bowl, stir together cornstarch, soy, and ginger. Add beef and stir to coat well. Let marinate for 10 minutes.

Meanwhile, prepare Cooking Sauce and set aside. Also cut cabbage crosswise into ¾-inch slices.

Place a wok over high heat. When wok is hot, add 2 tablespoons of the oil. When oil is hot, add meat mixture. Stir-fry until meat is browned (1½ to 2 minutes); set aside.

Add remaining 2 tablespoons oil to wok. When oil is hot, add garlic and bell pepper. Stir-fry for about 30 seconds. Add cabbage and stir-fry until cabbage is bright green and tender-crisp to bite (about 2 minutes).

Return meat mixture to wok. Stir Cooking Sauce and add, then stir until sauce boils and thickens. Mix in onions. Makes 2 or 3 servings.

Cooking Sauce. Stir together 1 tablespoon *each* **cornstarch** and **sugar**, ½ cup **regular-strength beef broth**, and 1 tablespoon *each* **soy sauce** and **dry sherry.**

Per serving: 386 calories, 29 g protein, 14 g carbohydrates, 23 g total fat, 65 mg cholesterol, 912 mg sodium

Beef with Bok Choy

Preparation time: About 10 minutes

Marinating time: 15 minutes

Cooking time: About 12 minutes

Crisp bok choy and sweet sesame seeds complement strips of steak in this simple entrée. As you prepare the bok choy, remember to keep stems and leaves separate—they go into the wok at different times.

      Cooking Sauce (recipe follows)
¾ pound lean boneless beef steak (such as top round, flank, or sirloin)
1 tablespoon soy sauce
1 medium-size head bok choy
2 to 3 teaspoons sesame seeds
¼ cup salad oil
1 clove garlic, minced or pressed
¼ cup water

Prepare Cooking Sauce and set aside.

Cut beef with the grain into 1½-inch-wide strips; then cut each strip across the grain into ⅛-inch-thick slanting slices. Place meat in a bowl, stir in soy, and let marinate for 15 minutes.

Meanwhile, cut bok choy leaves from stems. Cut stems diagonally into ¼-inch slices; coarsely shred leaves. Set stems and leaves aside separately; you should have 6 to 8 cups *total* lightly packed stems and leaves.

Place a wok over medium heat. When wok is hot, add sesame seeds and stir until golden (about 2 minutes); remove from wok and set aside. Increase heat to high. Add 2 tablespoons of the oil to wok; when oil is hot, add garlic and bok choy stems. Stir-fry for 1 to 2 minutes. Add water, then cover and cook for 2 minutes; add bok choy leaves and cook, uncovered, stirring occasionally, just until leaves and stems are tender to bite (1 to 2 more minutes). Remove from wok and set aside.

Pour remaining 2 tablespoons oil into wok. When oil is hot, add meat; stir-fry until browned (1½ to 2 minutes). Return bok choy to wok. Stir sauce and add, then add sesame seeds. Cook, stirring, until sauce boils and thickens. Makes 2 or 3 servings.

Cooking Sauce. Stir together ¾ cup **regular-strength chicken broth,** 4 teaspoons **cornstarch,** 2 teaspoons **soy sauce,** 1 teaspoon minced **fresh ginger** or ½ teaspoon ground ginger, and 2 tablespoons **dry sherry.**

Per serving: 407 calories, 32 g protein, 14 g carbohydrates, 26 g total fat, 65 mg cholesterol, 1,081 mg sodium

Oyster Beef

Preparation time: About 15 minutes, plus 30 minutes to soak mushrooms

Marinating time: 15 minutes

Cooking time: About 7 minutes

This tasty beef dish gains subtle flavor from oyster sauce—a thick brown sauce sold in Asian markets and well-stocked supermarkets.

6 medium-size dried Oriental mushrooms
¾ pound lean boneless beef steak (such as top round, flank, or sirloin)
1 tablespoon *each* dry sherry and soy sauce
2 tablespoons water
¼ teaspoon sugar
2 teaspoons cornstarch
3½ tablespoons salad oil
      Cooking Sauce (recipe follows)
1 clove garlic, minced
½ teaspoon minced fresh ginger
½ cup sliced bamboo shoots
      Salt

Soak mushrooms in warm water to cover for 30 minutes, then drain. Cut off and discard stems; squeeze caps dry, thinly slice, and set aside.

Cut beef with the grain into 1½-inch-wide strips; then cut each strip across the grain into ⅛-inch-thick slanting slices. In a bowl, stir together sherry, soy, 1 tablespoon of the water, sugar, and cornstarch. Add beef and stir to coat, then stir in 1½ teaspoons of the oil and let marinate for 15 minutes.

Meanwhile, prepare Cooking Sauce and set aside.

Place a wok over high heat; when wok is hot, add 2 tablespoons of the oil. When oil begins to heat, add garlic and ginger and stir once. Add beef mixture and stir-fry until meat is browned (1½ to 2 minutes); remove from wok and set aside.

Pour remaining 1 tablespoon oil into wok. When oil is hot, add bamboo shoots and mushrooms; stir-fry for 1 minute. Add remaining 1 tablespoon water, cover, and cook for 2 minutes. Return meat mixture to wok. Stir Cooking Sauce, add to wok, and stir until sauce boils and thickens. Season to taste with salt. Makes 4 servings.

Cooking Sauce. Stir together 2 tablespoons **oyster sauce,** 1 tablespoon **cornstarch,** and ½ cup **regular-strength chicken broth.**

Per serving: 268 calories, 22 g protein, 9 g carbohydrates, 16 g total fat, 49 mg cholesterol, 787 mg sodium

Asparagus Beef

Follow directions for **Oyster Beef**, but substitute 1 pound **asparagus** for mushrooms and bamboo shoots. To prepare asparagus, snap off and discard tough ends of spears, then cut spears into ½-inch slanting slices.

Two-Onion Beef

Follow directions for **Oyster Beef**, but substitute 1 large **onion** and 12 **green onions** (including tops) for mushrooms and bamboo shoots. Cut onion in half, then thinly slice; cut green onions into 1½-inch lengths. After removing beef from wok, stir-fry sliced onion for 1 minute. Then add green onions and stir-fry for 30 seconds before returning beef to wok.

Beef & Broccoli

Preparation time: About 20 minutes

Marinating time: 15 minutes

Cooking time: About 15 minutes

Ginger and ground red pepper heat up the hearty sauce that coats beef strips and tender broccoli. Make the cooking sauce while the beef marinates.

- ¾ pound broccoli
- 1 pound lean boneless beef steak (such as top round, flank, or sirloin)
- 2 tablespoons soy sauce
- 1 clove garlic, minced or pressed
  Cooking Sauce (recipe follows)
- ¼ cup salad oil
- 2 tablespoons water

Cut off and discard tough ends of broccoli stalks; peel stalks, if desired. Cut tops into small flowerets; slice stalks ¼ inch thick. Set aside.

Cut beef with the grain into 1½-inch-wide strips, then cut each strip across the grain into ¼-inch-thick slanting slices. In a bowl, mix beef, soy, and garlic. Let marinate for 15 minutes. Meanwhile, prepare Cooking Sauce and set aside.

Place a wok over high heat; when wok is hot, add 1 tablespoon of the oil. When oil is hot, add half the meat mixture and stir-fry until meat is browned (2 to 3 minutes); remove from wok and set aside. Repeat to brown remaining meat, using 1 tablespoon more oil.

Pour remaining 2 tablespoons oil into wok. When oil is hot, add broccoli and stir-fry for about 1 minute. Add water, cover, and cook, stirring fre-

quently, until broccoli is tender-crisp to bite (about 3 more minutes). Stir Cooking Sauce, then add to wok along with meat; stir until sauce boils and thickens. Makes 3 or 4 servings.

Cooking Sauce. Stir together 1½ tablespoons **cornstarch,** ¼ teaspoon **ground ginger,** a dash of **ground red pepper** (cayenne), 2 tablespoons **dry sherry,** and 1¼ cups **regular-strength beef broth.**

Per serving: 318 calories, 29 g protein, 8 g carbohydrates, 19 g total fat, 65 mg cholesterol, 879 mg sodium

Steak Paprikash

Preparation time: About 10 minutes

Cooking time: About 15 minutes

A traditional slow-simmered dish from central Europe is easily adapted to stir-frying—with delicious results (and a considerable savings of time).

- 6 slices bacon
- 1½ pounds lean boneless beef steak (such as top round, flank, or sirloin), cut across the grain into ¼-inch-thick slices
- 1 large onion, thinly sliced
- 1 small head green cabbage (about 1½ lbs.), coarsely shredded
- 1 tablespoon paprika
- 2 tablespoons water
- 1 cup *each* sour cream and plain yogurt
- 2 tablespoons all-purpose flour
- 2 tablespoons minced parsley

Place a wok over medium heat; when wok is hot, add bacon. Cook, turning as needed, until crisp (about 3 minutes). Lift from wok, drain, crumble, and set aside. Pour off and discard all but 2 tablespoons of the drippings.

Place wok with bacon drippings over high heat. When fat is hot, add half the beef and stir-fry just until browned (2 to 3 minutes); with a slotted spoon, transfer meat to a bowl. Repeat to brown remaining beef.

Add onion, cabbage, and paprika to wok. Stir-fry for 1 minute; then add water, cover, and cook for 4 more minutes.

Stir together sour cream, yogurt, and flour; then stir into cabbage mixture. Add meat and any juices and stir just until hot. Top with bacon and parsley. Makes 4 servings.

Per serving: 565 calories, 50 g protein, 23 g carbohydrates, 31 g total fat, 138 mg cholesterol, 375 mg sodium

(Pictured on facing page)

Tomato Beef

Preparation time: About 20 minutes

Marinating time: 15 minutes

Cooking time: About 7 minutes

Tender strips of beef and crisply cooked vegetables are tossed with a curry-flavored sauce for this easy Cantonese dish.

- ¾ **pound lean boneless beef steak (such as top round, flank, or sirloin)**
- 2 **teaspoons** *each* **cornstarch and soy sauce**
- 1 **tablespoon** *each* **dry sherry and water**
- ¼ **cup salad oil**
  Cooking Sauce (recipe follows)
- ½ **teaspoon minced fresh ginger**
- 1 **clove garlic, minced**
- 2 **large stalks celery, cut into ¼-inch-thick slanting slices**
- 1 **medium-size onion, cut into wedges, layers separated**
- 1 **green bell pepper, seeded and cut into 1-inch squares**
- 3 **medium-size tomatoes,** *each* **cut into 6 wedges**
  Salt

Cut beef with the grain into 1½-inch-wide strips; then cut each strip across the grain into ⅛-inch-thick slanting slices. In a bowl, stir together cornstarch, soy, sherry, and water. Add meat and stir to coat, then stir in 1½ teaspoons of the oil and let marinate for 15 minutes.

Meanwhile, prepare Cooking Sauce and set aside.

Place a wok over high heat; when wok is hot, add 2 tablespoons of the oil. When oil begins to heat, add ginger and garlic and stir once. Add meat mixture and stir-fry until meat is browned (1½ to 2 minutes); remove from wok and set aside.

Pour remaining 1½ tablespoons oil into wok. When oil is hot, add celery and onion and stir-fry for 1 minute. Add bell pepper and stir-fry for 1 minute, adding a few drops of water if wok appears dry. Add tomatoes and stir-fry for 1 minute. Return meat to wok. Stir Cooking Sauce, pour into wok, and stir until sauce boils and thickens. Season to taste with salt. Makes 4 servings.

Cooking Sauce. Stir together 1 tablespoon *each* **soy sauce, Worcestershire,** and **cornstarch;** 3 tablespoons **catsup;** 1 teaspoon **curry powder;** and ½ cup **water.**

Per serving: 308 calories, 22 g protein, 16 g carbohydrates, 18 g total fat, 48 mg cholesterol, 679 mg sodium

Beef with Snow Peas

Preparation time: About 25 minutes

Marinating time: 2 hours

Cooking time: About 8 minutes

This spicy stir-fry of beef and snow peas owes its complex flavors to a meat marinade of soy, sherry, sesame oil, hoisin sauce, and Tientsin preserved vegetables. You'll find the preserved vegetables—called *chong choy*— in Asian markets.

- 1 **pound lean boneless beef steak (such as top round, flank, or sirloin)**
  Spicy Marinade (recipe follows)
- ¼ **cup salad oil**
- ¾ **pound Chinese pea pods (also called snow or sugar peas) or sugar snap peas, ends and strings removed; or 2 packages (6 oz.** *each***) frozen Chinese pea pods, thawed and drained**
- 1 **tablespoon water**
- 1 **tablespoon soy sauce**
- 1 **teaspoon sugar**
- 1 **small onion, cut into slivers**

Cut beef into 1-inch chunks. With a mallet, pound each piece to a thickness of about ¼ inch. Prepare marinade; stir in beef, then cover and refrigerate for at least 2 hours or until next day.

Place a wok over high heat; when wok is hot, add 2 tablespoons of the oil. When oil is hot, add fresh pea pods. Stir-fry for about 3 minutes; add water, cover, and cook until pea pods are tender-crisp to bite—about 30 seconds. (If using frozen pea pods, simply stir-fry for 30 seconds *total*.) Transfer to a serving dish. Return wok to heat and add remaining 2 tablespoons oil; when oil is hot, add beef and marinade. Stir-fry until meat is browned (2 to 3 minutes). Stir in soy, sugar, and onion; cook for 1 more minute. Makes about 4 servings.

Spicy Marinade. Stir together 2 tablespoons **salad oil** and 1 tablespoon *each* **soy sauce, catsup, dry sherry, cornstarch, hoisin sauce,** and **sesame oil.** If desired, stir in 1 tablespoon **Tientsin preserved vegetables.** Then stir in 1 teaspoon **Worcestershire** and 1 clove **garlic,** minced or pressed.

Per serving: 436 calories, 29 g protein, 14 g carbohydrates, 29 g total fat, 65 mg cholesterol, 764 mg sodium

A visual feast of appetizing color, Tomato Beef
(recipe on facing page) shows off the wok's magic with
fresh ingredients. A touch of curry gives the spicy
sauce memorable flavor.

The Tabletop Wok

If your guests like to participate in making a meal, you'll want to introduce them to these easy and delicious variations on the popular Asian hot-pot tradition. To present the meal, you'll need one electric wok (or a regular wok with a portable heat source) for every six guests. If serving more than six, set up a second table and wok. Set the wok in the middle of the table and fill it with boiling broth, then offer trays of cut-up meats and vegetables and let guests choose and cook their own portions.

Mizutaki

1½ **pounds lean boneless beef sirloin, trimmed of excess fat and cut across the grain into ¼-inch-thick slanting slices**

6 **chicken thighs (1½ to 2 lbs.** *total***) or 3 whole chicken breasts (about 1 lb.** *each***), skinned, boned, and cut across the grain into ¼-inch-thick slices**

1 **pound carrots, cut into ¼-inch-thick slanting slices**

¾ **pound cauliflower (about ½ head), cut into flowerets, each floweret sliced in half lengthwise**

6 **to 8 green onions (including tops), cut into 2-inch lengths**

½ **pound fresh shiitake or button mushroom caps, cut into ¼-inch-thick slices**

1 **pound spinach or watercress, stems and any yellow or wilted leaves removed, green leaves rinsed well**

½ **pound medium or firm tofu (bean curd), drained and cut into ½-inch cubes**

Mizutaki Sauce (recipe follows)

6 **to 8 cups hot cooked rice**

8 **cups regular-strength beef broth**

Arrange beef, chicken, vegetables, and tofu on trays. Place next to wok in center of table.

Prepare Mizutaki Sauce; pour into 6 small bowls (1 for each diner). Fill 6 more small bowls with rice.

Place an electric wok in center of table. Pour broth into wok and bring to a boil; adjust heat to keep broth simmering. Let guests fill wok with some of each food, starting with the slower-cooking carrots and cauliflower and ending with meats. Cover wok. Let foods simmer until chicken is no longer pink in center; cut to test (3 to 5 minutes).

Uncover wok; let guests remove portions with chopsticks, tongs, or strainer ladles, a bite at a time. Dip each bite in Mizutaki Sauce, then eat with rice. As wok is emptied, let guests add more food and cook it to taste.

At the end of the meal, add the enriched broth to sauce cups; stir broth and sauce together, then sip mixture as soup. Makes 6 servings.

Mizutaki Sauce. In a blender or food processor, combine 1 **egg,** 2 tablespoons **rice wine vinegar** or white wine vinegar, and ¼ teaspoon **dry mustard;** whirl until blended. With motor running, pour in 1 cup **salad oil** in a slow, steady stream. Pour mixture into a bowl; stir in ½ cup **sour cream,** 2 tablespoons **soy sauce,** 2 tablespoons **mirin** (sweet sake) or dry sherry, and ⅓ cup **regular-strength beef broth.** Makes about 2 cups.

Chicken & Vegetable One-pot Meal

Mushroom Bundles (directions follow)

Carrot Bundles (directions follow)

Spinach Rolls (directions follow)

Peanut Sauce (recipe follows)

1½ **to 2 pounds skinned, boned chicken breasts**

1½ **to 2 pounds mustard greens, tough stems removed, leaves rinsed well and chilled**

2 **large cans (49½ oz.** *each***) regular-strength chicken broth**

½ **cup finely chopped green onions (white part only)**

2 **limes,** *each* **cut into 4 wedges**

1 **tablespoon crushed dried hot red chiles**

Prepare Mushroom Bundles, Carrot Bundles, Spinach Rolls. Prepare Peanut Sauce and set aside.

Rinse chicken, pat dry, and cut into 1- by 2-inch strips no thicker than 1 inch. Arrange chicken, mustard greens, Mushroom Bundles, Carrot Bundles, and Spinach Rolls on trays.

Place an electric wok in center of table. Pour half the broth into wok and bring to a boil; adjust heat to keep broth simmering. Place trays of foods alongside. Place onions, limes, chiles, and Peanut Sauce in separate containers for each guest. Guests add foods to broth, removing vegetables when hot (about 1 minute) and chicken when no longer pink in center, cut to test (2 to 4 minutes). Add remaining broth as needed.

Let guests flavor their portions of Peanut Sauce to taste with onions, a squeeze of lime, and chiles. Dip vegetables and chicken into sauce to eat. At the end of the meal, ladle hot broth into cups, add Peanut Sauce to taste, and sip broth. Makes 6 servings.

Mushroom Bundles. Divide 2 bags (3½ oz. *each*) **enoki mushrooms** into 6 equal portions, laying mushrooms parallel.

Cut 6 green stems (tops) from about 2 **green onions**; reserve white part to chop for flavoring Peanut Sauce. Immerse stems in **boiling water** until limp (about 30 seconds); drain and let cool. Tie each portion of mushrooms with an onion stem. Cut off and discard brown, woody ends of mushrooms.

Carrot Bundles. Peel 2 medium-size **carrots**; trim off ends. Cut each carrot crosswise into thirds; cut each third into thin sticks. Divide sticks into 12 equal portions, laying them parallel. Cut 12 green stems (tops) from about 4 **green onions**; reserve white part to chop for flavoring Peanut Sauce. Immerse stems in **boiling water** until limp (about 30 seconds); drain and let cool. Tie each portion of carrots with an onion stem.

Spinach Rolls. Discard stems and any yellow or wilted leaves from 2 pounds **spinach**; rinse green leaves well and set aside. Cut 4 large outer **napa cabbage** leaves, *each* 9 to 10 inches long. Immerse cabbage leaves in **boiling water** until limp (about 2 minutes). Lift from water; drain, lay flat, and pat dry. Trim thick part of rib from center of each leaf, making a V-shaped cut.

Add spinach to boiling water and cook until limp (about 2 minutes); drain. Let cool; firmly squeeze out moisture with your hands.

On a muslin cloth, lay 2 cabbage leaves side by side (stems in opposite directions), with edges overlapping by several inches. Lay half the spinach along outer edge of cabbage leaves. Form a roll by lifting cloth with 1 hand (from spinach side); smooth roll with other hand. Make roll tight so it will hold its shape when heated in broth. Form another roll with remaining cabbage and spinach. Cut rolls crosswise into 1½-inch slices.

Peanut Sauce. Blend ⅔ cup **creamy peanut butter**, 2 tablespoons **soy sauce**, 4 teaspoons **distilled white vinegar**, and 2 teaspoons **sugar**. Slowly whisk in 1 cup **regular-strength chicken broth.** Makes 1¾ cups.

Udon-suki

Pork Balls (recipe follows)
Prepared vegetables (suggestions follow)

12 **small live hard-shell clams, scrubbed well, rinsed in cold water**

3 **packages (about 7 oz. *each*) fresh udon noodles or about 6 ounces dried udon or spaghetti**
    Boiling salted water

1 **tablespoon salad oil**

2 **large cans (49½ oz. *each*) regular-strength chicken broth**

Prepare Pork Balls and vegetables. Set aside with clams.

Shortly before serving, immerse fresh noodles in boiling salted water until tender to bite (2 to 3 minutes); drain. (Or cook dried noodles according to package directions; drain.) Mix noodles with oil and place in a bowl.

Place an electric wok in center of table. Pour half the broth plus pan juices from Pork Balls into wok; bring to a boil. Place half the clams in broth. Cover and cook until broth returns to a boil; reduce heat and simmer for 3 minutes. Then

add about half the Pork Balls and half the vegetables; continue to simmer until clams pop open. Let guests remove cooked ingredients and noodles to individual bowls; then ladle some of the hot broth into each bowl. Repeat to prepare second servings. Makes 4 to 6 servings.

Pork Balls. Toast ¼ cup **pine nuts** in a small frying pan over medium heat until golden (about 4 minutes), shaking pan frequently. Place in a bowl and add 1 pound **lean ground pork**, 1 **egg**, 2 tablespoons **all-purpose flour**, 1 tablespoon **soy sauce**, and ½ teaspoon grated **fresh ginger**. Mix well. Shape into balls, using about 1 tablespoon meat mixture for each; arrange slightly apart on a rimmed baking sheet. Bake in a 475° oven until no longer pink in center; cut to test (about 15 minutes). Reserve any pan juices to add to broth. Makes about 3 dozen meatballs.

Prepared vegetables. You'll need a total of 6 to 8 cups vegetables.

■ *Carrots or celery.* Cut into ¼-inch-thick slanting slices. Immerse in boiling water until tender to bite (about 5 minutes); drain.

■ *Daikon or turnips.* Peel and cut crosswise into ¼-inch-thick slices. Immerse in boiling water until tender to bite (3 minutes for daikon, 4 minutes for turnips); drain.

■ *Chinese pea pods* (also called snow or sugar peas) or sugar snap peas. Remove and discard ends and strings. Immerse in boiling water until tender to bite (about 30 seconds); drain.

■ *Dried Oriental mushrooms or fresh button mushrooms.* Soak dried mushrooms in warm water to cover for 30 minutes; drain. Cut off and discard stems; squeeze caps dry and leave whole. Cut fresh mushrooms lengthwise into ¼-inch-thick slices.

Fajitas in a wok? Yes—when you make this hearty
stir-fried version of the Southwestern barbecue classic. Fun, delicious,
and quick, Fajitas Stir-fry (recipe on facing page)
is sure to become a favorite.

(Pictured on facing page)

Fajitas Stir-fry

Preparation time: About 30 minutes

Cooking time: About 7 minutes

In this quick version of fajitas, the steak is stir-fried instead of grilled. You wrap the meat in warm flour tortillas—or crisp iceberg lettuce leaves.

- 1 **pound lean boneless beef steak (such as top round, flank, or sirloin)**
- 2 **tablespoons salad oil**
- 2 **cloves garlic, minced or pressed**
- 1 **large onion, thinly sliced and separated into rings**
- 2 or 3 **fresh jalapeño chiles, seeded and minced**
- 1 **large red bell pepper, seeded and cut into thin strips**
- 2 **teaspoons ground cumin**
- 3 **tablespoons lime juice**
- 1 **teaspoon cornstarch**
- 2 **medium-size Roma-type tomatoes, diced**
  Salt and pepper
  Lime wedges
  Sour cream (optional)
- 1 **large ripe avocado, pitted, peeled, and diced**
- 8 **warm flour tortillas (8-inch diameter); or 8 large iceberg lettuce leaves, chilled**
  Homemade or purchased salsa (optional)

Cut beef with the grain into 1-inch-wide strips; then cut each strip across the grain into ⅛-inch-thick slices. Set aside.

Place a wok over high heat; when wok is hot, add 1 tablespoon of the oil. When oil is hot, add meat. Stir-fry until meat is browned (1½ to 2 minutes); transfer meat to a bowl with a slotted spoon.

Add remaining 1 tablespoon oil to wok, then add garlic, onion, chiles, and bell pepper. Stir-fry until onion is soft (about 3 minutes). Stir together cumin, lime juice, and cornstarch; add to wok. Return meat to wok, add tomatoes, and stir until mixture is hot and juices boil. Season to taste with salt and pepper, then pour fajitas into a serving dish; garnish with lime wedges. Offer sour cream (if desired) and avocado in separate dishes.

Spoon meat mixture onto tortillas or lettuce leaves; add sour cream, avocado, and a squeeze of lime to taste. Fold up and eat out of hand. Accompany with salsa, if desired. Makes 4 servings.

Per serving: 612 calories, 34 g protein, 49 g carbohydrates, 32 g total fat, 65 mg cholesterol, 76 mg sodium

Beef & Rice in Lettuce

Preparation time: About 10 minutes

Marinating time: 1½ hours

Cooking time: 8 minutes

Accompany tender soy-marinated steak strips with steamed rice—then wrap both meat and rice in lettuce for an eat-out-of-hand entrée. (You'll find instructions for steaming short-grain rice on page 77.)

- 1 **tablespoon sesame seeds**
- 2½ **tablespoons soy sauce**
- 1 **tablespoon *each* sugar and sesame oil**
- 2 **tablespoons thinly sliced green onion (including top)**
- 1 **teaspoon *each* minced garlic and minced fresh ginger**
- 1 **pound lean boneless beef steak (such as top round, flank, or sirloin)**
- 2 to 3 **tablespoons salad oil**
  About 2 cups steamed short-grain rice (such as pearl) or medium-grain rice
- 20 to 32 **red leaf lettuce leaves**
  Korean hot red pepper paste (optional)

Place a wok over medium heat. When wok is hot, add sesame seeds and stir until golden (about 2 minutes). Pour out of wok; crush thoroughly with a mortar and pestle or whirl briefly in a blender. Then pour into a bowl and stir in soy, sugar, sesame oil, onion, garlic, and ginger.

Cut beef across the grain into ⅛-inch-thick slices; add to soy mixture and stir to coat well. Cover and refrigerate for about 1½ hours. Drain, reserving marinade.

Place a wok over high heat; when wok is hot, add 2 tablespoons of the salad oil. When oil is hot, add about half the meat mixture and 1 to 2 tablespoons of the marinade. Stir-fry until meat is browned (1½ to 2 minutes). Remove from wok and keep warm. Repeat to brown remaining meat, adding more oil as needed and 1 to 2 tablespoons more marinade.

On each of 4 dinner plates, arrange about a fourth of the beef, about ½ cup of the rice, 5 to 8 lettuce leaves, and, if desired, a dab of red pepper paste. To eat, fill a lettuce leaf with meat, rice, and red pepper paste (if used). Roll up and eat out of hand. Makes 4 servings.

Per serving: 409 calories, 30 g protein, 30 g carbohydrates, 18 g total fat, 65 mg cholesterol, 706 mg sodium

Sirloin Tips & Vegetables

Preparation time: About 10 minutes

Marinating time: About 30 minutes

Cooking time: About 8 minutes

Thin sirloin strips and vegetables, enhanced with ginger and hoisin, are served over spinach for an outstanding entrée. A red wine marinade both flavors and tenderizes the meat. You may use either fresh or frozen spinach; cook it just before you start to stir-fry.

About 1 pound sirloin tips
¼ **cup dry red wine**
2 **tablespoons soy sauce**
1 **clove garlic, minced or pressed**
1 **teaspoon minced fresh ginger**
2 **tablespoons salad oil**
1 **cup thinly sliced celery**
½ **pound mushrooms, thinly sliced**
1 **can (about 8 oz.) water chestnuts, drained and sliced**
½ **cup thinly sliced green onions (including tops)**
2 **tablespoons hoisin sauce**
Hot cooked spinach

Cut beef across the grain into ⅛-inch-thick strips and place in a shallow dish. Stir together wine, soy, garlic, and ginger; pour over meat and let marinate for about 30 minutes.

Place a wok over high heat; when wok is hot, add oil. When oil is hot, add meat mixture and stir-fry until meat is browned (1½ to 2 minutes). Remove meat from wok and set aside. Immediately add celery, mushrooms, water chestnuts, onions, and hoisin. Stir-fry until celery is tender-crisp to bite (2 to 3 minutes). Return meat to wok; stir until heated through. Serve immediately over spinach. Makes 4 servings.

Per serving: 305 calories, 25 g protein, 14 g carbohydrates, 16 g total fat, 68 mg cholesterol, 352 mg sodium

Burgundy Beef

Preparation time: About 10 minutes

Marinating time: About 15 minutes

Cooking time: About 7 minutes

Nobody would describe *boeuf bourguignon* as a classic stir-fry—but this bold beef dish can in fact be made quite successfully in a wok. Wine and herbs flavor the distinctive sauce.

1 **pound lean boneless beef steak (such as top round, flank, or sirloin)**
¼ **pound mushrooms, thinly sliced**
½ **cup dry red wine**
2 **tablespoons salad oil**
¼ **teaspoon *each* dry chervil, dry tarragon, and salt**
⅛ **teaspoon dry marjoram leaves**
1½ **tablespoons all-purpose flour**

Cut beef with the grain into 2-inch-wide strips; then cut each strip across the grain into ⅛-inch-thick slanting slices. Combine meat and mushrooms in a bowl; stir in wine and let marinate at room temperature for about 15 minutes (or cover and refrigerate for up to 3 hours).

Drain meat and mushrooms, reserving marinade. Place a wok over high heat; when wok is hot, add oil. When oil begins to heat, add chervil, tarragon, salt, and marjoram. Then add meat and mushrooms and stir-fry just until meat is browned (1½ to 2 minutes).

Sprinkle meat mixture with flour, then blend in reserved marinade. Stir until sauce is slightly thickened. Makes 4 servings.

Per serving: 235 calories, 27 g protein, 4 g carbohydrates, 12 g total fat, 65 mg cholesterol, 197 mg sodium

Picadillo

Preparation time: About 5 minutes

Marinating time: 15 minutes

Cooking time: About 15 minutes

Picadillo is a South American specialty—"minced meat" (here, ground beef) served with a sweet and sour sauce and such traditional ingredients as olives, raisins, and bell peppers.

1 **pound lean ground beef**
1½ **tablespoons distilled white vinegar**
1 **clove garlic, minced or pressed**
1 **teaspoon ground cumin**
2 **tablespoons salad oil**
1 **small onion, chopped**
1 **small green bell pepper, seeded and cut into thin strips**
1 **can (8 oz.) tomato sauce**
½ **cup water**
½ **teaspoon cracked bay leaves**
6 **pimento-stuffed green olives, sliced**
1 **tablespoon raisins**
Salt and pepper
1 **can (4 oz.) shoestring potatoes**

In a bowl, combine beef, vinegar, garlic, and cumin; mix well and let stand for 15 minutes.

Place a wok over medium-high heat; when wok is hot, add 1 tablespoon of the oil. When oil is hot, add meat mixture; cook, stirring, until meat is browned (about 3 minutes). Lift out and set aside; spoon out and discard any fat.

Pour remaining 1 tablespoon oil into wok; when oil is hot, add onion and bell pepper and stir-fry until onion is soft (about 4 minutes). Stir in tomato sauce, water, bay leaves, olives, and raisins. Bring to a boil; then reduce heat and simmer, uncovered, until slightly reduced (about 5 minutes). Add meat mixture and cook until heated through (about 2 more minutes). Season to taste with salt and pepper. Mound on a rimmed platter; surround with potatoes. Makes 4 servings.

Per serving: 378 calories, 22 g protein, 16 g carbohydrates, 26 g total fat, 69 mg cholesterol, 525 mg sodium

Lettuce Tacos

Preparation time: About 25 minutes

Cooking time: 8 to 10 minutes

Crisp lettuce leaves make a light, cool, change-of-pace wrapper for this spicy meat and vegetable mixture.

    1   medium-size head iceberg lettuce (about 1 lb.)
    1   tablespoon salad oil
    2   medium-size carrots, coarsely chopped
    1   large zucchini (7 to 8 inches long), cut into ¼-inch cubes
    1   cup fresh corn kernels cut from cob or 1 cup frozen whole-kernel corn, thawed and drained
    1   pound lean ground beef
    2   cloves garlic, minced or pressed
    1   tablespoon chili powder
    1   teaspoon ground cumin
    1   cup thinly sliced green onions (including tops)
    1   can (6 oz.) spicy tomato cocktail
    1   tablespoon cornstarch
        Salt
    ½   cup shredded jack cheese

Separate leaves from lettuce; rinse and shake dry. Arrange on a serving plate, cover, and refrigerate.

Place a wok over high heat; when wok is hot, add oil. When oil is hot, add carrots; stir-fry for 1 minute. Add zucchini and corn; stir-fry for 1 more minute, then remove vegetables with a slotted spoon and set aside.

Crumble beef into wok; cook, stirring, until browned (2 to 3 minutes). Spoon off and discard all but 1 tablespoon of the fat. Then add garlic, chili powder, cumin, and onions to meat; cook, stirring, just until onions begin to soften. Return carrot mixture to wok and stir until heated through.

Mix tomato cocktail and cornstarch; add to wok and cook, stirring, until sauce boils and thickens. Season to taste with salt. Transfer to a serving bowl; sprinkle with cheese.

To serve, spoon beef mixture onto chilled lettuce leaves. Makes 4 servings.

Per serving: 451 calories, 28 g protein, 24 g carbohydrates, 28 g total fat, 85 mg cholesterol, 342 mg sodium

Five-spice Pork & Potatoes

Preparation time: About 10 minutes

Cooking time: About 25 minutes

Russet potatoes and thin, tender pork strips soak up the fragrance and flavor of Chinese five-spice. The bottled spice blend is sold in many markets, but if you can't find it, you can easily make your own.

    3   large russet potatoes (about 1½ lbs. *total*)
    2   tablespoons salad oil
    1   pound lean boneless pork (such as shoulder or butt), trimmed of excess fat and cut into ¼- by 1- by 3-inch strips
    2   cloves garlic, minced or pressed
    1½ cups water
    3   tablespoons soy sauce
    2   teaspoons sugar
    1¼ teaspoons Chinese five-spice; or ½ teaspoon ground ginger, ¼ teaspoon *each* ground cinnamon and crushed anise seeds, and ⅛ teaspoon *each* ground allspice and ground cloves
    ⅓   cup thinly sliced green onions (including tops)

Peel potatoes and cut crosswise into ½-inch-thick slices; cut large slices in half. Set aside.

Place a wok over high heat; when wok is hot, add oil. When oil is hot, add pork and garlic. Stir-fry until pork is browned (2 to 3 minutes). Add potatoes, water, soy, sugar, and five-spice. Bring to a boil; then reduce heat, cover, and simmer, stirring occasionally, until potatoes are tender when pierced (about 20 minutes). Garnish with onions. Makes 3 or 4 servings.

Per serving: 359 calories, 26 g protein, 28 g carbohydrates, 16 g total fat, 76 mg cholesterol, 867 mg sodium

(Pictured on facing page)

Twice-cooked Pork

Preparation time: About 5 minutes

Cooking time: About 45 minutes to simmer; about 6 minutes to stir-fry

The pork in this spicy Szechwan dish really is cooked twice—first simmered, then stir-fried (if you like, you can even do the cooking on different days). Sweet and hot bean sauces add a distinctive flavor—but if you can't find them, you may use hoisin sauce and chiles with equally tasty results.

> 1 **pound lean boneless pork (such as shoulder or butt), in 1 piece**
> 1 **tablespoon dry sherry**
> 1 **thin, quarter-size slice fresh ginger, crushed with the side of a cleaver**
> 3 **green onions (including tops)**
> 2 **teaspoons hot bean sauce; or 2 small dried hot red chiles, crumbled**
> 4 **teaspoons sweet bean sauce or hoisin sauce**
> 1 **tablespoon soy sauce**
> 1 **teaspoon sugar**
> 2 **small green bell peppers or 1 *each* small green and red bell pepper**
> 3 **tablespoons salad oil**
> ½ **teaspoon salt**
> 2 **cloves garlic, minced**
> 1 **teaspoon minced fresh ginger**

Place pork, sherry, and ginger slice in a 2-quart pan. Cut 1 of the green onions in half crosswise and add to pork, then add enough water to barely cover meat. Bring to a simmer; cover and simmer until meat is tender when pierced (about 45 minutes).

Lift meat from broth and refrigerate until cold. Then cut into 1½-inch-square pieces about ⅛ inch thick. (The fatty parts of the meat are considered a delicacy, but remove them if you wish.)

In a bowl, combine hot bean sauce, sweet bean sauce, soy, and sugar. Seed bell peppers and cut into 1-inch squares; cut remaining 2 green onions into 1-inch lengths.

Place a wok over high heat; when wok is hot, add 2 tablespoons of the oil. When oil is hot, add bell peppers and stir-fry for 1½ minutes, adding a few drops of water if wok appears dry. Sprinkle with salt and stir once, then remove peppers from wok. Add remaining 1 tablespoon oil to wok. When oil begins to heat, add garlic and minced ginger and stir once; then add pork and stir-fry for 1 minute. Add bean sauce mixture and toss until pork is coated with sauce. Return bell peppers to wok along with onion. Stir for 30 seconds to heat through. Makes 3 or 4 servings.

Per serving: 302 calories, 24 g protein, 8 g carbohydrates, 20 g total fat, 76 mg cholesterol, 790 mg sodium

Hawaiian Pork

Preparation time: About 15 minutes

Cooking time: About 20 minutes

Emerald-green snow peas and bright bell peppers add color and crisp texture to this richly flavored version of sweet and sour pork.

> **Sweet-Sour Sauce (recipe follows)**
> 2 **pounds lean boneless pork (such as shoulder or butt), trimmed of excess fat and cut into ¾-inch cubes**
> 1 **egg, beaten**
> **About ½ cup cornstarch**
> **About 6 tablespoons salad oil**
> 1 ***each* small green and red bell pepper, seeded and cut into 1-inch squares**
> 1 **small onion, cut into wedges, layers separated**
> ¼ **pound Chinese pea pods (also called snow or sugar peas) or sugar snap peas, ends and strings removed; or 1 package (6 oz.) frozen Chinese pea pods, thawed and drained**

Prepare Sweet-Sour Sauce; set aside.

Dip pork cubes in beaten egg, drain briefly, and roll in cornstarch to coat lightly; shake off excess.

Place a wok over high heat; when wok is hot, add 2 tablespoons of the oil. When oil is hot, add half the pork; stir-fry until evenly browned (5 to 7 minutes). Lift pork from wok and set aside. Repeat to brown remaining meat, adding more oil as needed.

Add remaining oil (about 2 tablespoons) to wok. Add bell peppers and onion; stir-fry until vegetables are tender-crisp to bite (about 2 minutes). Add pea pods; then stir sauce and add. Stir until sauce boils and thickens; return pork to wok and stir until heated through. Makes 6 to 8 servings.

Sweet-Sour Sauce. Stir together ½ cup *each* **cider vinegar,** firmly packed **brown sugar,** and **catsup;** ¼ cup *each* **cornstarch** and **unsweetened pineapple juice;** and 2 tablespoons **soy sauce.**

Per serving: 408 calories, 24 g protein, 33 g carbohydrates, 20 g total fat, 110 mg cholesterol, 535 mg sodium

Instead of going out for Chinese food, you'll soon choose to
stay home and dine on spicy Twice-cooked Pork (recipe on
facing page). It really does involve double-cooking the pork,
but the flavor is well worth the extra time.

Pork Tenderloin Normandy

Preparation time: About 15 minutes

Cooking time: About 10 minutes

Apple slices, onion, and sliced pork mingle in a creamy sauce sparked with Dijon mustard. A sprinkle of raisins adds a sweet finishing touch.

- ½ teaspoon *each* salt and dry oregano leaves
- ⅛ teaspoon pepper
- 3 tablespoons all-purpose flour
  About ¾ pound pork tenderloin, cut into ⅛-inch-thick, 1½-inch-wide slices
- ¼ cup butter or margarine
- 1 large onion, chopped
- 1 large Golden Delicious apple, cored and thinly sliced
- 2 tablespoons Dijon mustard
- 1 cup milk
- 2 tablespoons raisins
  Chopped parsley

Combine salt, oregano, pepper, and flour. Dredge pork in flour mixture; shake off excess. Set remaining flour mixture aside.

Place a wok over medium-high heat; when wok is hot, add 2 tablespoons of the butter. When butter is melted, add pork and stir-fry until browned (2 to 3 minutes); remove pork from wok and set aside.

Add remaining 2 tablespoons butter to wok; when butter is melted, add onion and stir-fry until soft (about 3 minutes). Add apple, then sprinkle in remaining flour mixture; stir-fry for about 1 minute. Stir in mustard and milk; bring to a boil, then return meat to wok and stir-fry for about 2 minutes. Stir in raisins and sprinkle with parsley. Makes 3 or 4 servings.

Per serving: 318 calories, 21 g protein, 22 g carbohydrates, 16 g total fat, 95 mg cholesterol, 686 mg sodium

Pork with Baby Corn

Preparation time: About 20 minutes

Marinating time: 15 minutes

Cooking time: About 8 minutes

Baby sweet corn is a treat in this quick Cantonese entrée. Sold canned or bottled, the tiny, tender ears of corn are available in Asian markets and in the imported food section of most supermarkets.

- 1 teaspoon *each* cornstarch and soy sauce
- 1 tablespoon dry sherry
- ¼ teaspoon pepper
- 1 pound lean boneless pork (such as shoulder or butt), trimmed of excess fat and cut into ⅛- by 1- by 2-inch strips
- ¼ cup salad oil
  Cooking Sauce (recipe follows)
- 2 cloves garlic, minced
- 1 small onion, cut into wedges, layers separated
- ¼ pound mushrooms, thinly sliced
- 1 can (about 1 lb.) whole baby sweet corn, drained
- 8 green onions (including tops), cut into 2-inch lengths

In a bowl, stir together cornstarch, soy, sherry, and pepper. Add pork and stir to coat. Stir in 1 teaspoon of the oil. Let marinate for 15 minutes. Meanwhile, prepare Cooking Sauce and set aside.

Place a wok over high heat; when wok is hot, add 2 tablespoons of the oil. When oil begins to heat, add garlic and stir once. Then add half the pork mixture and stir-fry until meat is lightly browned (1½ to 2 minutes); remove from wok. Repeat to brown remaining meat, using 1 tablespoon more oil.

Pour remaining 2 teaspoons oil into wok. When oil is hot, add onion pieces and mushrooms and stir-fry for 1 minute, adding a few drops of water if wok appears dry. Return meat mixture to wok, then add corn and green onions; stir-fry for 30 seconds. Stir Cooking Sauce, add to wok, and stir until sauce boils and thickens. Makes 4 servings.

Cooking Sauce. Stir together 1½ tablespoons **cornstarch**, 1 teaspoon *each* **sugar** and **vinegar**, ¼ teaspoon **salt**, 1 tablespoon **soy sauce**, and ¾ cup **regular-strength chicken broth** or water.

Per serving: 435 calories, 27 g protein, 32 g carbohydrates, 24 g total fat, 76 mg cholesterol, 1,064 mg sodium

Yu-shiang Pork

Preparation time: About 15 minutes

Marinating time: 15 minutes

Cooking time: About 8 minutes

Yu-shiang pork doesn't taste like fish—but because the seasonings used are typical of Szechwan fish cookery, the dish is often called fish-flavored pork.

1 teaspoon cornstarch
¼ teaspoon salt
  Dash of white pepper
1 tablespoon dry sherry
¾ pound lean boneless pork (such as shoulder or butt), trimmed of excess fat and cut into matchstick pieces
3½ tablespoons salad oil
  Cooking Sauce (recipe follows)
2 cloves garlic, minced
1 teaspoon minced fresh ginger
3 or 4 small dried hot red chiles
⅔ cup sliced bamboo shoots, cut into matchstick pieces
10 green onions (including tops), cut into 2-inch lengths

In a bowl, combine cornstarch, salt, white pepper, and sherry. Add pork and stir to coat; then stir in 1½ teaspoons of the oil. Let marinate for 15 minutes. Meanwhile, prepare Cooking Sauce; set aside.

Place a wok over high heat. When wok is hot, add 2 tablespoons of the oil. When oil begins to heat, add garlic, ginger, and chiles; stir once. Add pork mixture and stir-fry until meat is lightly browned (2 to 3 minutes); remove from wok.

Pour remaining 1 tablespoon oil into wok. When oil is hot, add bamboo shoots and onions and stir-fry for 1 minute. Return pork mixture to wok. Stir Cooking Sauce, pour into wok, and stir until sauce boils and thickens. Makes 4 servings.

Cooking Sauce. Stir together 1 tablespoon *each* **sugar, vinegar,** and **dry sherry;** 2 tablespoons **soy sauce;** 3 tablespoons **regular-strength chicken broth** or water; and 2 teaspoons **cornstarch.**

Per serving: 299 calories, 19 g protein, 13 g carbohydrates, 17 g total fat, 57 mg cholesterol, 766 mg sodium

Sweet & Sour Pork

Preparation time: About 15 minutes

Cooking time: About 25 minutes

Here's one Chinese dish that's familiar to just about everybody. Crisp, juicy chunks of pork and a colorful medley of vegetables and fruit combine in a tangy, ginger-spiked sauce.

  Sweet & Sour Sauce (recipe follows)
2 pounds lean boneless pork (such as shoulder or butt), trimmed of excess fat and cut into 1-inch cubes
1 egg, beaten
  About ½ cup cornstarch

  About 5 tablespoons salad oil
1 medium-size onion, cut into 1-inch cubes
2 medium-size carrots, cut into ¼-inch-thick slanting slices
1 clove garlic, minced or pressed
2 tablespoons water
1 green bell pepper, seeded and cut into 1-inch squares
½ cup fresh or drained canned pineapple chunks
2 medium-size tomatoes, cut into 1-inch cubes

Prepare Sweet & Sour Sauce; set aside.

Dip pork cubes in beaten egg, drain briefly, and roll in cornstarch to coat lightly; shake off excess.

Place a wok over medium-high heat. When wok is hot, add 3 tablespoons of the oil. When oil is hot, add half the pork and stir-fry until evenly browned (about 7 minutes); lift pork from wok and set aside. Repeat to brown remaining meat, adding more oil as needed.

Scrape away and discard any browned particles from sides and bottom of wok, but leave oil in wok. If necessary, add more oil to wok to make about 2 tablespoons total. Place wok over high heat. When oil is hot, add onion, carrots, and garlic; stir-fry for about 1 minute. Add water and bell pepper; cover and cook, stirring frequently, for about 2 minutes. Add pineapple, tomatoes, and pork; stir Sweet & Sour Sauce, then add. Stir until mixture boils and thickens (about 1 minute). Makes 6 servings.

Sweet & Sour Sauce. Stir together 1 tablespoon **cornstarch** and ⅓ cup firmly packed **brown sugar.** Then stir in ½ teaspoon minced **fresh ginger** or ¼ teaspoon ground ginger, 1 tablespoon *each* **soy sauce** and **dry sherry,** and ¼ cup *each* **wine vinegar** and **regular-strength chicken or beef broth.**

Per serving: 474 calories, 32 g protein, 31 g carbohydrates, 25 g total fat, 147 mg cholesterol, 358 mg sodium

Rich flavors mingle in Papaya & Sausage Sauté
(recipe on facing page). Brought together in a spicy honey glaze,
hearty bites of Italian sausage and smooth papaya slices
make an exquisite entrée.

Sausage Etouffée

Preparation time: About 25 minutes

Cooking time: About 35 minutes

Extra-rich, spicy, and filling! This Cajun entrée starts with a "black roux": a blend of flour and oil cooked until deep brown, then blended with minced vegetables.

- 1 cup Black Roux (recipe follows)
- ½ pound bacon, chopped
- 1 medium-size eggplant (¾ to 1 lb.), cut into ½-inch cubes
- ½ cup *each* chopped onion, chopped green bell pepper, and chopped celery
- 1 clove garlic, minced or pressed
- 1 pound kielbasa (Polish sausage), cut into ½-inch-thick slices
- ½ teaspoon black pepper
- ⅛ teaspoon ground red pepper (cayenne)
- 1½ cups water
  Salt
- ½ cup sliced green onions (including tops)

Prepare roux; set aside.

Place a wok over medium heat; when wok is hot, add bacon and cook until crisp (about 3 minutes). Lift out with a slotted spoon and set aside; spoon out and discard all but 3 tablespoons of the drippings. Add eggplant to wok; stir often until eggplant is soft when pressed (about 5 minutes). Add bacon, chopped onion, bell pepper, celery, and garlic; stir-fry until onion is soft (about 4 minutes). Add sausage and stir-fry until hot. Mix in roux, black pepper, red pepper, and water; bring to a boil over high heat. Season to taste with salt, sprinkle with green onions, and serve. Makes 4 to 6 servings.

Black Roux. In a bowl, mix 1 cup **salad oil** and 1 cup **all-purpose flour** until smoothly blended. Place a wok over medium-high heat; when wok is hot, add oil-flour mixture. Using a spoon with a long wooden or heat-resistant handle, stir until mixture is dark brown to red-brown in color and smells darkly toasted (about 15 minutes); if it begins to smell burned, immediately remove wok from heat, let cool, discard roux, and start again.

All at once add ¾ cup *each* finely chopped **onion** and finely chopped **green bell pepper** and ⅓ cup finely chopped **celery** to hot roux. Then remove wok from heat and stir until roux is no longer bubbly (2 to 3 minutes).

Per serving: 791 calories, 18 g protein, 26 g carbohydrates, 69 g total fat, 67 mg cholesterol, 884 mg sodium

(Pictured on facing page)

Papaya & Sausage Sauté

Preparation time: About 10 minutes

Cooking time: About 12 minutes

If you like meat and fruit together, be sure to try this unusual dish: succulent papaya slices and sausage rounds tumbled in a spicy honey glaze. When papayas aren't in season (or if you can't find them at the market), try making the sauté with apples instead.

- 1¼ pounds mild Italian sausages, cut into ½-inch-thick slices
- 2 tablespoons *each* lemon juice and honey
- ½ teaspoon *each* ground ginger, ground coriander, and curry powder
- 2 medium-size papayas (about 1 lb. *each*), peeled, seeded, and cut lengthwise into ½-inch-thick slices
  Green onions (roots and any wilted tops trimmed) and minced green onion tops (optional)

Place a wok over high heat; when wok is hot, add sausage. Stir-fry until browned (about 3 minutes). Discard all but 3 tablespoons of the drippings. Push sausage to side of wok; stir lemon juice, honey, ginger, coriander, and curry powder into drippings at bottom of wok. Then push sausage into spice mixture and toss to coat; transfer to a serving plate and keep warm.

Add papayas to wok. Cook over high heat, turning occasionally, until fruit is glazed and light brown (3 to 5 minutes). Arrange papayas around sausage. Garnish with whole and minced green onions, if desired. Makes about 4 servings.

Per serving: 499 calories, 22 g protein, 26 g carbohydrates, 35 g total fat, 88 mg cholesterol, 1,012 mg sodium

Apple & Sausage Sauté

Follow directions for **Papaya & Sausage Sauté,** but substitute 2 large **green-skinned apples,** cored and cut into ½-inch-thick slices, for papayas. Add ½ cup **toasted whole blanched almonds** along with apples.

Italian Veal with Peppers

Preparation time: About 15 minutes

Cooking time: About 15 minutes

Red and green bell peppers give this zesty entrée its great eye appeal. Quick preparation is another plus—making the dish takes only about half an hour from start to finish.

> 1 pound boneless veal, cut into ¼-inch-thick slices
> All-purpose flour
> About 3 tablespoons butter or margarine
> About 3 tablespoons salad oil
> 2 large red or green bell peppers (or 1 *each* large red and green bell pepper), seeded and cut into ½-inch-wide strips
> 1 teaspoon dry oregano leaves
> 1 clove garlic, minced or pressed
> ⅔ cup dry white wine
> Salt and pepper

Trim and discard any fat and membrane from veal; then cut meat into pieces about 1½ inches square. Dredge veal squares in flour to coat lightly; shake off excess. Set aside.

Place a wok over medium heat; when wok is hot, add 1 tablespoon *each* of the butter and oil. When butter is melted, add bell pepper strips, oregano, and garlic; stir-fry until peppers are soft when pierced (about 5 minutes). With a slotted spoon, transfer pepper mixture to a serving dish; keep warm.

Increase heat to medium-high; add 1 tablespoon *each* more butter and oil. When butter is melted, add about half the veal squares and stir-fry just until lightly browned on both sides (about 2 minutes). Arrange cooked veal in dish with bell peppers. Repeat to brown remaining veal squares, adding remaining butter and oil as needed to prevent sticking.

Pour wine into wok; bring to a boil. Boil, stirring to scrape browned bits free, until liquid is reduced by about half. Season sauce to taste with salt and pepper; pour over veal and peppers. Makes 4 servings.

Per serving: 383 calories, 23 g protein, 6 g carbohydrates, 29 g total fat, 104 mg cholesterol, 169 mg sodium

Veal & Asparagus Platter

Preparation time: About 15 minutes

Cooking time: About 25 minutes

Veal and fresh asparagus are topped with creamy mushroom sauce in an elegant entrée for entertaining. For a showy touch, you can flame the sauce with brandy.

> 1½ pounds boneless veal, cut into ¼-inch-thick slices
> Salt and pepper
> All-purpose flour
> About ¼ cup butter or margarine
> About 2 tablespoons salad oil
> 2 pounds asparagus
> ½ pound mushrooms, cut into ¼-inch-thick slices
> 2 tablespoons brandy (optional)
> ½ teaspoon *each* dry tarragon and dry mustard
> ⅔ cup half-and-half or light cream
> 1 tablespoon lemon juice

Trim and discard any fat and membrane from veal. Place veal between 2 sheets of wax paper on a cutting board or work surface. Pound with a flat-surfaced meat mallet until meat is about ⅛ inch thick. Cut into ¾-inch-wide strips; sprinkle lightly with salt and pepper, then dust with flour and shake off excess.

Place a wok over medium heat; when wok is hot, add 1 tablespoon *each* of the butter and oil. When butter is melted, add about half the veal and stir-fry until lightly browned (about 2 minutes). Transfer to a warm platter; keep warm. Repeat to brown remaining veal, adding about 1 tablespoon *each* more butter and oil as needed to prevent sticking.

Snap off and discard tough ends of asparagus. Rinse spears, then immerse in 1½ inches boiling water and cook, uncovered, just until tender to bite (5 to 7 minutes). Drain well; arrange on platter with veal.

Place wok over medium heat; when wok is hot, add remaining 2 tablespoons butter. When butter is melted, add mushrooms and stir-fry until lightly browned (about 3 minutes). Stir in 1 tablespoon flour; stir for 1 minute.

If using brandy, pour into a small pan. Warm over low heat until bubbly; carefully ignite (not beneath an exhaust fan or near flammable items) and pour into wok. When flames die down, add tarragon, mustard, and half-and-half. Stir until sauce is bubbly and thickened. Remove from heat, stir in lemon juice, and pour over veal and asparagus. Makes 6 servings.

Per serving: 367 calories, 27 g protein, 8 g carbohydrates, 26 g total fat, 111 mg cholesterol, 170 mg sodium

Green Beans with Lamb Sauce

Preparation time: About 15 minutes

Cooking time: About 30 minutes

Crisp green beans topped with a tomato-lamb sauce and dusted with Parmesan make an especially colorful entrée. Another time, try serving the sauce over steamed asparagus.

1 can (2 oz.) anchovy fillets
2 tablespoons salad oil
1 medium-size onion, minced
1 pound lean ground lamb
1 can (about 14 oz.) pear-shaped tomatoes
¼ pound cooked ham, minced
1 tablespoon drained capers
¼ teaspoon crushed dried hot red chiles
2 pounds green beans, ends removed
⅓ cup grated Parmesan cheese

Drain anchovy fillets. Set 3 fillets aside; mince remaining anchovies and set aside separately.

Place a wok over high heat; when wok is hot, add oil. When oil is hot, add onion and stir-fry until soft (about 3 minutes).

Crumble in lamb; stir-fry until browned (about 5 minutes). Spoon off and discard fat. With scissors, snip tomatoes in can into chunks. Add tomatoes and their liquid, minced anchovies, ham, capers, and chiles to meat mixture. Reduce heat and simmer, uncovered, stirring often, until sauce is almost dry (about 20 minutes).

Meanwhile, immerse beans in 1½ inches boiling water; cover and boil until tender-crisp to bite (5 to 10 minutes). Drain, arrange on a warm platter, and keep warm.

Spoon lamb sauce over beans; sprinkle with cheese and top with whole anchovy fillets. Makes 4 servings.

Per serving: 416 calories, 37 g protein, 20 g carbohydrates, 22 g total fat, 107 mg cholesterol, 939 mg sodium

Quick Lamb Curry

Preparation time: About 10 minutes

Cooking time: About 20 minutes

This is a mild curry, but if you enjoy fiery flavors, you can boost the heat with cayenne pepper. Complement the dish with your choice of condiments—raisins, coconut, peanuts, and more.

1 tablespoon salad oil
1 pound lean ground lamb
2 cloves garlic, minced or pressed
1 large onion, chopped
1 medium-size carrot, thinly sliced
1 small green bell pepper, seeded and cut into ½-inch-wide strips
1 tablespoon curry powder
½ teaspoon *each* ground ginger and ground cumin
1 small apple, peeled, cored, and thinly sliced
1 can (14½ oz.) regular-strength beef broth
Salt and ground red pepper (cayenne)
Condiments (suggestions follow)

Place a wok over medium heat; when wok is hot, add oil. When oil is hot, crumble in lamb and cook, stirring, until meat is browned (about 5 minutes). Spoon off and discard all but 2 tablespoons of the fat. Add garlic, onion, carrot, bell pepper, curry powder, ginger, and cumin; stir-fry until onion is soft (about 4 minutes). Add apple and stir-fry for 1 minute.

Stir in broth and simmer, uncovered, until vegetables are tender when pierced and sauce is slightly thickened (about 10 minutes). Season to taste with salt and red pepper. Serve with condiments of your choice. Makes 4 servings.

Condiments. Choose 3 or 4 of the following: sliced **bananas, chutney, plain yogurt,** chopped **peanuts,** shredded **coconut, raisins.**

Per serving: 226 calories, 23 g protein, 11 g carbohydrates, 8 g total fat, 79 mg cholesterol, 504 mg sodium

Chicken & Turkey

(Pictured on facing page)

Chicken with Black Bean Sauce

Preparation time: About 15 minutes

Marinating time: 15 minutes

Cooking time: About 10 minutes

Depending on your preference, you can make this Cantonese dish with asparagus or bell peppers. Serve with hot rice and garnish with cilantro sprigs, if you like.

> 1 teaspoon *each* cornstarch and soy sauce
> 4 teaspoons water
> 2 teaspoons dry sherry
> 1 whole chicken breast (about 1 lb.), skinned, boned, and cut into bite-size pieces
> 3½ tablespoons salad oil
> Cooking Sauce (recipe follows)
> 1 pound red or green bell peppers or 1 pound asparagus
> 2 teaspoons fermented salted black beans, rinsed, drained, and finely chopped
> 1 large clove garlic, minced
> 1 medium-size onion, cut into wedges, layers separated

In a bowl, stir together cornstarch, soy, 1 teaspoon of the water, and sherry. Add chicken and stir to coat; then stir in 1½ teaspoons of the oil and let marinate for 15 minutes.

Meanwhile, prepare Cooking Sauce; set aside. Seed bell peppers and cut into 1-inch squares. (Or snap off and discard tough ends of asparagus; cut spears into ½-inch slanting slices.)

Place a wok over high heat; when wok is hot, add 2 tablespoons of the oil. When oil begins to heat, add black beans and garlic; stir once. Add chicken mixture and stir-fry until meat is no longer pink in center; cut to test (about 3 minutes). Remove from wok and set aside.

Pour remaining 1 tablespoon oil into wok; when oil is hot, add bell peppers and onion and stir-fry for 1 minute. Add remaining 1 tablespoon water and cook, uncovered, until vegetables are tender-crisp to bite—2 to 4 more minutes. (If using asparagus, add 2 tablespoons water; cook, covered, for 3 to 4 minutes.) Return chicken to wok. Stir Cooking Sauce, pour into wok, and stir until sauce boils and thickens. Makes 2 or 3 servings.

Cooking Sauce. Stir together 1 tablespoon *each* **soy sauce** and **cornstarch,** ¼ teaspoon **sugar,** and ½ cup **regular-strength chicken broth** or water.

Per serving: 320 calories, 25 g protein, 14 g carbohydrates, 18 g total fat, 57 mg cholesterol, 791 mg sodium

Jeweled Chicken

Preparation time: About 15 minutes

Cooking time: About 7 minutes

Fragrant lychees, spicy crystallized ginger, and slices of preserved kumquat bejewel this sweet-sour stir-fry. Look for the fruits in the gourmet or specialty foods section of your supermarket.

> 1 egg white
> Cornstarch
> 2 whole chicken breasts (about 1 lb. *each*), skinned, boned, and cut into ½- by 2-inch strips
> ¼ cup soy sauce
> 1 can (about 20 oz.) lychees
> 2 tablespoons *each* vinegar and sugar
> ¼ cup salad oil
> 1½ tablespoons minced crystallized ginger
> Fresh cilantro (coriander) sprigs
> Sliced kumquats preserved in syrup

In a bowl, beat together egg white and 2 tablespoons cornstarch. Add chicken and stir to coat. Set aside.

In another bowl, gradually blend soy with 1 tablespoon cornstarch. Drain lychees, reserving 6 tablespoons of the syrup; add reserved syrup to soy mixture along with vinegar and sugar.

Place a wok over high heat; when wok is hot, add 2 tablespoons of the oil. When oil is hot, add half the chicken mixture and stir-fry until meat is no longer pink in center; cut to test (about 3 minutes). Remove from wok and set aside. Repeat to cook remaining chicken, adding remaining 2 tablespoons oil.

Return all chicken to wok; blend in ginger, drained lychees, and soy mixture. Stir until sauce boils and thickens. Garnish with cilantro and kumquats. Makes 4 servings.

Per serving: 456 calories, 37 g protein, 43 g carbohydrates, 16 g total fat, 86 mg cholesterol, 1,190 mg sodium

In Chicken with Black Bean Sauce (recipe on facing page),
tender morsels of breast meat contrast with brilliant bell pepper chunks.
Garlic, fermented black beans, and a soy-based sauce contribute to this
Cantonese feast of color and flavor.

Sweet & Sour Chicken in Pineapple Shells

Preparation time: About 30 minutes

Cooking time: About 10 minutes

Pineapple shells make attractive individual serving dishes for hot rice and a stir-fry of chicken, pepper strips, and juicy pineapple chunks.

> 2 **small pineapples (about 3 lbs.** *each***)**
> **Sweet & Sour Sauce (recipe follows)**
> 3 **tablespoons salad oil**
> 1 **clove garlic, minced or pressed**
> 1¾ **pounds chicken breasts, skinned, boned, and cut into ½- by 2-inch strips**
> 1 **medium-size onion, thinly sliced**
> 1 **medium-size green bell pepper, seeded and cut into thin strips**
> **About 4 cups hot cooked rice**
> **Fresh cilantro (coriander) sprigs (optional)**

Cut each pineapple in half lengthwise, cutting through crown. With a curved, serrated knife such as a grapefruit knife, cut fruit from peel, leaving shells intact; turn shells upside down to drain. Trim away core from fruit, then cut fruit into chunks about ½ inch thick. You'll need 3 cups pineapple chunks; reserve any remaining fruit for another use.

Just before cooking, drain the 3 cups pineapple chunks; reserve juice for another use. Also prepare Sweet & Sour Sauce and set aside.

Place a wok over high heat; when wok is hot, add 1 tablespoon of the oil. When oil is hot, add garlic and half the chicken and stir-fry until chicken is no longer pink in center; cut to test (about 3 minutes). Remove from wok and set aside. Repeat to cook remaining chicken, adding 1 tablespoon more oil.

Pour remaining 1 tablespoon oil into wok. When oil is hot, add onion and bell pepper. Stir-fry until vegetables are tender-crisp to bite (about 2 minutes).

Return chicken to wok. Stir Sweet & Sour Sauce; pour into wok along with pineapple. Stir until sauce boils and thickens.

Spoon equal portions of the chicken mixture into each of the 4 pineapple shells, mounding mixture at 1 end of shells. Spoon about 1 cup of the rice alongside chicken in each shell. Garnish with cilantro, if desired. Pour any extra chicken mixture into a serving bowl; offer at the table. Makes 4 servings.

Sweet & Sour Sauce. Stir together 4 teaspoons **cornstarch;** ¼ cup *each* **sugar, wine vinegar,** and **regular-strength chicken broth;** 2 tablespoons minced **fresh cilantro** (coriander) or 1½ teaspoons dry cilantro leaves; 2 tablespoons **catsup;** 1 tablespoon *each* **soy sauce** and **dry sherry;** ½ teaspoon **ground ginger;** and ¼ teaspoon *each* **salt** and **crushed red pepper.**

Per serving: 603 calories, 36 g protein, 85 g carbohydrates, 13 g total fat, 75 mg cholesterol, 634 mg sodium

Hot & Sour Chicken

Preparation time: About 15 minutes

Cooking time: About 10 minutes

Peppery-hot foods are favored in the Chinese province of Hunan—a preference reflected in this spicy dish. Season the sauce with purchased red pepper flakes, if you like, or use crushed whole dried chiles (remove the seeds for a milder flavor).

> **Cooking Sauce (recipe follows)**
> 2 **teaspoons** *each* **cornstarch, dry sherry, and salad oil**
> ¼ **teaspoon pepper**
> 1½ **to 1¾ pounds chicken breasts, skinned, boned, and cut into ¾-inch cubes**
> 2 **to 3 tablespoons salad oil**
> 1 **tablespoon finely chopped garlic**
> 2 **teaspoons finely chopped fresh ginger**
> 1 **tablespoon fermented salted black beans, rinsed, drained, and patted dry**
> 1 **green bell pepper, seeded and cut into 1-inch squares**
> 1 **carrot, thinly sliced**
> 1 **can (about 8 oz.) sliced bamboo shoots, drained**

Prepare Cooking Sauce and set aside. In a bowl, stir together cornstarch, sherry, the 2 teaspoons oil, and pepper. Add chicken and stir to coat.

Place a wok over high heat; when wok is hot, add 2 tablespoons of the oil. When oil is hot, add chicken mixture; stir-fry for 2 minutes. Add 1 tablespoon more oil, if needed; then add garlic, ginger, and black beans. Stir-fry until chicken is lightly browned (about 2 more minutes). Then add bell pepper, carrot, and bamboo shoots; stir-fry for 2 minutes. Stir sauce and add; stir until sauce boils and thickens. Makes 4 servings.

Cooking Sauce. Stir together 2 teaspoons **cornstarch,** ½ teaspoon **crushed dried hot red chiles,** 2 tablespoons **soy sauce,** 2½ tablespoons **white wine vinegar,** and ½ cup **regular-strength chicken broth.**

Per serving: 302 calories, 32 g protein, 9 g carbohydrates, 15 g total fat, 75 mg cholesterol, 843 mg sodium

Chicken Breasts with Papaya & Chutney

Preparation time: About 15 minutes

Cooking time: About 10 minutes

A tangy, chutney-based glaze coats tender chicken and sweet papaya. Present this richly flavored entrée on a bed of hot cooked spinach.

- 3 **tablespoons salad oil**
- ½ **cup sliced almonds**
- 3 **whole chicken breasts (about 1 lb. *each*), skinned, boned, and split**
- 1 **large papaya**
- 1½ **tablespoons lime or lemon juice**
- ½ **cup Major Grey's chutney, finely chopped**
- ½ **cup regular-strength chicken broth**
- 1 **teaspoon cornstarch**
- ½ **teaspoon *each* paprika and ground ginger**
- 2 **tablespoons butter or margarine**
  White pepper
  Hot cooked spinach

Place a wok over medium heat; when wok is hot, add 1 tablespoon of the oil. When oil is hot, add almonds and stir until golden (about 2 minutes). Remove from wok and set aside.

Rinse chicken and pat dry. Cut each breast half across the grain into ½-inch-wide strips; set aside.

Peel and halve papaya; remove seeds. Cut each papaya half lengthwise into quarters, then cut each piece in half crosswise. Place in a bowl, add lime juice, and stir until fruit is coated. In another bowl, stir together chutney, broth, cornstarch, paprika, and ginger.

Place wok over medium-high heat. When wok is hot, add 1 tablespoon *each* of the butter and oil. When butter is melted, add half the chicken and stir-fry until meat is no longer pink in center; cut to test (about 3 minutes). Remove from wok and set aside. Repeat to cook remaining chicken, adding remaining 1 tablespoon *each* butter and oil. Return all chicken to wok.

Stir chutney mixture and add to chicken. Bring to a boil and stir until thickened (about 2 minutes). Add papaya and stir gently just until fruit is glazed and heated through. Season to taste with white pepper.

To serve, spoon chicken mixture over spinach; sprinkle with almonds. Makes 6 servings.

Per serving: 388 calories, 36 g protein, 23 g carbohydrates, 17 g total fat, 96 mg cholesterol, 267 mg sodium

Watercress Chicken with Mushrooms

Preparation time: About 15 minutes

Cooking time: About 15 minutes

Vivid fresh watercress, mushrooms, and chunks of chicken breast combine in this simple stir-fry. For extra taste and texture, add a few teaspoons of toasted sesame seeds.

- ½ **pound watercress**
  Cooking Sauce (recipe follows)
- 2 **whole chicken breasts (about 1 lb. *each*), skinned, boned, and cut into 1-inch chunks**
- 2 **cloves garlic, minced or pressed**
- ¼ **teaspoon *each* pepper and ground ginger**
- 2 **to 3 teaspoons sesame seeds (optional)**
- 5 **tablespoons salad oil**
- ½ **pound mushrooms, sliced**

Pluck watercress leaves from stems and lightly pack in a measuring cup. Coarsely chop thinnest stems and add to leaves; discard thick stems. You should have about 4 cups lightly packed watercress.

Prepare Cooking Sauce and set aside. Sprinkle chicken chunks evenly with garlic, pepper, and ginger; set aside.

Place a wok over medium heat. When wok is hot, add sesame seeds (if used) and stir until golden (about 2 minutes); pour out of wok and set aside.

Increase heat to high; pour 2 tablespoons of the oil into wok. When oil is hot, add half the chicken and stir-fry until no longer pink in center; cut to test (about 3 minutes). Remove chicken from wok and set aside. Repeat to cook remaining chicken, using 1 tablespoon more oil.

Pour remaining 2 tablespoons oil into wok. When oil is hot, add mushrooms and stir-fry for about 3 minutes. Add watercress and toasted sesame seeds (if used); stir-fry for about 30 seconds.

Add chicken; stir Cooking Sauce and add. Stir until sauce boils and thickens. Makes 3 or 4 servings.

Cooking Sauce. Stir together 1 teaspoon *each* **cornstarch** and firmly packed **brown sugar,** 1 tablespoon **dry sherry,** and 2½ tablespoons **soy sauce.**

Per serving: 351 calories, 38 g protein, 7 g carbohydrates, 19 g total fat, 86 mg cholesterol, 764 mg sodium

Once wok and ingredients are ready, it takes just minutes
to produce tantalizing Chicken & Snow Peas (recipe on facing page).
Crisp, emerald green pea pods share the spotlight with velvety
mushrooms and juicy chicken.

42

(Pictured on facing page)

Chicken & Snow Peas

Preparation time: About 20 minutes, plus 30 minutes to soak mushrooms

Marinating time: About 15 minutes

Cooking time: About 10 minutes

Use either thin, flat Chinese pea pods (often sold as snow or sugar peas) or the thicker, crisper sugar snap peas in this classic Cantonese dish.

- **4 dried Oriental mushrooms**
- **2 teaspoons** *each* **soy sauce, cornstarch, dry sherry, and water**
  Dash of white pepper
- **1½ pounds chicken breasts, skinned, boned, and cut into bite-size pieces**
- **3½ tablespoons salad oil**
  Cooking Sauce (recipe follows)
- **1 small clove garlic, minced or pressed**
- **½ cup sliced bamboo shoots**
- **¼ pound Chinese pea pods (also called snow or sugar peas) or sugar snap peas, ends and strings removed; or 1 package (6 oz.) frozen Chinese pea pods, thawed and drained**

Soak mushrooms in warm water to cover for 30 minutes, then drain. Cut off and discard stems; squeeze caps dry, thinly slice, and set aside.

In a bowl, mix soy, cornstarch, sherry, water, and white pepper. Add chicken and stir to coat, then stir in 1½ teaspoons of the oil. Let marinate for 15 minutes. Prepare Cooking Sauce; set aside.

Place a wok over high heat; when wok is hot, add 1 tablespoon of the oil. When oil begins to heat, add garlic and stir once. Add half the chicken mixture and stir-fry until meat is no longer pink in center; cut to test (about 3 minutes). Remove chicken from wok and set aside. Repeat to cook remaining chicken, adding 1 tablespoon more oil.

Pour remaining 1 tablespoon oil into wok. When oil is hot, add mushrooms and bamboo shoots. Stir-fry for 1 minute, adding a few drops of water if wok appears dry. Add pea pods and stir-fry for 3 minutes (30 seconds if using frozen pea pods), adding a few drops more water if wok appears dry. Return chicken to wok. Stir Cooking Sauce, pour into wok, and stir until sauce boils and thickens. Makes 3 or 4 servings.

Cooking Sauce. Stir together ½ cup **water,** 1 tablespoon **dry sherry,** 2 tablespoons **oyster sauce** or soy sauce, ¼ teaspoon **sugar,** 1 teaspoon **sesame oil,** and 1 tablespoon **cornstarch.**

Per serving: 294 calories, 28 g protein, 12 g carbohydrates, 15 g total fat, 65 mg cholesterol, 604 mg sodium

Almond Chicken

Follow directions for **Chicken & Snow Peas,** but first place wok over medium heat; when wok is hot, add 1 tablespoon **salad oil.** When oil is hot, add ½ cup **blanched almonds** and stir until golden (about 2 minutes); remove from wok and set aside. Stir in almonds just before serving.

Fruited Chicken Stir-fry

Preparation time: About 15 minutes

Cooking time: About 15 minutes

Slices of plum compete for attention with the chicken and vegetables in this tempting dish. The sweet-sour sauce is a bit out of the ordinary; it's based on peach nectar and lemon juice rather than the usual pineapple juice and vinegar.

- **Cooking Sauce (recipe follows)**
- **3 medium-size firm-ripe Santa Rosa-type plums**
- **3 to 4 tablespoons salad oil**
- **2 teaspoons minced fresh ginger**
- **2 whole chicken breasts (about 1 lb.** *each***), skinned, boned, and cut into ½- by 2-inch strips**
- **1 large green bell pepper, seeded and cut into 1-inch squares**
- **1 medium-size onion, cut into 1-inch cubes**

Prepare Cooking Sauce and set aside. Halve and pit plums; cut each half into ½-inch-thick wedges. Set aside.

Place a wok over high heat; when wok is hot, add 2 tablespoons of the oil. When oil is hot, add ginger and half the chicken. Stir-fry until meat is no longer pink in center; cut to test (about 3 minutes). Remove from wok and set aside. Repeat to cook remaining chicken, adding 1 tablespoon more oil if needed.

Pour remaining 1 tablespoon oil into wok. When oil is hot, add bell pepper and onion and stir-fry until tender-crisp to bite (about 4 minutes). Remove from wok. Add plums; stir-fry until softened (about 2 minutes). Stir sauce, pour into wok, and stir until boiling. Add chicken, bell pepper, and onion; stir until hot. Makes 4 servings.

Cooking Sauce. Stir together 1 cup **peach nectar,** ¼ cup **lemon juice,** 1 tablespoon **cornstarch,** 2 tablespoons **soy sauce,** and ½ teaspoon *each* **dry mustard** and crushed **anise seeds.**

Per serving: 345 calories, 36 g protein, 22 g carbohydrates, 13 g total fat, 86 mg cholesterol, 619 mg sodium

Chicken Pocket Sandwiches

Preparation time: About 10 minutes

Cooking time: About 15 minutes

A garlicky mixture of diced chicken breast, anchovies, and ripe olives makes a delicious stuffing for pocket breads—or for hollowed-out crusty rolls, if you like.

- 1 to 2 tablespoons salad oil
- 1 to 2 tablespoons butter or margarine
- 2 cloves garlic, minced or pressed
- ¼ to ½ teaspoon crushed red pepper
- 2 whole chicken breasts (about 1 lb. *each*), skinned, boned, and cut into ½-inch chunks
- 3 tablespoons *each* chopped parsley and drained, chopped capers
- 3 or 4 anchovy fillets, finely chopped
- 1 can (2¼ oz.) sliced ripe olives, drained
- ½ cup dry red wine
  Salt and black pepper
- 4 pocket breads, halved crosswise

Place a wok over medium-high heat. When wok is hot, add 1 tablespoon *each* of the oil and butter. When butter is melted, add garlic, red pepper, and half the chicken. Stir-fry until chicken is no longer pink in center; cut to test (about 3 minutes). Remove from wok and set aside; repeat to cook remaining chicken, adding more oil and butter as needed.

Return all chicken to wok. Stir in parsley, capers, anchovies, olives, and wine. Cook, stirring occasionally, until almost all liquid has evaporated (about 5 minutes). Season to taste with salt and black pepper.

Fill each bread half with an eighth of the chicken mixture. Makes about 4 servings.

Per serving: 434 calories, 41 g protein, 38 g carbohydrates, 12 g total fat, 96 mg cholesterol, 808 mg sodium

Kung Pao Chicken

Preparation time: About 10 minutes

Marinating time: 15 minutes

Cooking time: About 10 minutes

If you're fond of Chinese food and fiery flavors, you're almost certain to enjoy this Szechwan specialty. Chinese chefs often leave the charred whole chiles in the dish, but you can remove them if you prefer.

- 1 tablespoon *each* dry sherry and cornstarch
- ½ teaspoon salt
- ⅛ teaspoon white pepper
- 1½ pounds chicken breasts, skinned, boned, and cut into ½-inch chunks
- ¼ cup salad oil
  Cooking Sauce (recipe follows)
- 4 to 6 small dried hot red chiles
- ½ cup salted peanuts
- 1 teaspoon *each* minced garlic and grated fresh ginger
- 2 green onions (including tops), cut into 1½-inch lengths

In a bowl, stir together sherry, cornstarch, salt, and white pepper. Add chicken and stir to coat, then stir in 1 tablespoon of the oil and let marinate for 15 minutes. Meanwhile, prepare Cooking Sauce and set aside.

Place a wok over medium heat; when wok is hot, add 1 tablespoon of the oil. When oil is hot, add chiles and peanuts and stir until chiles just begin to char. (If chiles become completely black, discard them. Remove peanuts from wok and set aside; repeat with new oil and chiles.) Remove peanuts and chiles from wok; set aside.

Pour 1 tablespoon more oil into wok and increase heat to high. When oil begins to heat, add garlic and ginger and stir once, then add half the chicken mixture. Stir-fry until meat is no longer pink in center; cut to test (about 3 minutes). Remove from wok and set aside. Repeat to cook remaining chicken, adding remaining 1 tablespoon oil.

Return all chicken to wok; add peanuts, chiles, and onions. Stir Cooking Sauce and pour into wok; stir until sauce boils and thickens. Makes 4 servings.

Cooking Sauce. Stir together 2 tablespoons **soy sauce**, 1 tablespoon *each* **white wine vinegar** and **dry sherry**, 3 tablespoons **regular-strength chicken broth** or water, and 2 tablespoons *each* **sugar** and **cornstarch**.

Per serving: 425 calories, 32 g protein, 21 g carbohydrates, 25 g total fat, 65 mg cholesterol, 1,069 mg sodium

Chicken with Eggplant

Preparation time: About 15 minutes

Cooking time: About 20 minutes

The strips of chicken and eggplant are mild—but the sauce is spicy with dried chiles and grated fresh ginger. For even hotter flavor, add a few extra chiles.

1 medium-size eggplant (¾ to 1 lb.), cut into ¾- by 3-inch strips
Boiling water

1 tablespoon cornstarch

2 tablespoons soy sauce

1 to 1¼ pounds chicken breasts or thighs, skinned, boned, and cut into ½- by 2-inch strips

6 tablespoons salad oil

1 or 2 small dried hot red chiles, split in half and seeded

1 clove garlic, minced or pressed

1 teaspoon grated fresh ginger or ½ teaspoon ground ginger

¼ cup water

1 can (about 8 oz.) water chestnuts, drained and sliced

3 tablespoons regular-strength chicken broth or water

1 tablespoon dry sherry
Sliced green onions (including tops) or chopped parsley (optional)

Place eggplant in a bowl and pour boiling water over it to cover. Let stand for about 7 minutes; then drain and pat dry.

In another bowl, stir together cornstarch and soy; add chicken and stir to coat. Set aside.

Place a wok over high heat; when wok is hot, add ¼ cup of the oil. When oil is hot, add chiles. When chiles begin to brown, remove them from wok with a wire skimmer and discard them. Add garlic, ginger, eggplant, and 2 tablespoons of the water to wok; stir-fry for about 2 minutes. Add remaining 2 tablespoons water, cover, and cook, stirring frequently, until eggplant is tender when pierced (about 10 minutes). Remove from wok.

Pour remaining 2 tablespoons oil into wok; when oil is hot, add chicken mixture and water chestnuts. Stir-fry until meat is no longer pink in center; cut to test (about 3 to 5 minutes). Add broth, sherry, and eggplant mixture; cook for about 1 minute. Sprinkle with onions, if desired. Makes about 3 servings.

Per serving: 387 calories, 31 g protein, 21 g carbohydrates, 20 g total fat, 71 mg cholesterol, 856 mg sodium

Thai Chicken & Basil Stir-fry

Preparation time: 10 to 15 minutes, plus 30 minutes to soak mushrooms

Cooking time: About 15 minutes

An unusual combination of coconut milk, aromatic fish sauce, and fresh basil enhances chicken strips and succulent mushrooms. When you buy fish sauce, look for the Thai variety, labeled *nam pla;* the Vietnamese version, *nuoc mam,* is somewhat stronger-tasting.

6 dried Oriental mushrooms, *each* 2 to 3 inches in diameter
Cooking Sauce (recipe follows)

2 to 3 tablespoons salad oil

1 medium-size onion, thinly sliced

3 cloves garlic, minced or pressed

2 tablespoons minced fresh ginger

2 pounds chicken breasts, skinned, boned, and cut into ¼-inch-wide strips

1½ cups lightly packed slivered fresh basil leaves

5 green onions (including tops), cut into 1-inch lengths

Soak mushrooms in warm water to cover for 30 minutes, then drain. Cut off and discard stems; squeeze caps dry, cut into ¼-inch slivers, and set aside.

Prepare Cooking Sauce and set aside.

Place a wok over high heat; when wok is hot, add 2 tablespoons of the oil. When oil is hot, add sliced onion, garlic, and ginger; stir-fry until onion is soft (about 4 minutes). Remove vegetables from wok and set aside.

Add half the chicken to wok and stir-fry until meat is tinged with brown (about 3 minutes). Remove from wok; set aside with cooked onion mixture. Repeat to brown remaining chicken, adding 1 tablespoon more oil if needed.

Pour Cooking Sauce into wok and boil until reduced by a third. Return onion mixture and chicken to wok. Add basil, mushrooms, and green onions; stir to heat through. Makes 4 or 5 servings.

Cooking Sauce. Stir together ¾ cup **canned or thawed frozen coconut milk,** 3 tablespoons *each* **soy sauce** and **rice wine vinegar,** 1½ tablespoons **fish sauce** (*nam pla*) or soy sauce, and ½ to 1 teaspoon **crushed dried hot red chiles.**

Per serving: 321 calories, 31 g protein, 12 g carbohydrates, 17 g total fat, 68 mg cholesterol, 1,011 mg sodium

(Pictured on facing page)

Minced Chicken in Lettuce

Preparation time: About 15 minutes, plus 30 minutes to soak
mushrooms

Marinating time: 15 minutes

Cooking time: About 10 minutes

For an informal meal, serve minced chicken, mushrooms, bamboo shoots, and water chestnuts to wrap
in chilled lettuce leaves and eat out of hand. Because
there's not much sauce in the chicken mixture—just
enough to hold the ingredients together—the lettuce
stays crisp.

 8 medium-size dried Oriental mushrooms
 1 teaspoon *each* cornstarch and soy sauce
 2 teaspoons *each* dry sherry and water
 ½ teaspoon salt
   Dash of white pepper
 1½ pounds chicken breasts, skinned,
   boned, and minced
 ¼ cup salad oil
   Cooking Sauce (recipe follows)
 1 teaspoon minced fresh ginger
 2 cloves garlic, minced
 2 green onions (white part only), minced
 1 can (about 8 oz.) sliced bamboo shoots,
   drained and minced
 1 can (about 8 oz.) water chestnuts,
   drained and minced
   Hoisin sauce
   About 30 iceberg lettuce leaves, chilled

Soak mushrooms in warm water to cover for 30 minutes, then drain. Cut off and discard stems; squeeze
caps dry, mince, and set aside.

In a bowl, stir together cornstarch, soy, sherry,
water, salt, and white pepper. Add chicken and
stir to coat, then stir in 1½ teaspoons of the oil and
let marinate for 15 minutes. Meanwhile, prepare
Cooking Sauce and set aside.

Place a wok over high heat; when wok is hot,
add 2 tablespoons of the oil. When oil is hot, add
chicken and stir-fry until no longer pink (about 3
minutes). Remove from wok and set aside.

Pour remaining 1½ tablespoons oil into wok.
When oil begins to heat, add ginger, garlic, and
onions and stir once. Then add mushrooms, bamboo
shoots, and water chestnuts and stir-fry for 2 minutes. Return chicken to wok. Stir Cooking Sauce,
pour into wok, and stir until sauce boils and
thickens.

To eat, spread a little hoisin on a lettuce leaf,
top with some of the hot chicken mixture, and fold

lettuce to enclose; eat out of hand. Makes 4 to 6
servings.

Cooking Sauce. Stir together 1 teaspoon **soy sauce,**
1 tablespoon **dry sherry,** 2 tablespoons *each* **oyster
sauce** and **water,** 1 teaspoon **sesame oil,** ½ teaspoon
sugar, and 2 teaspoons **cornstarch.**

*Per serving: 225 calories, 19 g protein, 13 g carbohydrates, 11 g total fat,
43 mg cholesterol, 601 mg sodium*

Many-spice Chicken

Preparation time: About 10 minutes

Cooking time: About 5 minutes

The distinctive flavor of this stir-fry comes from anise-
flavored liqueur and a seasoning blend of eight dried
herbs and spices. The liqueur is readily available in
liquor stores; you'll find it sold under several names,
including *ouzo* and *pastis* (avoid the syrupy cordial
anisette). If you don't enjoy the licoricelike taste of
anise, use dry sherry in place of liqueur; you'll end
up with an equally good—though different—dish.

 ¼ cup salad oil
 2 tablespoons anise-flavored liqueur or
   dry sherry
 2 tablespoons minced fresh ginger
 1 teaspoon *each* minced garlic and soy
   sauce
 3 tablespoons thinly sliced green onions
   (including tops)
 ¼ teaspoon *each* dry mustard, chili powder,
   pepper, dry oregano leaves, dry sage
   leaves, dry thyme leaves, ground cloves,
   and ground cinnamon
 ¼ teaspoon *each* salt, sugar, and all-
   purpose flour
 1 whole chicken breast (about 1 lb.),
   skinned, boned, and cut into bite-size
   pieces
   Chopped parsley

In a small bowl, stir together 2 tablespoons of the oil,
liqueur, ginger, garlic, soy, onions, mustard, chili
powder, pepper, oregano, sage, thyme, cloves,
cinnamon, salt, sugar, and flour. Set aside.

Place a wok over high heat; when wok is hot,
add remaining 2 tablespoons oil. When oil is hot,
add chicken and stir-fry until meat is no longer pink
in center; cut to test (about 3 minutes). Add liqueur
mixture and stir constantly until mixture boils and
thickens (about 1 minute). Sprinkle with parsley.
Makes 2 servings.

*Per serving: 479 calories, 35 g protein, 9 g carbohydrates, 29 g total fat,
86 mg cholesterol, 543 mg sodium*

Spread a little hoisin sauce on a crisp lettuce leaf, add a topping of hot,
savory chicken and vegetables—then wrap up and eat out of hand.
Egg rolls and grapes are good-tasting accompaniments for Minced Chicken
in Lettuce (recipe on facing page).

Chicken with Two-tone Pears

Preparation time: About 15 minutes

Cooking time: About 15 minutes

Slices of golden- and red-skinned pears add an especially handsome touch to this dish. If you can't find red pears, just use two yellow ones—but in any case, look for richly fragrant fruit with flesh that's tender but still slightly firm to the touch.

Cooking Sauce (recipe follows)

3 tablespoons **salad oil**

2 cloves **garlic**, minced or pressed

2 **whole chicken breasts** (about 1 lb. *each*), skinned, boned, and cut into bite-size pieces

2 stalks **celery**, thinly sliced

3 **green onions** (including tops), cut into 2-inch lengths

1 can (about 8 oz.) sliced **bamboo shoots**, drained

¼ pound **Chinese pea pods** (also called snow or sugar peas) or sugar snap peas, ends and strings removed; or 1 package (6 oz.) frozen Chinese pea pods, thawed and drained

1 *each* small red and yellow **pear**, quartered, cored, and cut into ½-inch-thick slices

Salt

½ cup salted roasted **cashews**

Prepare Cooking Sauce and set aside.

Place a wok over high heat; when wok is hot, add 1 tablespoon of the oil. When oil is hot, add garlic and half the chicken. Stir-fry until chicken is no longer pink in center; cut to test (about 3 minutes). Remove from wok and set aside. Repeat to cook remaining chicken, adding 1 tablespoon more oil.

Pour remaining 1 tablespoon oil into wok. When oil is hot, add celery, onions, and bamboo shoots; stir-fry for about 1 minute. Add pea pods and stir-fry for 3 minutes (30 seconds if using frozen pea pods), adding a few drops of water if wok appears dry. Add pears and chicken; stir Cooking Sauce and add. Stir until sauce boils and thickens. Season to taste with salt; garnish with cashews. Makes 6 servings.

Cooking Sauce. Stir together 4 teaspoons **cornstarch**, 1 teaspoon **sugar**, 2 teaspoons minced **fresh ginger**, 2 tablespoons *each* **soy sauce** and **dry sherry**, and ¾ cup **regular-strength chicken broth**.

Per serving: 297 calories, 27 g protein, 17 g carbohydrates, 14 g total fat, 57 mg cholesterol, 616 mg sodium

Chicken & Garlic Stir-fry

Preparation time: About 45 minutes

Chilling time for pickles: At least 1 day

Cooking time: About 5 minutes

Pickled garlic or shallots add sparkle to this dish. You'll need to make the pickles at least a day in advance (or up to 2 months ahead, if you like), but actual cooking time is extra-short—just 5 minutes.

Our pickle recipe yields 3 cups—more than you'll need for this stir-fry. Try using leftover pickles in salads; the liquid is good in dressings.

⅓ cup **Garlic or Shallot Pickles** (recipe follows), drained

Cooking Sauce (recipe follows)

2 tablespoons **salad oil**

1 **whole chicken breast** (about 1 lb.), skinned, boned, and cut into ¼- by 3-inch strips

4 **green onions** (including tops), cut into 2-inch lengths

At least 1 day ahead, prepare Garlic or Shallot Pickles and refrigerate.

Prepare Cooking Sauce and set aside.

Place a wok over high heat; when wok is hot, add oil. When oil is hot, add chicken and stir-fry until lightly browned (about 2 minutes). Add onions; then stir Cooking Sauce and add. Continue to stir until sauce boils and thickens. Stir in pickles. Serve immediately. Makes 3 servings.

Garlic or Shallot Pickles. Peel 3 cups (about 1 lb.) **garlic** cloves or small shallots. Cut any garlic cloves or shallots that are thicker than ¾ inch in half lengthwise.

In a 2- to 3-quart pan, combine 1½ cups **distilled white vinegar**, ⅓ cup **sugar**, and ½ teaspoon **salt**.

Bring to a boil over high heat, stirring until sugar is dissolved. Drop garlic into boiling vinegar mixture and cook, uncovered, stirring occasionally, for 1 minute. Let cool.

Place pickles and their liquid in a jar, cover tightly, and refrigerate for at least 1 day or for up to 2 months. Makes about 3 cups.

Cooking Sauce. Stir together ½ cup **regular-strength chicken broth,** 2 teaspoons **cornstarch,** and 1 table-spoon *each* **soy sauce** and **liquid from garlic pickles.**

Per serving: 324 calories, 27 g protein, 32 g carbohydrates, 11 g total fat, 57 mg cholesterol, 236 mg sodium

Cashew Chicken

Preparation time: About 15 minutes

Cooking time: About 8 minutes

Cashew chicken is adaptable—you can use peanuts, almonds, or walnut halves in place of the cashews, or substitute another favorite vegetable for the bell pepper.

      Cooking Sauce (recipe follows)
1 tablespoon soy sauce
1 teaspoon cornstarch
1 whole chicken breast (about 1 lb.), skinned, boned, and cut into bite-size pieces
3 tablespoons salad oil
½ cup salted roasted cashews
1 medium-size green bell pepper, seeded and cut into 1-inch squares
1 medium-size onion, cut into 8 wedges, layers separated
½ teaspoon finely minced fresh ginger or ¼ teaspoon ground ginger

Prepare Cooking Sauce and set aside. In a bowl, stir together soy and cornstarch; add chicken and stir to coat. Set aside.

Place a wok over medium-high heat; when wok is hot, add 2 tablespoons of the oil. When oil is hot, add cashews and stir until browned (about 1 minute). Remove with a slotted spoon and set aside. Add chicken mixture and stir-fry until meat is no longer pink in center; cut to test (about 3 minutes). Remove from wok and set aside.

Pour remaining 1 tablespoon oil into wok; when oil is hot, add bell pepper, onion, and ginger and stir-fry until pepper is tender-crisp to bite (about 4 minutes). Return chicken to wok. Stir Cooking Sauce and pour into wok; stir until sauce boils and thickens. Stir in cashews. Makes 2 servings.

Cooking Sauce. Stir together ½ teaspoon **cornstarch,** a dash of **liquid hot pepper seasoning,** ¾ teaspoon *each* **sugar** and **white wine vinegar,** 1 teaspoon **dry sherry** or water, and 1 tablespoon **soy sauce.**

Per serving: 579 calories, 42 g protein, 19 g carbohydrates, 38 g total fat, 86 mg cholesterol, 1,335 mg sodium

Coq au Vin Sauté

Preparation time: About 15 minutes

Cooking time: About 25 minutes

Here's a quick and easy adaptation of a classic French dish. The robust sauce is flavored with red wine and Dijon mustard.

1 tablespoon salad oil
⅓ pound lean boneless pork (such as shoulder or butt), trimmed of excess fat and cut into ½-inch cubes
2 whole chicken breasts (about 1 lb. *each*), skinned, boned, and cut into ½- by 2-inch strips
1 large onion, finely chopped
½ pound small mushrooms, thinly sliced
1 can (14½ oz.) regular-strength chicken broth
1 cup dry red wine
2 tablespoons Dijon mustard
1 teaspoon *each* cornstarch and water, stirred together
2 tablespoons chopped parsley

Place a wok over medium-high heat; when wok is hot, add oil. When oil is hot, add pork and stir-fry until well browned (about 7 minutes). Lift out meat and set aside; leave drippings in wok.

Add half the chicken to wok. Stir-fry until meat is no longer pink in center; cut to test (3 to 4 minutes). Remove from wok and set aside. Repeat to cook remaining chicken.

Increase heat to high. Add onion and mushrooms; stir-fry until onion is soft (about 3 minutes). Remove vegetables from wok and set aside. Pour broth into wok, bring to a boil, and boil until reduced to 1 cup. Stir in wine and mustard and bring to a boil. Add pork, reduce heat, and simmer for 5 minutes.

Return chicken and vegetables to wok along with cornstarch-water mixture. Bring to a boil, stirring until slightly thickened. Sprinkle with parsley. Makes about 4 servings.

Per serving: 314 calories, 44 g protein, 9 g carbohydrates, 11 g total fat, 111 mg cholesterol, 806 mg sodium

A rosemary sprig tops robust Italian-inspired Chicken in
Tomato Sauce (recipe on facing page). This speedy version of classic
chicken *cacciatore* can be ready in just half an hour. If you like,
serve it atop low-calorie zucchini instead of pasta.

(Pictured on facing page)
Chicken in Tomato Sauce

Preparation time: About 15 minutes

Cooking time: About 30 minutes

Cut into 2-inch chunks, chicken cooks quickly in a rich, brandied tomato sauce. Serve on a bed of zucchini sticks (just follow directions for Zucchini Sticks on page 99, cutting zucchini into noodle-thin strips).

To make easy work of cutting the chicken, use a well-sharpened heavy knife or cleaver.

- 1 frying chicken (3 to 3½ lbs.), cut up
- 2 tablespoons salad oil
  Salt and pepper
- 2 tablespoons brandy
- 1 small onion, finely chopped
- ¼ pound mushrooms, sliced
- 1 fresh rosemary sprig (2 to 3 inches long) or 1 teaspoon dry rosemary
- 1 tablespoon all-purpose flour
- ½ cup dry white wine
- 1 can (about 14 oz.) pear-shaped tomatoes
  Fresh rosemary sprigs (optional)

Pull off and discard all visible fat from chicken pieces, then rinse chicken and pat dry. With a heavy knife or cleaver, cut each chicken piece through bones into 2-inch lengths.

Place a wok over medium-high heat; when wok is hot, add oil. When oil is hot, add thickest dark-meat pieces of chicken and cook, turning, until browned on both sides (about 5 minutes). Add remaining chicken. Continue to cook, turning, until pieces are well browned on both sides and meat near thighbone is no longer pink; cut to test (about 15 more minutes). Season to taste with salt and pepper.

Add brandy; when liquid bubbles, carefully ignite (not beneath an exhaust fan or near flammable items), then shake wok until flames die down. Lift out chicken pieces. Spoon off and discard all but about 1 tablespoon of the drippings.

Add onion, mushrooms, and 1 rosemary sprig (or 1 teaspoon dry rosemary) to drippings in wok; stir-fry until onion is soft (about 4 minutes). Sprinkle in flour and stir until golden. Blend in wine and bring to a boil. Add tomatoes (break up with a spoon) and their liquid; bring to a simmer. Return chicken to wok and stir gently just until heated through. Garnish with rosemary, if desired. Makes 4 servings.

Per serving: 518 calories, 50 g protein, 8 g carbohydrates, 31 g total fat, 154 mg cholesterol, 308 mg sodium

Cuban Chicken

Preparation time: About 15 minutes

Cooking time: About 1 hour

Raisins, olives, and chopped peppers join chicken pieces and potato chunks in this colorful stew. You may accompany chicken and sauce with Orange-scented Rice and a crisp salad.

- 1 frying chicken (3 to 3½ lbs.), cut up
- 2 tablespoons salad oil
- 2 cloves garlic, minced or pressed
- 1 large onion, chopped
- 1 large green bell pepper, seeded and chopped
- 4 small thin-skinned potatoes, cut into 1-inch chunks
- ¾ teaspoon *each* dry oregano leaves and ground cumin
- 1 can (15 oz.) tomato sauce
- ⅓ cup dry white wine
- ½ cup *each* raisins and pitted ripe olives
  Orange-scented Rice (recipe follows), optional
- 1 cup frozen peas, thawed and drained

Rinse chicken and pat dry. Place a wok over medium-high heat; when wok is hot, add oil. When oil is hot, add half the chicken pieces; cook, turning, until browned on all sides (about 15 minutes). Remove from wok and set aside. Repeat to brown remaining chicken. Spoon off and discard all but 2 tablespoons of the drippings.

Add garlic, onion, and bell pepper to drippings in wok. Stir-fry until onion is soft (about 4 minutes). Add potatoes, oregano, cumin, tomato sauce, wine, raisins, olives, and chicken. Bring to a boil. Then reduce heat, cover, and simmer, turning chicken once, until meat near thighbone is no longer pink; cut to test (about 35 minutes). Meanwhile, prepare Orange-scented Rice and keep warm.

Skim and discard fat from chicken stew, then stir in peas and cook just until hot. Accompany chicken and sauce with Orange-scented Rice, if desired. Makes about 4 servings.

Orange-scented Rice. In a 2-quart pan, combine 1 cup *each* **regular-strength chicken broth** and **fresh orange juice;** stir in grated **peel of 1 orange.** Bring to a boil; add 1 cup **long-grain white rice,** stir once, and reduce heat to low. Cover and simmer until liquid is absorbed (about 20 minutes).

Per serving: 727 calories, 55 g protein, 51 g carbohydrates, 35 g total fat, 154 mg cholesterol, 965 mg sodium

Garlic Celebration Chicken

Preparation time: About 20 minutes

Cooking time: About 1¼ hours

Simmered in white wine and vermouth and seasoned with basil and plenty of garlic, this hearty entrée is a good choice for a cool-weather meal. Wedges of ripe tomato make a pretty, fresh-tasting garnish.

    1 frying chicken (3 to 3½ lbs.), cut up
    4 slices bacon, chopped
    2 medium-size onions, chopped
    5 cloves garlic, minced or pressed
    1 cup dry white wine
    ¼ cup dry vermouth or dry white wine
    1 tablespoon dry basil
    1 teaspoon poultry seasoning
      Salt and pepper
    1 tablespoon *each* cornstarch and water,
      stirred together
    2 medium-size tomatoes, cut into wedges

Rinse chicken and pat dry; set aside.

Place a wok over medium-high heat; when wok is hot, add bacon and stir-fry until crisp (about 2 minutes). Lift out bacon with a slotted spoon, leaving drippings in wok; drain bacon and set aside.

Add half the chicken to wok; cook, turning, until browned on all sides (about 15 minutes). Remove from wok and set aside. Repeat to brown remaining chicken.

Add onions and garlic to wok and stir-fry until onions are soft (about 4 minutes). Spoon off and discard any fat from wok; add wine, vermouth, basil, poultry seasoning, bacon, and chicken pieces. Bring

to a boil over high heat. Then reduce heat, cover, and simmer, turning once, until meat near thighbone is no longer pink; cut to test (about 35 minutes).

Arrange chicken on a platter; keep warm. Skim and discard fat from pan juices, then season to taste with salt and pepper. Stir cornstarch-water mixture into pan juices; continue to stir until sauce is thickened. Garnish chicken with tomatoes; pass sauce at the table. Makes about 4 servings.

Per serving: 505 calories, 51 g protein, 12 g carbohydrates, 27 g total fat, 159 mg cholesterol, 256 mg sodium

Indian Pan-roasted Chicken

Preparation time: About 10 minutes

Cooking time: About 35 minutes

Despite the name, this handsome, spice-fragrant whole chicken isn't really roasted; it's braised in a broth seasoned with cumin, cardamom, cinnamon, and pepper. Garnish the bird with juicy orange slices and sprigs of fresh cilantro.

      Seasoned Broth (recipe follows)
    1 frying chicken (3 to 3½ lbs.)
      Pepper
    3 tablespoons salad oil
    2 dry bay leaves
    1 cinnamon stick (about 3 inches long)
    6 whole cloves
    5 whole black peppercorns
    3 cloves garlic, minced or pressed
      Orange slices
      Fresh cilantro (coriander) sprigs

Prepare Seasoned Broth and set aside.

Remove chicken neck and giblets; reserve for other uses, if desired. Remove and discard skin from entire chicken; pull off and discard lumps of fat. Rinse chicken inside and out, pat dry, and sprinkle lightly with pepper. Tie ends of drumsticks together.

Place a wok over medium-high heat; when wok is hot, add oil. When oil is hot, add bay leaves, cinnamon stick, cloves, and peppercorns; then add chicken and cook, uncovered, turning occasionally with long-handled tongs, until browned on all sides (about 10 minutes). Stir in Seasoned Broth and garlic; bring to a boil. Then reduce heat, cover, and simmer, turning chicken occasionally, until meat near thighbone is no longer pink; cut to test (20 to 25 more minutes).

Transfer chicken to a serving dish. Skim and discard any fat from pan juices; pour juices over chicken. Garnish with orange slices and cilantro. Makes about 4 servings.

Seasoned Broth. In a bowl, combine 1 cup **regular-strength chicken broth**, 2 teaspoons *each* **soy sauce** and **Worcestershire**, 1 teaspoon **ground cumin**, ¼ teaspoon **ground red pepper** (cayenne), and ⅛ teaspoon **ground cardamom**.

Per serving: 530 calories, 49 g protein, 3 g carbohydrates, 35 g total fat, 154 mg cholesterol, 596 mg sodium

Turkey Chili

Preparation time: About 15 minutes

Cooking time: About 45 minutes

An alternative to traditional beef chili is this version made with chunks of turkey. At the table, offer lime wedges, cheese, chopped tomato, and green onions to embellish individual servings.

- 2 **tablespoons salad oil**
- 1 **onion, chopped**
- 1 **small green bell pepper, seeded and chopped**
- 1 **clove garlic, minced or pressed**
- 1½ **pounds turkey breast, skinned, boned, and cut into bite-size chunks**
- 1 **small can (about 8 oz.) tomatoes, drained and chopped**
- 2 **cans (about 15 oz. *each*) kidney beans, drained**
- 1 **can (15 oz.) tomato sauce**
- 2 **tablespoons soy sauce**
- 1½ **tablespoons chili powder**
- ½ **teaspoon *each* ground cumin, dry sage leaves, and dry thyme leaves**
   Garnishes (suggestions follow)

Place a wok over medium-high heat; when wok is hot, add oil. When oil is hot, add onion, bell pepper, and garlic; stir-fry until onion is soft (about 4 minutes). Remove from wok and set aside.

Increase heat to high. Add half the turkey and stir-fry until no longer pink in center; cut to test (about 3 minutes). Remove from wok and set aside. Repeat to cook remaining turkey.

Return all turkey and vegetables to wok. Then add tomatoes, beans, tomato sauce, soy, chili powder, cumin, sage, and thyme. Bring to a boil; reduce heat, cover, and simmer until chili is thick and flavors are well blended (about 30 minutes; uncover for last 5 minutes).

To serve, ladle hot chili into bowls; offer garnishes to embellish individual servings. Makes 4 servings.

Garnishes. Offer **lime wedges**, sliced **green onions** (including tops), shredded **jack or Cheddar cheese**, and chopped **tomatoes**.

Per serving: 476 calories, 47 g protein, 50 g carbohydrates, 11 g total fat, 84 mg cholesterol, 2,074 mg sodium

Turkey & Green Bean Stir-fry

Preparation time: About 15 minutes

Cooking time: About 15 minutes

Readily available turkey breast is a nice alternative to chicken in stir-fry dishes; though not as velvety-textured as chicken, it's every bit as tasty. This easy-to-prepare dish features turkey with fresh green beans and celery; if you like, offer toasted almonds or sesame seeds to sprinkle on top.

   Cooking Sauce (recipe follows)
- 1 **egg white**
- 2 **tablespoons soy sauce**
- 2 **pounds turkey breast, skinned, boned, and cut into ¼- by 2-inch strips**
- ¼ **cup salad oil**
- ½ **pound green beans (ends removed), cut into 2-inch pieces**
- ½ **cup thinly sliced celery**
- ½ **cup thinly sliced onion, separated into rings**
- 6 **tablespoons water or dry sherry**
- 1 **or 2 cloves garlic, minced or pressed**

Prepare Cooking Sauce; set aside.

In a bowl, beat together egg white and soy; add turkey and stir to coat. Set aside. Place a wok over high heat; when wok is hot, add 2 tablespoons of the oil. When oil is hot, add beans, celery, and onion; stir-fry for about 1 minute, then add water. Cover and cook, stirring occasionally, until beans are tender-crisp to bite (about 4 minutes).

Remove vegetables from wok, then add remaining 2 tablespoons oil. When oil is hot, add garlic and half the turkey. Stir-fry until meat is no longer pink in center; cut to test (about 3 minutes). Remove from wok. Repeat to cook remaining turkey; return all turkey to wok along with green bean mixture. Stir Cooking Sauce, pour into wok, and stir until sauce boils and thickens. Makes 4 servings.

Cooking Sauce. Mix 1 tablespoon *each* **cornstarch** and **soy sauce**, 2 tablespoons **dry sherry**, ½ teaspoon **ground ginger**, and ½ cup **water**.

Per serving: 376 calories, 45 g protein, 10 g carbohydrates, 17 g total fat, 111 mg cholesterol, 922 mg sodium

Fish & Shellfish

(Pictured on facing page)

Sweet & Sour Fish

Preparation time: About 15 minutes

Cooking time: 12 minutes

Sweet-sour sauce is just as good with fish as it is with pork or chicken. Here, the familiar red sauce enhances a combination of bell pepper squares, tomato, and chunks of turbot or halibut.

- Sweet-Sour Sauce (recipe follows)
- About ⅓ cup cornstarch
- 2 pounds turbot or halibut fillets, cut into ½-inch squares
- About 6 tablespoons salad oil
- 1 clove garlic, minced or pressed
- 1 onion, cut into 1-inch cubes
- 1 medium-size green bell pepper, seeded and cut into ½-inch thick strips
- 1 medium-size tomato, cut into 1-inch cubes
- Fresh cilantro (coriander) or Italian parsley (optional)

Prepare Sweet-Sour Sauce and set aside.

Place cornstarch in a bag, add fish pieces, and shake to coat completely; shake off excess.

Place a wok over medium-high heat; when wok is hot, add 2 tablespoons of the oil. When oil is hot, add some of the fish; stir-fry until fish is browned on all sides and flakes when prodded (about 2 minutes). Remove from wok and keep warm. Repeat to cook remaining fish, adding about 2 tablespoons more oil.

Increase heat to high and pour 2 tablespoons more oil into wok. When oil is hot, add garlic, onion, and bell pepper; stir-fry for 2 minutes. Stir Sweet-Sour Sauce; pour into wok and stir in tomato. Bring to a boil, stirring. Return fish and any accumulated juices to wok; stir to combine. Garnish with cilantro, if desired. Makes 4 servings.

Sweet-Sour Sauce. Stir together 1 tablespoon **cornstarch** and ¼ cup **sugar.** Stir in 2 tablespoons *each* **soy sauce** and **catsup,** ¼ cup **distilled white vinegar,** and ½ cup **regular-strength chicken broth.**

Per serving: 736 calories, 35 g protein, 31 g carbohydrates, 52 g total fat, 104 mg cholesterol, 915 mg sodium

Lemony Fish with Asparagus

Preparation time: About 10 minutes

Cooking time: About 5 minutes

Bright green asparagus and delicate white-fleshed fish are flavored with fresh lemon in this simple and speedy entrée.

- 1 pound asparagus
- 2 teaspoons *each* cornstarch, lemon juice, and salad oil
- ¾ pound orange roughy, sea bass, or halibut fillets, *each* about ½ inch thick, cut into 1- by 3-inch strips
- 3 tablespoons salad oil
- 1 large clove garlic, minced or pressed
- 2 tablespoons regular-strength chicken broth or water
- 2 tablespoons lemon juice

Snap off and discard tough ends of asparagus; cut spears into ½-inch slanting slices. Set aside.

In a bowl, stir together cornstarch, the 2 teaspoons lemon juice, and the 2 teaspoons oil. Add fish and stir gently until evenly coated.

Place a wok over medium-high heat; when wok is hot, add 2 tablespoons of the oil. When oil is hot, add fish and stir-fry until opaque (about 2 minutes); remove fish from wok and set aside.

Pour remaining 1 tablespoon oil into wok. When oil begins to heat, add garlic and stir-fry for about 30 seconds. Then add asparagus and stir-fry for 1 minute. Stir together broth and the 2 tablespoons lemon juice; pour into wok, cover, and cook, stirring often, until asparagus is tender-crisp to bite (2 to 3 more minutes). Return fish and any accumulated juices to wok and stir just until heated through. Makes 3 or 4 servings.

Per serving: 199 calories, 16 g protein, 4 g carbohydrates, 13 g total fat, 40 mg cholesterol, 294 mg sodium

Lemony Fish with Fennel

Follow directions for **Lemony Fish with Asparagus,** but substitute 1 large **fennel** bulb for asparagus. To prepare fennel, trim off and discard stalks, reserving a few of the feathery leaves for garnish. Cut away and discard base; cut bulb in half lengthwise, then thinly slice crosswise. (Fennel may need to cook for a few more minutes than asparagus.) Garnish dish with reserved fennel leaves.

Ready in minutes from your wok, Sweet & Sour Fish
(recipe on facing page) is a seafood lover's symphony of contrasts.
Nuggets of fish, onion, green pepper, and tomato
harmonize in a tangy sauce.

Charcoal Cooking

When the barbecue season arrives, don't overlook your wok, whether you plan to cook at the beach or on the patio. The wok's shape makes it a practical choice for charcoal cooking: the curved bowl rests easily in a barbecue. (You can also use your wok on a camp stove, if you like.)

Presented here are two great outdoor meals, both easily made in a wok. Adventurous guests who enjoy getting involved in the cooking will appreciate the Mongolian Barbecue; the Patio Paella is a little more traditional from a Western standpoint, but no less adventurous in flavor.

Patio Paella

You'll need a two-handled wok to make this colorful dish, since a one-handled wok won't nest into a barbecue. (If you like, you may also prepare the dish on a camp stove, using either a one- or two-handled wok. Follow the directions given here, cooking over high heat until you add the seafood; then reduce heat to low and cover the wok with its lid.)

> **Bell Pepper Sauce (recipe follows)**
> ¾ **pound linguisa sausage, cut into ½-inch-thick slanting slices**
> 1½ **pounds chicken thighs, cut in half along bone**
> 2½ **cups short-grain rice (such as pearl)**
> ½ **teaspoon ground turmeric**
> ¼ **teaspoon ground saffron or ½ teaspoon saffron threads**
> 6 **cups regular-strength chicken broth**

> 1½ **pounds firm-textured white-fleshed fish (cut into 1-inch chunks), tenderized giant squid (calamari) steaks (cut into ¼-inch strips), or medium-size raw shrimp (shelled and deveined); or some of each**
> **Shellfish (choices follow)**
> 1 **package (10 oz.) frozen tiny peas**
> 2 **lemons, *each* cut into 6 wedges**

Prepare Bell Pepper Sauce and set aside.

Mound and ignite 50 charcoal briquets on fire grate of a barbecue (at least 22 inches wide) with lid; open dampers. When coals are lightly covered with gray ash (about 30 minutes), push them out to form a circle just large enough to accommodate a metal ring stand in the center. To maintain heat, scatter 12 more briquets over coals; also scatter 12 more briquets over coals at 30-minute intervals throughout remainder of cooking time until directed otherwise.

Set a 2-handled 14- to 16-inch wok on stand.

Add linguisa to wok; with tongs or a long-handled slotted spoon, stir frequently until meat is browned on all sides (about 1 minute), pushing sausage slices up sides of wok where wok is hottest. Transfer sausage to a plate, leaving drippings in wok.

Add chicken to wok; turn to coat in drippings, then push up onto wok sides. Turn frequently until golden brown (10 to 15 minutes). Transfer to plate with sausage.

Add Bell Pepper Sauce to wok; stir frequently until pepper softens. Add rice, turmeric, and saffron; cook, stirring frequently, until rice begins to turn opaque (about 10 minutes). Add broth and cook, stirring often, for 10 minutes.

Lay chicken, sausage (and any accumulated juices), fish, and shellfish on rice. Scatter peas over top. (From this point on, add no more briquets.) Cover barbecue and close dampers; cook until rice is tender to bite and clams (if used) pop open (about 20 minutes). Remove lid. If coals are almost extinguished, push as far from wok as possible. If coals are still hot, lift wok and stand from barbecue and set on a counter to serve. Offer lemon wedges. Makes 6 to 8 servings.

Bell Pepper Sauce. Mix ¼ cup chopped **onion;** 1 small **green bell pepper,** seeded and cut into ¼-inch-wide strips; 1 large ripe **tomato,** seeded and diced; and 1 small clove **garlic,** minced or pressed.

Shellfish. Purchase 2½ pounds *total* of 1 kind or combine any of the following.

- *Spiny lobster.* Buy cooked tails or whole lobster. Rinse shells. Twist tail off whole lobster, reserving head section to use for decoration. With scissors, snip out underside shell of tail. Pull meat free, cut into ½-inch pieces, and return to shell.

- *Dungeness crab.* Buy cooked crab in the shell, cleaned and cracked.

- *Small live hard-shell clams or mussels.* Scrub shells under running water; pull off mussel beards.

Mongolian Barbecue

If you're serving a group of 12 to 16, cooking will go more quickly with two or three cooking stations (consider borrowing an extra barbecue or two).

- **3 to 5 seasoning sauces (choices and recipes follow)**
- **3 or 4 meat, poultry, or seafood selections (choices follow)**
- **6 to 8 vegetables (choices follow)**
  Salad oil
- **24 to 36 spring roll wrappers or 8 to 12 cups hot cooked rice**

Up to 2 days ahead, prepare seasoning sauces; cover and refrigerate. Up to a day ahead, prepare meats and vegetables; cover and refrigerate.

About 45 minutes before serving, mound and ignite enough charcoal briquets on fire grate of each barbecue you're using to make a solid bed of hot coals to fit underneath wok. Set cooking grill in place 2 to 4 inches above coals; set wok on cooking grill.

While coals are heating, arrange meat and vegetables on platters or baskets and set them out alongside bowls of seasoning sauce. Place a small pitcher of oil, a wide spatula, and a potholder at each cooking station.

Also heat spring roll wrappers: separate wrappers, fold into quarters, and wrap in a clean towel. Place on a rack in a pan about 1 inch above simmering water. Cover and steam until hot (about 5 minutes). To keep warm, leave wrappers on rack over simmering water in an electric wok, or wrap in a thick cloth napkin and transfer to a basket.

Let each guest fill a plate with a selection of meats, vegetables, and sauces, drizzle hot wok with about 2 tablespoons oil, and add the plateful of food. Stir-fry until meat is lightly browned and vegetables are tender-crisp to bite (2 to 3 minutes). Use spatula to scoop food from wok to plate. To eat, wrap foods in a warm spring roll wrapper (or eat with rice). If pan becomes thickly coated with juices, pour in a little water and swish it around with a brush; then discard water and continue cooking. Makes 12 to 16 servings.

Meat, poultry, or seafood selections. Use 3 or 4 of the following: 1 pound **lean boneless beef steak** (such as top round, flank, or sirloin), trimmed of excess fat and cut across the grain into 1⁄8-inch-thick, 3-inch-long slanting slices; 1 pound **lamb shoulder chops,** trimmed of excess fat and bone, then cut across the grain into 1⁄8-inch-thick, 3-inch-long slanting slices; 1 pound **Chinese barbecued pork** or unseasoned cooked pork, cut into 1⁄8- by 3-inch strips; 2 pounds **chicken breasts,** skinned, boned, and cut into 1⁄4- by 3-inch strips; 1 pound **large raw shrimp** (shelled and deveined, if desired).

Vegetables. Choose 6 to 8 of the following: 1 pound **spinach,** tough stems and yellow or wilted leaves removed and green leaves rinsed well; 1 pound **bok choy,** leaves and stems cut into 1⁄2-inch slanting slices; 1 pound **napa cabbage,** cut crosswise into 1⁄2-inch-wide strips; 2 large **onions,** thinly sliced; 1⁄2 pound **Chinese long beans** or green beans, cut into 3-inch lengths; 1⁄2 pound **bean sprouts;** 1⁄2 pound **lotus root,** peeled and thinly sliced (to preserve color, keep immersed in water until shortly before serving, then drain well); 1⁄2 pound **fresh shiitake or button mushrooms,** thinly sliced; 1⁄2 pound **mustard greens,** leaves and stems cut crosswise into 1⁄2-inch-wide strips; 1⁄2 pound **zucchini** or fresh loofa gourd (Chinese okra), cut into 1⁄2-inch slanting slices; 1⁄2 pound **Japanese or regular eggplant,** cut into 1⁄4-inch-thick, 2-inch-wide slices; 1⁄2 pound **Chinese bitter melon,** seeds and white pith removed and melon cut into 1⁄8-inch-thick slices.

Seasoning sauces. Choose 3 to 5 of the following. All sauces can be made up to 2 days ahead and stored, covered, in the refrigerator. Before using, bring to room temperature and stir well.

- *Mustard Sauce.* Stir together 1⁄4 cup **dry mustard,** 3 tablespoons **water,** 3 tablespoons **honey,** 1 tablespoon **vinegar,** and 1⁄8 teaspoon **ground turmeric.**

- *Singapore Hot Sauce.* Stir together 1⁄4 cup **crunchy peanut butter;** 1⁄3 cup **vinegar;** 3 tablespoons *each* **soy sauce** and minced **garlic;** 2 tablespoons minced **green onion** (including top); 2 tablespoons **sesame oil** or salad oil; 1 tablespoon *each* minced **fresh ginger** and **dry sherry;** 1 teaspoon **sugar;** and 1⁄2 to 1 teaspoon **crushed dried hot red chiles.** Stir in 1⁄2 cup **regular-strength chicken broth.**

- *Teriyaki Sauce.* Stir together 1 cup **soy sauce,** 1⁄2 cup **honey,** 2 teaspoons minced **fresh ginger,** and 5 cloves **garlic,** minced or pressed.

- *Sweet & Sour Sauce.* Stir together 1 cup **unsweetened pineapple juice;** 1⁄4 cup *each* **sugar,** minced **crystallized ginger,** and **cider vinegar;** 2 tablespoons **soy sauce;** and 3⁄4 cup **canned plum sauce** (or fruit chutney whirled in a blender until smooth).

- *Garlic Miso Sauce.* Stir together 1⁄4 cup **miso** (fermented soybean paste), 3 tablespoons **sake** or dry sherry, 1 tablespoon **honey,** 1 tablespoon **sesame oil** or salad oil, and 4 cloves **garlic,** thinly sliced.

Because squid toughens if heated too long, Chinese
chefs traditionally score it to hasten cooking. The crosshatching shows in
Squid & Pea Stir-fry (recipe on facing page), here served atop individual
cakes of Pan-fried Noodles.

Lime & Chile Monkfish with Corn

Preparation time: About 10 minutes

Cooking time: 10 minutes

Often called "poor man's lobster," monkfish is valued for its delicate flavor and lean, firm flesh.

Monkfish fillets are encased in a tough membrane; you can have the membrane removed at the fish market or do the job yourself, using a sharp knife.

Lime-Chile Sauce (recipe follows)
1½ pounds monkfish fillets
3 tablespoons salad oil
1 cup fresh corn cut from cob or 1 cup frozen whole-kernel corn, thawed and drained
2 tablespoons chopped fresh cilantro (coriander)

Prepare Lime-Chile Sauce; set aside.

Remove and discard membrane from fish. Rinse fish and pat dry, then cut into 1-inch chunks. Place a wok over high heat; when wok is hot, add 2 tablespoons of the oil. When oil is hot, add half the fish; stir-fry until fish flakes when prodded (about 2 minutes). Remove from wok and set aside. Repeat to cook remaining fish, adding remaining 1 tablespoon oil.

Pour Lime-Chile Sauce into wok and bring to a boil, stirring constantly. Add corn and stir until heated through (2 to 3 minutes). Return fish and any accumulated juices to wok; mix gently to heat. Pour onto a warm platter and sprinkle with cilantro. Makes 4 servings.

Lime-Chile Sauce. Stir together ⅓ cup **lime juice;** 3 tablespoons **regular-strength chicken broth;** 1 clove **garlic,** minced or pressed; 1 **small fresh Fresno or jalapeño chile,** minced; ½ teaspoon *each* **ground cumin, pepper,** and **sugar;** and 1 teaspoon **cornstarch.**

Per serving: 268 calories, 26 g protein, 11 g carbohydrates, 13 g total fat, 43 mg cholesterol, 88 mg sodium

Teriyaki Monkfish

Follow directions for **Lime & Chile Monkfish with Corn,** but omit Lime-Chile Sauce. Instead, use this teriyaki sauce: stir together ¼ cup **regular-strength chicken or beef broth,** 2 tablespoons *each* **dry sherry** and **soy sauce,** 2 teaspoons **sugar,** and 1 teaspoon **cornstarch.** Also omit corn; instead, use 1 cup **cooked fresh shelled peas** or 1 cup frozen peas, thawed and drained.

(Pictured on facing page)

Squid & Pea Stir-fry

Preparation time: About 30 minutes

Cooking time: 7 minutes

Its flavor is sweet and delicate—but squid quickly toughens if it's cooked too long. To eliminate the risk of overcooking, start by scoring the squid.

Pan-fried Noodles (recipe follows)
1 pound squid
2 tablespoons salad oil
½ teaspoon minced fresh ginger
1 cup shelled peas (about 1 lb. unshelled)
½ cup regular-strength chicken broth
1 teaspoon soy sauce
1 tablespoon oyster sauce
¼ teaspoon sugar
2 teaspoons cornstarch and 1 tablespoon water, stirred together

Prepare Pan-fried Noodles and keep warm.

To clean each squid, gently pull on body to separate it from hood. Then pull out and discard long, clear quill from hood. Scoop out and discard contents of hood; rinse out hood. Set aside.

With a sharp knife, sever body between eyes and tentacles. Discard eyes and attached material. Pop out and discard hard black beak in center of tentacles. Rinse and drain tentacles; pat dry and set aside.

Pull off and discard thin, speckled membrane from hood; rinse and drain hood. Slit hood lengthwise and open flat. Make ½-inch-wide diagonal cuts across inside of hood. Repeat in opposite direction. Cut scored hood in about 2-inch-square pieces.

Place a wok over medium-high heat; when wok is hot, add 1 tablespoon of the oil. When oil begins to heat, add ginger; stir once. Add squid; stir-fry until edges curl (1½ to 2 minutes). Remove from wok.

Pour remaining 1 tablespoon oil into wok. When oil is hot, add peas and stir-fry for 1 minute. Add broth, soy, oyster sauce, and sugar; bring to a boil and boil for 1 minute. Stir cornstarch-water mixture; pour into wok and stir until sauce boils and thickens. Return squid to wok, stir, and serve at once, over Pan-fried Noodles. Makes 3 or 4 servings.

Pan-fried Noodles. Heat 2 tablespoons **salad oil** in a frying pan over medium-high heat. Spread 8 ounces **Chinese wheat flour noodles,** cooked and drained, in pan in a layer 1 inch thick. Cook until brown on bottom. Turn noodles over in 1 piece; add 1 tablespoon more **salad oil** and cook until browned on other side. Serve whole or in wedges.

Per serving: 473 calories, 27 g protein, 49 g carbohydrates, 19 g total fat, 49 mg cholesterol, 458 mg sodium

Squid & Vegetable Stir-fry

Preparation time: About 35 minutes

Cooking time: 10 minutes

Quick stir-frying makes the squid in this savory vegetable mélange as tender as it's tasty. Garlic, ginger, and beef broth give the dish its robust flavor.

Cooking Sauce (recipe follows)
1 pound squid
3 tablespoons salad oil
2 cloves garlic, minced or pressed
2 teaspoons finely minced fresh ginger
1 medium-size onion, thinly sliced
¼ pound mushrooms, sliced
1 cup sliced celery
1 green bell pepper, seeded and thinly sliced

Prepare Cooking Sauce and set aside. Clean squid as directed for Squid & Pea Stir-fry (page 59). Slit squid hoods in half lengthwise, then cut crosswise into ¾-inch-wide strips. Leave tentacles whole or cut each into 2 or 3 pieces.

Place a wok over high heat; when wok is hot, add 2 tablespoons of the oil. When oil is hot, add garlic, ginger, and onion and stir-fry for 1 minute. Add mushrooms and stir-fry until mushrooms are soft (about 3 minutes). Remove mixture from wok and set aside.

Pour remaining 1 tablespoon oil into wok. When oil is hot, add squid and stir-fry until edges of hood pieces curl (1½ to 2 minutes). Add celery and bell pepper and stir-fry for 2 more minutes. Return mushroom mixture to wok; stir Cooking Sauce and add. Stir until sauce boils and thickens. Makes 4 servings.

Cooking Sauce. Stir together 1½ tablespoons **cornstarch**, 2 tablespoons **soy sauce**, 1 teaspoon *each* **sugar** and **vinegar**, and ½ cup **regular-strength beef broth**.

Per serving: 213 calories, 17 g protein, 11 g carbohydrates, 11 g total fat, 49 mg cholesterol, 596 mg sodium

Sautéed Oysters with Basil

Preparation time: About 10 minutes

Cooking time: 5 minutes

Made with just five ingredients, this dish could hardly be simpler or quicker. You just brown oysters in butter with a little chopped basil, then make a speedy sauce by stirring white wine into the pan juices.

½ pound shucked fresh oysters, drained
All-purpose flour
2 tablespoons butter or margarine
1 tablespoon chopped fresh basil or ½ teaspoon dry basil
2 tablespoons dry white wine

Cut any large oysters into bite-size pieces. Pat oysters dry with paper towels; dredge in flour and shake off excess. Place a wok over medium-high heat; when wok is hot, add butter. When butter is melted, add oysters and sprinkle with basil. Stir-fry until oysters are golden brown (about 3 minutes), then transfer to a serving dish.

Add wine to wok and cook until sauce is reduced to 1 tablespoon. Spoon sauce over oysters. Makes 2 servings.

Per serving: 209 calories, 9 g protein, 11 g carbohydrates, 14 g total fat, 115 mg cholesterol, 201 mg sodium

Gingered Oysters

Preparation time: About 10 minutes

Marinating time: 10 minutes

Cooking time: 5 minutes

Fresh ginger and a sprinkling of Chinese five-spice add a distinctive accent to plump stir-fried oysters. When purchasing fresh ginger, look for firm, unblemished roots with unwrinkled skin; pare off the khaki-colored peel before you slice the root.

10 ounces shucked fresh oysters, drained
⅛ teaspoon Chinese five-spice
1½ teaspoons cornstarch
4 teaspoons soy sauce
1½ tablespoons *each* dry sherry and water
10 green onions (including tops)
2 tablespoons salad oil
4 thin, dime-size slices fresh ginger

Cut any large oysters into bite-size pieces. In a bowl, stir together five-spice and 1 teaspoon *each* of the cornstarch and soy. Add oysters and stir to coat; let marinate for 10 minutes. Meanwhile, in another bowl, blend remaining ½ teaspoon cornstarch, remaining 1 tablespoon soy, sherry, and water; set aside. Also cut onions in half lengthwise, then cut crosswise into 1½-inch lengths.

Place a wok over medium-high heat; when wok is hot, add 1 tablespoon of the oil. When oil begins to heat, add ginger and stir-fry for 10 seconds; then add onions and stir-fry for 30 seconds. Remove ginger and onions from wok.

Reduce heat to medium. Pour remaining 1 tablespoon oil into wok. When oil is hot, add oysters and stir-fry until slightly firm (about 2 minutes). Return ginger and onions to wok. Stir cornstarch-sherry mixture; pour into wok and stir until sauce boils and thickens. Remove ginger, if desired. Makes 2 or 3 servings.

Per serving: 172 calories, 8 g protein, 9 g carbohydrates, 11 g total fat, 71 mg cholesterol, 530 mg sodium

Lobster Cantonese

Preparation time: About 15 minutes

Cooking time: 10 minutes

If you see "lobster sauce" on the menu in a Chinese restaurant, chances are it's something like the cooking sauce used in this dish. Though it doesn't contain lobster (it's just a mixture of broth, soy, sherry, and a little cornstarch and white pepper), it's traditionally used with lobster. The same sauce enhances other shellfish, too; try it with crab, scallops, or shrimp.

Cooking Sauce (recipe follows)
1½ **pounds raw lobster tails (thawed if frozen)**
3 **tablespoons salad oil**
2 **tablespoons fermented salted black beans, rinsed, drained, and finely chopped**
2 **cloves garlic, finely chopped**
1 **teaspoon minced fresh ginger**
¼ **pound lean boneless pork (such as shoulder or butt), trimmed of excess fat and finely chopped or ground**
1 **green onion (including top), thinly sliced**
1 **egg, lightly beaten**

Prepare Cooking Sauce and set aside. If you want to cook lobster in the shell, trim side fins; then cut tails in half lengthwise and devein. Cut large pieces in half crosswise. If you prefer to cook lobster out of the shell, remove meat from shell and cut into bite-size pieces.

Place a wok over high heat; when wok is hot, add oil. When oil begins to heat, add black beans, garlic, and ginger; stir once. Then add pork and stir-fry until no longer pink (about 2 minutes).

Add lobster and stir-fry until shells turn red or until shelled meat is opaque throughout; cut to test (3 to 4 minutes). Stir Cooking Sauce, add to wok, and stir until sauce boils and thickens. Add onion and egg; stir just until egg begins to set (about 30 seconds). Makes 3 or 4 servings.

Cooking Sauce. Stir together 1 tablespoon *each* **cornstarch, soy sauce,** and **dry sherry;** ½ cup **regular-strength chicken broth;** and a dash of **white pepper.**

Per serving: 297 calories, 29 g protein, 5 g carbohydrates, 17 g total fat, 184 mg cholesterol, 901 mg sodium

Crab Cantonese

Follow directions for **Lobster Cantonese,** but use 1 large **cooked crab in shell** (1½ to 2 lbs.), cleaned and cracked, in place of lobster. Cut body into quarters; leave legs and claws whole. Cook crab until heated through (3 to 4 minutes).

Shrimp Cantonese

Follow directions for **Lobster Cantonese,** but use 1 pound **medium-size raw shrimp** in place of lobster. Cut through backs of shells with scissors and devein, or remove shells and devein. Cook shrimp until they turn pink (about 3 minutes).

Scallops Cantonese

Follow directions for **Lobster Cantonese,** but use 1 pound **scallops** (thawed if frozen) in place of lobster. Rinse scallops and pat dry, then cut into ¼-inch-thick slices. Cook scallops just until opaque throughout; cut to test (about 3 minutes).

Crab in Black Bean Sauce

Preparation time: About 15 minutes

Cooking time: 5 minutes

If you cook crab in its shell, the meat stays especially succulent—and the preparation time stays brief. Like our Crab Curry (at right), this is finger food; it's a good choice for an informal meal.

> 1 **large cooked crab in shell (1½ to 2 lbs.), cleaned and cracked**
> 2 **tablespoons salad oil**
> 1½ **tablespoons fermented salted black beans, rinsed, drained, and finely chopped**
> 1 **large clove garlic, minced or pressed**
> ¾ **teaspoon minced fresh ginger**
> 1 **green bell pepper, seeded and cut into 1-inch squares**
> 1 **tablespoon *each* soy sauce and dry sherry**
> 2 **green onions (including tops), cut into 1-inch lengths**
> ⅓ **cup regular-strength chicken broth**

Cut crab body into quarters; leave legs and claws whole. Set aside.

Place a wok over high heat; when wok is hot, add oil. When oil begins to heat, add black beans, garlic, and ginger and stir once. Add bell pepper and stir-fry for 1 minute. Add crab, soy, sherry, onions, and broth; stir until crab is heated through (about 3 minutes). Makes 2 servings.

Per serving: 328 calories, 22 g protein, 7 g carbohydrates, 24 g total fat, 114 mg cholesterol, 1,248 mg sodium

Crab in Tomato-Garlic Sauce

Follow directions for **Crab in Black Bean Sauce,** but increase garlic to 3 cloves and omit black beans and ginger. Add 2 large **tomatoes,** peeled, seeded, and chopped, along with bell pepper. Omit soy, sherry, and broth; instead, use ½ cup **dry white wine.**

Crab in Cream Sauce

Follow directions for **Crab in Black Bean Sauce,** using 1 tablespoon minced **shallots** and 1 **red bell pepper,** seeded and cut into 1-inch squares, in place of the black beans, ginger, and green bell pepper. Substitute ¼ cup **whipping cream,** 2 tablespoon **dry white wine,** 1 teaspoon **Dijon mustard,** and 1 tablespoon chopped **parsley** for the soy, sherry, green onions, and broth.

(Pictured on facing page)

Crab Curry

Preparation time: About 15 minutes

Cooking time: 10 minutes

This mild Cantonese curry of crab and vegetables is appealing to the eye and fun to eat, too. Finger food can be messy, though, so pass a basket of damp cloths around the table at the end of the meal.

> **Cooking Sauce (recipe follows)**
> 1 **teaspoon *each* salt and sugar**
> 4 **teaspoons curry powder**
> ¼ **pound lean boneless pork (such as shoulder or butt), trimmed of excess fat and finely chopped or ground**
> 1 **large cooked crab in shell (1½ to 2 lbs.), cleaned and cracked**
> 3 **tablespoons salad oil**
> 1 **large clove garlic, minced**
> 1 **medium-size onion, cut into wedges, layers separated**
> 1 **medium-size green bell pepper, seeded and cut into 1-inch squares**
> 1 **egg, lightly beaten**

Prepare Cooking Sauce and set aside. Sprinkle salt, sugar, and curry powder over pork; mix well and set aside. Cut crab body into quarters; leave legs and claws whole. Set crab aside.

Place a wok over high heat. When wok is hot, add oil. When oil begins to heat, add garlic and stir once; then add seasoned pork and stir-fry until no longer pink (about 2 minutes). Add onion and bell pepper and stir-fry for 1 minute. Add crab and stir often until heated through (about 3 minutes). Stir Cooking Sauce, pour into wok, and stir until sauce boils and thickens. Add egg; stir just until egg begins to set (about 30 seconds). Makes 3 or 4 servings.

Cooking Sauce. Stir together ¾ cup **regular-strength chicken broth** and 1 tablespoon *each* **cornstarch, soy sauce,** and **dry sherry.**

Per serving: 252 calories, 18 g protein, 8 g carbohydrates, 16 g total fat, 145 mg cholesterol, 1,155 mg sodium

Shrimp Curry

Follow directions for **Crab Curry,** but use 1 pound **medium-size raw shrimp,** shelled and deveined, in place of crab. Stir-fry shrimp until they turn pink (about 3 minutes).

Use fingers—not forks or chopsticks—to enjoy Crab Curry
(recipe on facing page). Once you get started, it's hard to stop until
the last bite of this Cantonese specialty has disappeared! Pass around a
basket of hot, damp cloths after the meal.

Hot & Sour Shrimp

Preparation time: About 20 minutes

Cooking time: About 10 minutes

The pungent power of garlic and ginger comes through in this piquant shrimp and vegetable dish. Though it's a Szechwan recipe, it's not overwhelmingly spicy; if you want it hotter, increase the quantity of crushed red pepper.

- 1 pound medium-size raw shrimp, shelled and deveined
- 1 tablespoon dry sherry
  Cooking Sauce (recipe follows)
- 3 tablespoons salad oil
- 3 cloves garlic, minced or pressed
- 1½ tablespoons minced fresh ginger
- ¼ teaspoon crushed red pepper
- 2 large stalks celery, cut into ½-inch-thick slices
- ½ cup sliced bamboo shoots
- 2 green onions (including tops), thinly sliced

In a bowl, toss shrimp with sherry. Prepare Cooking Sauce and set aside.

Place a wok over high heat; when wok is hot, add 1½ tablespoons of the oil. When oil begins to heat, add garlic, ginger, and red pepper; stir once. Then add shrimp and stir-fry until shrimp turn pink (about 3 minutes). Remove from wok and set aside.

Pour remaining 1½ tablespoons oil into wok. When oil is hot, add celery and bamboo shoots and stir-fry for 1 minute. Stir Cooking Sauce, then pour into wok. Stir in shrimp and onions. Stir until sauce boils and thickens. Makes 3 or 4 servings.

Cooking Sauce. Stir together ¼ cup **distilled white vinegar,** 2 tablespoons **soy sauce,** 5 teaspoons **sugar,** and 2 teaspoons **cornstarch.**

Per serving: 236 calories, 21 g protein, 12 g carbohydrates, 12 g total fat, 131 mg cholesterol, 731 mg sodium

Shrimp & Cucumber Stir-fry

Preparation time: About 15 minutes

Cooking time: About 10 minutes

A winning combination of textures and tastes—crunchy cucumbers, succulent shrimp, and lively seasonings—makes this dish a standout.

   Cooking Sauce (recipe follows)
- 2 large cucumbers, peeled
- 3 tablespoons salad oil
- 2 tablespoons minced fresh ginger
- 1 clove garlic, minced or pressed
- ¼ cup minced green onions (including tops)
- 1 pound medium-size raw shrimp, shelled and deveined
  Salt

Prepare Cooking Sauce and set aside.

Cut cucumbers in half lengthwise; scrape out and discard seeds. Cut each cucumber half crosswise into ¼-inch-thick slices.

Place a wok over high heat; when wok is hot, add 1 tablespoon of the oil. When oil is hot, add cucumbers and 1 tablespoon of the ginger; stir-fry until cucumbers are tender-crisp to bite (about 3 minutes). Pour onto a platter and keep warm.

Pour remaining 2 tablespoons oil into wok; when oil is hot, add garlic, remaining 1 tablespoon ginger, onions, and shrimp. Stir-fry until shrimp turn pink (about 3 minutes). Stir Cooking Sauce, pour into wok, and stir until sauce boils and thickens. Season to taste with salt, then pour over cucumbers. Makes 3 or 4 servings.

Cooking Sauce. Stir together 3 tablespoons **dry sherry** or regular-strength chicken broth, 2 tablespoons **distilled white vinegar,** 1½ tablespoons **soy sauce,** 1 teaspoon **cornstarch,** and ½ teaspoon **sugar.**

Per serving: 224 calories, 21 g protein, 9 g carbohydrates, 12 g total fat, 131 mg cholesterol, 588 mg sodium

Shrimp Flambé

Preparation time: About 20 minutes

Cooking time: About 10 minutes

The assertive flavors of curry, paprika, garlic, and brandy blend beautifully in a rich-tasting sauce for shrimp. If you have an electric wok, you can flame the entrée right at the table.

2 tablespoons butter or margarine
2 cloves garlic, minced or pressed
1½ teaspoons curry powder
½ teaspoon paprika
⅓ cup thinly sliced green onions (including tops)
2 tablespoons finely chopped fresh cilantro (coriander)
1 pound medium-size raw shrimp, shelled, deveined, and butterflied
2 tablespoons *each* purchased teriyaki sauce and water
2 tablespoons brandy
3 or 4 slices French bread, toasted and buttered

Place a wok over medium heat; when wok is hot, add butter. When butter is melted, add garlic and curry powder; stir for 1 minute. Stir in paprika, onions, cilantro, and shrimp. Stir-fry until shrimp turn pink (about 3 minutes). Stir in teriyaki sauce and water and heat through. Also pour brandy into a small pan and warm over low heat until bubbly.

Carefully pour warm brandy over surface of shrimp mixture and ignite (not beneath an exhaust fan or near flammable items). When flames die down, spoon shrimp and juices evenly over toast. Makes 3 or 4 servings.

Per serving: 291 calories, 23 g protein, 23 g carbohydrates, 11 g total fat, 155 mg cholesterol, 829 mg sodium

Sautéed Shrimp in Mint Beurre Blanc

Preparation time: About 15 minutes

Cooking time: 10 minutes

Rich yet refreshing—that describes this dish. Juicy pink shrimp are cloaked in a minted wine and butter sauce that's lightly accented with lemon peel.

6 to 8 tablespoons butter or margarine
½ teaspoon grated lemon peel
1 cup lightly packed fresh mint leaves
1 pound medium-size raw shrimp, shelled and deveined
1 cup dry white wine
Lemon slices and fresh mint sprigs

In a food processor or blender, whirl 4 tablespoons of the butter, lemon peel, and mint leaves until well blended; scoop into a cup. If made ahead, cover and refrigerate until next day.

Place a wok over medium heat; when wok is hot, add 2 tablespoons of the remaining plain butter.

When butter is melted, add shrimp and stir-fry until shrimp turn pink (about 3 minutes). With a slotted spoon, lift out shrimp; keep warm.

Increase heat to high. Pour wine into wok, bring to a boil, and boil, stirring, until wine is reduced to ⅓ cup (about 5 minutes). Add mint butter all at once; stir quickly until melted and blended into sauce. For a thicker sauce, stir in 2 tablespoons more plain butter. Arrange shrimp in wok, or pour sauce into a serving dish and top with shrimp. Garnish with lemon slices and mint sprigs. Makes 4 servings.

Per serving: 304 calories, 20 g protein, 1 g carbohydrate, 24 g total fat, 193 mg cholesterol, 429 mg sodium

Shrimp with Asparagus & Tomatillos

Preparation time: About 20 minutes

Cooking time: About 10 minutes

Shrimp and asparagus take on a bit of Mexican flavor when you add diced tomatillos and fresh cilantro to the sauce. Tomatillos look and taste something like green tomatoes; they're sold in Mexican markets, specialty produce stores, and many well-stocked supermarkets.

1 pound asparagus
3 tablespoons butter or margarine
3 tablespoons olive oil or salad oil
1 cup diced celery
2 tomatillos *each* about 2 inches in diameter, husked, cored, and diced
½ cup chopped fresh cilantro (coriander)
1 tablespoon chopped fresh mint
1½ tablespoons lemon juice
1 pound medium-size raw shrimp, shelled and deveined
Salt and pepper

Snap off and discard tough ends of asparagus, then cut spears into ½-inch slanting slices. Set aside.

Place a wok over high heat; when wok is hot, add butter and oil. When butter is melted, add asparagus, celery, tomatillos, and cilantro. Stir-fry for 2 minutes. Add mint, lemon juice, and shrimp; stir-fry until shrimp turn pink and asparagus is tender-crisp to bite (3 to 5 more minutes). Season to taste with salt and pepper. Makes 4 servings.

Per serving: 291 calories, 22 g protein, 6 g carbohydrates, 21 g total fat, 154 mg cholesterol, 309 mg sodium

Pink shrimp and crunchy water chestnuts share the wok with
bright green snow peas in this quick, colorful stir-fry. When shelling
shrimp for Snow Peas with Shrimp (recipe on facing page), leave the
tails in place for a decorative look.

(Pictured on front cover)

Shrimp Pesto Stir-fry

Preparation time: 15 minutes

Cooking time: 12 minutes

Shrimp teams well with a pesto sauce redolent of basil. Make the pesto from fresh basil if you can find it, or use our quick version made with dried herbs.

Quick Pesto Sauce (recipe follows) or 2 tablespoons Fresh Pesto (page 88)

3 **tablespoons butter or margarine**

1 **carrot, cut into ¼-inch-thick slices**

1 **small onion, cut into 1-inch-square pieces**

1 **small zucchini, cut into ¼-inch-thick slices**

8 **to 10 small mushrooms, sliced**

½ **small green bell pepper, seeded and sliced lengthwise**

½ **small red bell pepper, seeded and sliced lengthwise**

¾ **pound medium-size raw shrimp, shelled and deveined**

Fresh basil sprigs (optional)

Grated Parmesan cheese (optional)

Hot cooked rice (optional)

Prepare Quick Pesto Sauce; set aside.

Place a wok over medium-high heat; when wok is hot, add 1 tablespoon of the butter. When butter is melted, add carrot and onion and stir-fry for 2 minutes. Add 1 tablespoon more butter, zucchini, mushrooms, and green and red bell pepper; stir-fry just until carrot is tender-crisp to bite (about 2 more minutes). Remove vegetables from wok and keep warm.

Add remaining 1 tablespoon butter to wok; when butter is melted, stir in Quick Pesto Sauce. Add shrimp and stir-fry until they turn pink (3 to 4 minutes). Return vegetables to wok and stir until vegetables are hot and coated with sauce.

Turn shrimp-vegetable mixture into a shallow serving dish; garnish with basil and sprinkle with cheese, if desired. Serve with rice, if desired. Makes 2 servings.

Quick Pesto Sauce. Stir together 1 tablespoon grated **Parmesan cheese,** 2 teaspoons *each* **dry basil** and **parsley flakes,** and 1 tablespoon **olive oil** or salad oil.

Per serving: 415 calories, 31 g protein, 11 g carbohydrates, 28 g total fat, 259 mg cholesterol, 444 mg sodium

Scallop Pesto Stir-fry

Follow directions for **Shrimp Pesto Stir-fry,** but in place of shrimp, use ½ to ¾ pound **scallops** (thawed if frozen). Rinse scallops and pat dry, then cut into ¼-inch-thick slices. Cook scallops until opaque throughout; cut to test (3 to 4 minutes).

(Pictured on facing page)

Snow Peas with Shrimp

Preparation time: About 20 minutes

Cooking time: 5 minutes

For a meal in minutes, try this snappy stir-fry of shrimp, water chestnuts, and sweet snow peas. If you like, leave the tails on the shrimp for an attractive presentation.

Cooking Sauce (recipe follows)

3 **tablespoons salad oil**

1 **clove garlic, minced or pressed**

1 **pound medium-size raw shrimp, shelled and deveined**

1½ **cups Chinese pea pods (also called snow or sugar peas) or sugar snap peas, ends and strings removed; or 1 package (6 oz.) frozen Chinese pea pods, thawed and drained**

1 **can (about 8 oz.) water chestnuts, drained and thinly sliced**

2 **or 3 green onions (including tops), thinly sliced**

Prepare Cooking Sauce and set aside.

Place a wok over high heat; when wok is hot, add oil. When oil is hot, add garlic and shrimp and stir-fry for about 1 minute. Add pea pods and stir-fry for about 3 minutes (30 seconds if using frozen pea pods). Add water chestnuts and onions; stir to mix. Stir Cooking Sauce and add; stir until sauce boils and thickens and shrimp turn pink. Makes 4 servings.

Cooking Sauce. Stir together 1 teaspoon **cornstarch** and ¼ teaspoon **ground ginger.** Stir in 2 tablespoons *each* **soy sauce** and **dry sherry** and ½ cup **regular-strength chicken broth.**

Per serving: 244 calories, 22 g protein, 11 g carbohydrates, 12 g total fat, 131 mg cholesterol, 850 mg sodium

Bahia Shrimp Sauté

Preparation time: 25 minutes

Cooking time: 20 minutes

A pungent blend of spices permeates an exotic Brazilian stir-fry of succulent pink shrimp and lightly cooked vegetables. Garnish each serving with peanuts and toasted coconut.

> **About ¾ pound spinach**
> ¼ **cup unsweetened flaked coconut**
> 3 **tablespoons salad oil**
> 1 **pound medium-size raw shrimp, shelled and deveined**
> 1 **medium-size onion, chopped**
> 1 **clove garlic, minced or pressed**
> ½ **pound green beans (ends removed), cut into 1-inch pieces**
> ¼ **teaspoon** *each* **ground ginger, ground cumin, ground coriander, crushed red pepper, and paprika**
> ¼ **cup water**
> **Salt and black pepper**
> ¼ **cup dry-roasted peanuts**

Discard spinach stems and any tough or wilted leaves. Rinse remaining leaves well, pat dry, and cut into short shreds. Set aside. Place a wok over medium heat; when wok is hot, add coconut and stir until golden. Pour out and set aside.

Increase heat to high. Pour 2 tablespoons of the oil into wok; when oil is hot, add shrimp. Stir-fry until shrimp turn pink (about 3 minutes). With a slotted spoon, lift out shrimp; set aside. Pour remaining 1 tablespoon oil into wok; when oil is hot, add onion and garlic and stir-fry until onion is soft.

Stir in beans, ginger, cumin, coriander, red pepper, and paprika. Stir-fry for 1 minute; then add water, cover, and cook, stirring often, until beans are tender-crisp to bite (about 4 more minutes). Add spinach and stir for 1 minute; then return shrimp to wok and cook just until heated through (about 1 more minute). Season to taste with salt and black pepper; sprinkle with coconut and peanuts. Makes 4 servings.

Per serving: 306 calories, 25 g protein, 12 g carbohydrates, 19 g total fat, 131 mg cholesterol, 324 mg sodium

Scallops & Shrimp in Béarnaise Cream

Preparation time: 15 minutes

Cooking time: 20 minutes

The sauce isn't true béarnaise, but the traditional ingredients are here: reduced vinegar, shallots, tarragon. You might accompany this elegant entrée with steamed broccoli, green beans, or another fresh green vegetable of your choice.

> 1 **pound scallops (thawed if frozen)**
> 2 **tablespoons butter or margarine**
> ½ **pound large raw shrimp, shelled, deveined, and split lengthwise**
> ⅓ **cup minced shallots**
> ¾ **cup tarragon wine vinegar or white wine vinegar**
> ½ **cup regular-strength chicken broth**
> ¼ **teaspoon dry tarragon**
> 1 **tablespoon Dijon mustard**
> ½ **cup whipping cream**
> **Salt and white pepper**

Rinse scallops and pat dry; cut any large scallops in half.

Place a wok over medium-high heat; when wok is hot, add butter. When butter is melted, add scallops and shrimp. Stir-fry just until shrimp turn pink and scallops are opaque throughout; cut to test (3 to 5 minutes). Lift out scallops and shrimp and keep warm.

Increase heat to high. Add shallots, vinegar, broth, and tarragon to wok. Bring to a boil; boil until reduced to ½ cup. Pour any accumulated juices from scallops and shrimp into wok along with mustard and cream. Boil until sauce is reduced to about ¾ cup. Add scallops and shrimp; stir until heated through. Season to taste with salt and white pepper. Makes 4 servings.

Per serving: 314 calories, 31 g protein, 9 g carbohydrates, 17 g total fat, 155 mg cholesterol, 586 mg sodium

Scallop & Shrimp Curry

Preparation time: 20 minutes

Cooking time: 20 minutes

Delightfully rich and spicy is this creamy curry of shrimp and scallops. If you use an imported curry powder from a spice shop (or mix up your own blend), you may want to adjust the amount used; imported powders are often hotter than domestic brands.

- ¾ pound scallops (thawed if frozen)
- ¼ cup butter or margarine
- 1 small onion, finely chopped
- 2 cloves garlic, minced or pressed
- 2 to 3 teaspoons curry powder
- 1 pound medium-size raw shrimp, shelled and deveined
- 1 cup whipping cream
- ½ cup dry white wine
- ½ teaspoon dry summer savory leaves
- 2 tablespoons water
- 1 tablespoon cornstarch
   Salt and pepper
   Hot cooked rice

Rinse scallops and pat dry; cut any large scallops in half. Set aside.

Place a wok over medium heat; when wok is hot, add 2 tablespoons of the butter. When butter is melted, add onion, garlic, and curry powder and stir-fry until onion is soft. Add remaining 2 tablespoons butter; when butter is melted, add scallops and shrimp. Stir-fry just until shrimp turn pink and scallops are opaque throughout; cut to test (3 to 5 minutes). With a slotted spoon, lift out scallops and shrimp; keep warm.

Add cream, wine, and summer savory to wok; blend water with cornstarch and stir into cream mixture. Cook, stirring, until sauce boils and thickens. Return scallops and shrimp to wok; stir until heated through. Season to taste with salt and pepper; serve over rice. Makes 4 to 6 servings.

Per serving: 312 calories, 24 g protein, 5 g carbohydrates, 22 g total fat, 172 mg cholesterol, 313 mg sodium

Scallops in Garlic Butter

Preparation time: About 10 minutes

Cooking time: About 10 minutes

Toasted almonds add a little crunch to a super-simple stir-fry of scallops seasoned with lemon peel and plenty of garlic.

- 1 to 1½ pounds scallops (thawed if frozen)
- 3 tablespoons sliced almonds
- ¼ cup butter
- 5 large cloves garlic, minced or pressed
- 2 tablespoons chopped parsley
- 1 teaspoon grated lemon peel

Rinse scallops and pat dry; then cut any large scallops in half. Set aside.

Place a wok over medium heat; when wok is hot, add almonds and stir until golden (about 2 minutes). Pour out of wok and set aside.

Add butter; when butter is melted, add garlic, parsley, and lemon peel and stir for about 1 minute. Add scallops (a portion at a time, if necessary) and stir-fry just until opaque throughout; cut to test (3 to 4 minutes). Transfer scallop mixture to a platter, top with almonds, and serve immediately. Makes 4 servings.

Per serving: 290 calories, 31 g protein, 6 g carbohydrates, 15 g total fat, 94 mg cholesterol, 393 mg sodium

Tarragon Scallop Sauté

Preparation time: About 10 minutes

Cooking time: About 10 minutes

If you like your scallops flavored with tarragon, try this easy stir-fry: just scallops, mushrooms, and shallots, seasoned with the dry herb and finished at the table with a squeeze of lemon.

- 1 pound scallops (thawed if frozen)
- 6 tablespoons butter or margarine
- ½ teaspoon dry tarragon
- 3 tablespoons chopped shallots or green onions (white part only)
- ½ pound mushrooms, sliced
- 2 tablespoons dry white wine
   Chopped parsley
   Lemon wedges

Rinse scallops, pat dry, and cut into bite-size pieces. Set aside.

Place a wok over medium-high heat; when wok is hot, add butter. When butter is melted, add tarragon, shallots, and mushrooms; stir-fry until mushrooms are soft. Push mushrooms to side of wok and add scallops. Stir-fry until scallops are opaque throughout; cut to test (3 to 4 minutes). Sprinkle wine over scallops and cook for 1 more minute; then stir together scallops and mushrooms. Garnish each serving with parsley and lemon wedges. Makes 3 or 4 servings.

Per serving: 276 calories, 21 g protein, 7 g carbohydrates, 18 g total fat, 88 mg cholesterol, 362 mg sodium

Sizzling Rice

In a cuisine that wastes little, Chinese cooks have devised many thrifty dishes. Sizzling rice is one example: the crust that forms on the pot bottom when rice is cooked is dried and deep-fried for use in recipes. "Sizzling" describes the sound made by the hot, crisp fried rice when it's dropped into soup or topped with a stir-fry.

Since saving rice crusts may take a long time, we recommend making a full batch of rice specifically for use in sizzling dishes. Start with short-grain rice; its sticky texture helps keep it in a clustered layer as it dries.

Sizzling Rice Wedges

Place 1 cup **short-grain rice** (such as pearl) in a 2-quart pan. Cover with **cold water;** stir and drain. Repeat until water is clear. Then add 1 cup **cold water** to drained rice. Cover and bring to a boil over high heat; reduce heat to low and simmer for 20 minutes. Turn off heat and let stand for 30 minutes.

Turn rice into a wok (a nonstick electric wok is best). Pack rice into an even layer about ½ inch thick. Cook over low heat for 1 hour; turn layer of rice over and continue to cook until rice is very dry (about 1 more hour). When rice crust is cool, cut it into 8 wedges and store airtight at room temperature for up to 3 months.

To cook sizzling rice, set wok in a ring stand over burner or element. Pour in **salad oil** to a depth of 1 inch. Heat oil to 375°F on a deep-frying thermometer. Cook rice wedges, 2 or 3 at a time, until golden (about 2 minutes); drain briefly on paper towels, then use while still hot in Sizzling Sweet & Sour Seafood (recipe follows) or any other sizzling dish.

(Pictured on facing page)

Sizzling Sweet & Sour Seafood

8 **Sizzling Rice Wedges (recipe at left)**
½ **pound scallops (thawed if frozen) Cooking Sauce (recipe follows) Salad oil**
2 **cloves garlic, minced**
1 **teaspoon minced fresh ginger**
½ **pound medium-size raw shrimp, shelled and deveined**
1 **carrot, very thinly sliced**
½ **cup sliced bamboo shoots**
1 **green bell pepper, seeded and cut into 1-inch squares**
5 **green onions (including tops), cut into 1½-inch lengths Salt**

Prepare Sizzling Rice Wedges, but do not fry. Set aside. Also rinse scallops and pat dry; cut any large ones in half. Prepare Cooking Sauce and set aside.

Place a wok over high heat; when wok is hot, add 1½ tablespoons oil. When oil begins to heat, add garlic and ginger and stir once. Then add shrimp and scallops and stir-fry until shrimp turn pink and scallops are opaque throughout; cut to test (about 3 minutes). Remove from wok and set aside.

Pour 1½ tablespoons more oil into wok. When oil is hot, add carrot and bamboo shoots and stir-fry for 3 minutes, adding a few drops of water if wok appears dry. Add bell pepper and onions; stir-fry for 1 minute. Return shrimp and scallops to wok. Stir Cooking Sauce, pour into wok, and stir until sauce boils and thickens. Season to taste with salt.

Turn off heat; cover seafood mixture and keep hot while you fry Sizzling Rice Wedges as directed at left. Turn seafood mixture into a preheated bowl. Bring hot rice wedges to the table on a platter and immediately pour seafood mixture over them. Makes 3 or 4 servings.

Cooking Sauce. Stir together ⅓ cup *each* **sugar, white wine vinegar,** and **regular-strength chicken broth;** 2 tablespoons **soy sauce;** 1 tablespoon **dry sherry;** and 1½ tablespoons **cornstarch.**

Per serving: 462 calories, 24 g protein, 50 g carbohydrates, 19 g total fat, 88 mg cholesterol, 768 mg sodium

Along with the flavor, appearance, and aroma of foods, Chinese chefs appreciate
the sounds of cooking. Sizzling Sweet & Sour Seafood
(recipe on facing page) makes appetizing music when spooned atop
Sizzling Rice Wedges hot from the wok.

Noodles, Rice & Tofu

Soft-fried Noodles

Preparation time: About 10 minutes

Cooking time: About 15 minutes

A sweet-hot sauce melds all the flavors in this Thai dish of rice noodles, pork, shrimp, and vegetables. You may see rice noodles sold as *mai fun;* they're available in many well-stocked supermarkets.

    Sweet-Hot Sauce (recipe follows)
    Soy-Pepper Sauce (recipe follows)
6 ounces dried thin rice noodles (rice sticks)
    About 3 quarts boiling salted water
5 tablespoons salad oil
¼ pound medium-size raw shrimp, shelled, deveined, and chopped
1 medium-size onion, chopped
½ pound lean ground pork
2 cloves garlic, minced or pressed
1 medium-size carrot, shredded
2 eggs, lightly beaten
¼ cup finely chopped roasted peanuts
    Garnishes: ⅓ pound bean sprouts, coarsely chopped; 3 green onions (including tops), cut into thin strips; and 1 lime, cut into wedges

Prepare Sweet-Hot Sauce and Soy-Pepper Sauce; set both aside. Cook noodles in about 3 quarts boiling salted water until barely tender to bite (2 to 4 minutes). Drain, rinse with cold water, and drain again.

Place a wok over high heat. When wok is hot, add 1 tablespoon of the oil; when oil is hot, add shrimp and stir-fry until pink (1 to 2 minutes). Remove from wok and set aside.

Pour 1 tablespoon more oil into wok; when oil is hot, add onion and crumble in pork. Stir-fry until pork is lightly browned (about 4 minutes). Add garlic and carrot and stir-fry for 1 more minute. Add 2 tablespoons more oil; add drained noodles and stir until heated through.

Make a well in center of noodle mixture and pour in remaining 1 tablespoon oil. Pour eggs into well. Cook, stirring (keep eggs in well), just until eggs begin to set; then stir eggs into noodle mixture.

Return shrimp to wok and add Sweet-Hot Sauce; stir to blend. Pour into a serving dish and sprinkle with peanuts. Surround with garnishes and serve with Soy-Pepper Sauce. Makes 3 or 4 servings.

Sweet-Hot Sauce. Stir together 2 teaspoons *each* **distilled white vinegar** and **water,** ½ teaspoon **crushed red pepper,** 2 tablespoons **fish sauce** (*nam pla*) or soy sauce, and 1 tablespoon *each* minced **fresh cilantro (coriander)** and **sugar.**

Soy-Pepper Sauce. Stir together 6 tablespoons **soy sauce** and ½ to ¾ teaspoon **crushed red pepper.**

Per serving: 566 calories, 27 g protein, 47 g carbohydrates, 30 g total fat, 208 mg cholesterol, 2,232 mg sodium

Noodles & Beef with Black Bean Sauce

Preparation time: About 10 minutes

Marinating time: 15 minutes

Cooking time: 25 minutes

Pungent fermented black beans, thin strips of beef, and egg noodles make a hearty dish with a decidedly Oriental accent. Black beans are widely available in supermarkets; you'll find them in jars or small plastic bags.

4 ounces dried medium-wide noodles
    Boiling salted water
¼ cup salad oil
½ pound lean boneless beef steak (such as top round, flank, or sirloin)
1 teaspoon *each* cornstarch, dry sherry, and soy sauce
1 tablespoon water
    Cooking Sauce (recipe follows)
2 tablespoons fermented salted black beans, rinsed, drained, and finely chopped
2 large cloves garlic, minced or pressed
1 teaspoon minced fresh ginger
¼ teaspoon crushed red pepper
1 green bell pepper, seeded and cut into 1-inch squares
2 green onions (including tops), cut into 1-inch lengths

Following package directions, cook noodles in boiling salted water until barely tender to bite. Drain, rinse with cold water, and drain again. Toss noodles with 1 tablespoon of the oil.

Cut beef with the grain into 1½-inch-wide strips; then cut each strip across the grain into ⅛-inch-thick slanting slices. In a bowl, stir together cornstarch, sherry, soy, and the 1 tablespoon water. Add beef and stir to coat; then stir in 1½ teaspoons of the oil. Let marinate for 15 minutes. Meanwhile, prepare Cooking Sauce and set aside.

Place a wok over high heat; when wok is hot, add 1 tablespoon of the oil. When oil begins to heat, add drained noodles and stir-fry until heated through. Remove from wok; then add remaining 1½ tablespoons oil to wok. When oil begins to heat, add black beans, garlic, ginger, and red pepper; stir once. Add beef and stir-fry for 2 minutes. Add bell pepper and onions and stir-fry for 1 more minute, adding a few drops of water if vegetables stick to wok. Stir Cooking Sauce, pour into wok, and stir until sauce boils and thickens. Return noodles to wok and toss lightly to mix. Makes 2 servings.

Cooking Sauce. Stir together ½ cup **water** and 1 tablespoon *each* **cornstarch** and **soy sauce**.

Per serving: 678 calories, 36 g protein, 52 g carbohydrates, 36 g total fat, 118 mg cholesterol, 1,185 mg sodium

(Pictured on page 74)

Bahmi Goreng

Preparation time: 15 minutes

Cooking time: 35 minutes

Indonesian *bahmi goreng* is a great way to dress up leftovers; you just combine shredded cooked meat with noodles, an assortment of vegetables, and savory seasonings. The result is always appealing and sometimes elegant enough for a party—as in this version, topped with a lattice of golden egg shreds and served with sweet-hot peanut sauce.

Egg Shreds (recipe follows)
Peanut Sauce (recipe follows)
2 tablespoons soy sauce
¼ teaspoon anchovy paste (optional)
4 cups shredded cooked chicken, pork, or beef
8 ounces dried medium-wide noodles
Boiling salted water
2 tablespoons salad oil
4 cloves garlic, minced or pressed
½ to 1 teaspoon crushed red pepper
2 medium-size onions, cut in half, then thinly sliced
3 cups thinly sliced celery
About ⅔ lb. cabbage, coarsely chopped

2 cups Chinese pea pods (also called snow or sugar peas) or sugar snap peas, ends and strings removed; or 1 package (6 oz.) frozen Chinese pea pods, thawed and drained
2 large tomatoes, coarsely chopped
Salt
Red bell pepper strips, celery leaves, cooked Chinese pea pods (optional)

Prepare Egg Shreds and Peanut Sauce; set aside.

In a bowl, stir together soy, anchovy paste (if used), and chicken; set aside. Following package directions, cook noodles in boiling salted water until barely tender to bite; drain and keep warm.

Place a wok over medium-high heat; when wok is hot, add oil. When oil is hot, add garlic, red pepper, onions, and celery. Stir-fry until vegetables are tender-crisp to bite (about 3 minutes). Add chicken mixture; reduce heat to medium and stir-fry for 3 more minutes. Add cabbage and fresh pea pods and stir-fry for 2 minutes (if using frozen pea pods, add for last 30 seconds). Add drained noodles and tomatoes and stir until heated through. Season to taste with salt. Turn onto a large platter and arrange Egg Shreds on top in a lattice design. Garnish with bell pepper strips, celery leaves, and pea pods, if desired. At the table, pass Peanut Sauce. Makes 6 servings.

Egg Shreds. Beat 2 **eggs** with a pinch of **salt**. Place a 10-inch frying pan with a nonstick finish over medium heat. When pan is hot, brush with ¼ teaspoon **salad oil**. Pour in half the beaten eggs; swirl pan to cover entire bottom. When egg sheet is lightly browned on bottom and set on top (45 seconds to 1 minute), flip it over and cook for 5 more seconds. Slide out of pan; let cool. Repeat with remaining eggs to make 1 more sheet, brushing pan with ¼ teaspoon **salad oil**. Let sheets cool; then cut in half, stack, and cut crosswise into ¼-inch-wide strips. Cover and refrigerate until ready to use or for up to 3 days.

Peanut Sauce. In a 1½-quart pan, combine 1 cup **unsweetened pineapple juice,** ⅔ cup **crunchy peanut butter,** and 2 cloves **garlic** (minced or pressed). Bring to a boil over medium heat, stirring. Remove from heat and stir in 2 tablespoons firmly packed **brown sugar,** 1 tablespoon **soy sauce,** and ¼ to ½ teaspoon **crushed red pepper.** Let cool to room temperature. If made ahead, cover and refrigerate for up to 3 days; serve at room temperature. Makes about 2 cups.

Per serving of Bahmi Goreng: 463 calories, 38 g protein, 41 g carbohydrates, 16 g total fat, 210 mg cholesterol, 996 mg sodium

Per tablespoon Peanut Sauce: 40 calories, 2 g protein, 3 g carbohydrates, 3 g total fat, 0 mg cholesterol, 54 mg sodium

As a star attraction at your next summer party, Bahmi Goreng
(recipe on page 73) will delight your guests. A lattice of tender,
golden Egg Shreds conceals a feast of marvelous flavors
from Indonesia.

Asian-style Pasta Primavera

Preparation time: About 20 minutes, plus 30 minutes to soak mushrooms

Cooking time: 30 minutes

Linguine is tossed with asparagus and favorite Asian vegetables in this light dish. You can adjust the recipe to suit available ingredients: Swiss chard can substitute for the bok choy, and button mushrooms can take the place of shiitakes.

　　3　tablespoons sesame seeds
　　8　large dried Oriental or fresh shiitake mushrooms (about 3 inches in diameter); or ½ pound fresh button mushrooms
　½　pound *each* asparagus and bok choy
　　6　ounces dried linguine
　　　Boiling salted water
　　2　tablespoons salad oil
　　2　cloves garlic, minced or pressed
　　1　tablespoon very finely chopped fresh ginger
　½　pound Chinese pea pods (also called snow or sugar peas) or sugar snap peas, ends and strings removed; or 1 package (6 oz.) frozen Chinese pea pods, thawed and drained
　¼　cup dry sherry
　　1　cup regular-strength chicken broth
　　2　tablespoons soy sauce
　　1　teaspoon *each* sugar and white wine vinegar

Place a wok over medium heat; when wok is hot, add sesame seeds and stir until golden (about 2 minutes). Pour out of wok and set aside.

If using dried mushrooms, soak in warm water to cover for 30 minutes, then drain. Cut off and discard stems; squeeze caps dry and thinly slice. Or trim any tough stems from fresh shiitake mushrooms; thinly slice caps. (Simply slice fresh button mushrooms thinly.)

Snap off and discard tough ends of asparagus; cut asparagus spears and bok choy stems and leaves into ½-inch slanting slices. Set vegetables aside.

Following package directions, cook linguine in boiling salted water until barely tender to bite; drain well. Place in a large, shallow serving bowl and keep warm.

Place wok over high heat; when wok is hot, add oil. When oil is hot, add garlic and ginger; stir-fry until lightly browned (about 30 seconds). Add mushrooms, asparagus, bok choy, fresh pea pods, and sherry. Cover and cook, stirring once or twice, until vegetables are bright green and tender-crisp to bite (about 2 minutes; if using frozen pea pods, add for last 30 seconds). Spoon over noodles.

Add broth, soy, sugar, and vinegar to wok; bring to a boil, stirring. Pour over noodles and vegetables. Sprinkle with sesame seeds, then mix lightly. Serve immediately. Makes 4 servings.

Per serving: 347 calories, 12 g protein, 51 g carbohydrates, 12 g total fat, 0 mg cholesterol, 806 mg sodium

(Pictured on page 159)

Italian Stir-fried Pasta

Preparation time: About 10 minutes

Cooking time: About 15 minutes

Dinner can be on the table in under half an hour when you serve this dish of *al dente* pasta mixed with onion, bell pepper, and small shrimp and topped with plenty of Parmesan cheese.

　　6　ounces dried linguine or other thin pasta
　　　Boiling salted water
　　2　tablespoons olive oil
　　1　small onion, cut into bite-size pieces
　　1　medium-size green bell pepper, seeded and cut into bite-size pieces
　¼　to ½ teaspoon crushed dried hot red chiles
　½　to 1 teaspoon dry oregano leaves
　　1　tablespoon butter or margarine
　　2　ounces (about 18) Chinese pea pods (also called snow or sugar peas) or sugar snap peas, ends and strings removed; or ½ package (6-oz. size) frozen Chinese pea pods, thawed and drained
　¾　pound small cooked, shelled shrimp
　　　About ½ cup grated Parmesan cheese

Following package directions, cook linguine in boiling salted water until barely tender to bite; drain well and pour onto a hot platter.

While pasta is cooking, place a wok over high heat; when wok is hot, add oil. When oil is hot, add onion, bell pepper, chiles, and oregano. Stir-fry until vegetables are tender to bite (about 5 minutes).

Reduce heat to medium-high. Add butter to wok; when butter is melted, add pea pods and stir-fry for 1 minute (30 seconds if using frozen pea pods). Add shrimp, stir well, and remove wok from heat.

Spoon hot stir-fried mixture over drained pasta and serve at once. Offer cheese to sprinkle on individual servings. Makes 2 servings.

Per serving: 856 calories, 62 g protein, 72 g carbohydrates, 34 g total fat, 302 mg cholesterol, 732 mg sodium

Noodles with Pork & Peanut Sauce

Preparation time: About 10 minutes

Cooking time: About 10 minutes

For a quick meal, toss together hot noodles, spicy peanut sauce, mustard greens, and chunks of browned ground pork. You can brown the meat while the pasta is cooking.

    Peanut Sauce (recipe follows)
3   tablespoons salad oil
1   pound lean ground pork, pinched into
    1-inch lumps
    About 4 quarts boiling salted water
8   ounces dried capellini or dried thin rice
    noodles (rice sticks)
4   cloves garlic, minced or pressed
1   medium-size onion, cut lengthwise into
    slender strips
1½ cups lightly packed slivered mustard
    greens

Prepare Peanut Sauce and set aside.

Place a wok over high heat; when wok is hot, add 2 tablespoons of the oil. When oil is hot, add pork. Stir-fry gently until pork is well browned (about 5 minutes).

Meanwhile, add remaining 1 tablespoon oil to about 4 quarts boiling salted water; then drop in noodles. Return to a boil; then boil, uncovered, until noodles are barely tender to bite (about 4 minutes for capellini, 2 to 4 minutes for rice noodles). Drain.

To pork, add garlic, onion, Peanut Sauce, and 1

cup of the mustard greens; stir until boiling. Stir pork mixture into drained noodles; top with remaining ½ cup mustard greens. Makes 4 servings.

Peanut Sauce. Stir together ¼ cup *each* **soy sauce** and **regular-strength chicken or beef broth,** 2 tablespoons **creamy peanut butter,** 2 tablespoons **hoisin sauce** or tart jam, and 2 teaspoons **sugar.**

Per serving: 579 calories, 30 g protein, 57 g carbohydrates, 25 g total fat, 77 mg cholesterol, 1,477 mg sodium

Korean Bean Threads & Beef

Preparation time: About 20 minutes, plus 30 minutes to soak bean threads and mushrooms

Cooking time: 10 minutes

Here's a complete meal to cook in a wok. If you want to extend it to four servings, serve it with steamed rice and small side dishes of *kim chee*—hot, pungent pickled cabbage, available in Asian markets.

3   ounces dried bean threads
3   medium-size dried Oriental mushrooms
3   tablespoons sesame seeds
¾   pound lean boneless beef steak (such as
    top round, flank, or sirloin)
1   tablespoon sesame oil
¼   teaspoon black pepper
½   teaspoon crushed red pepper
2   cloves garlic, minced or pressed
2   tablespoons soy sauce
3   tablespoons salad oil
1   small green bell pepper, seeded and cut
    into thin strips
1   medium-size carrot, shredded
6   green onions (including tops), cut into
    2-inch lengths
¼   pound bean sprouts
⅓   cup regular-strength beef broth
1   teaspoon *each* sugar and vinegar
    Salt

Soak bean threads in warm water to cover for 30 minutes. Drain, then cut into 2-inch lengths. Also soak mushrooms in warm water to cover for 30 minutes, then drain. Cut off and discard stems; squeeze caps dry and thinly slice. Set bean threads and mushrooms aside.

Place a wok over medium heat; when wok is hot, add sesame seeds and stir until golden (about 2 minutes). Pour out of wok and set aside.

Cut beef with the grain into 1½-inch-wide strips; then cut each strip across the grain into ⅛-inch-thick slanting slices. In a bowl, stir together sesame oil, black pepper, red pepper, garlic, and 1 tablespoon of the soy. Add beef and stir to coat.

Place wok over high heat. When wok is hot, add 1 tablespoon of the salad oil. When oil is hot, add beef mixture and stir-fry until meat is browned (1½ to 2 minutes); remove from wok and set aside.

Pour remaining 2 tablespoons salad oil into wok; add bell pepper, carrot, mushrooms, onions, and bean sprouts. Stir-fry for 2 minutes. Remove from wok; set aside.

Add broth, sugar, vinegar, remaining 1 tablespoon soy, and bean threads to wok. Cook, stirring frequently, until liquid is absorbed (about 2 minutes). Return meat and vegetable mixtures to wok and stir in 2 tablespoons of the sesame seeds. Turn onto a platter and sprinkle with remaining 1 tablespoon sesame seeds. Makes 3 or 4 servings.

Per serving: 396 calories, 24 g protein, 29 g carbohydrates, 21 g total fat, 49 mg cholesterol, 646 mg sodium

Rice & Bean Sprouts

Preparation time: 5 minutes

Cooking time: About 35 minutes

Stickier in texture than the familiar long-grain white rice, short-grain rice is favored by Korean, Japanese, and Filipino cooks. Here, hot steamed rice is combined with crunchy bean sprouts and characteristic Korean seasonings of soy and sesame for a filling side dish.

- 2 cups hot Steamed Short-grain Rice (recipe follows)
- 3 tablespoons sesame seeds
- 1 tablespoon salad oil
- 2 green onions (including tops), minced
- 1 clove garlic, minced or pressed
- 1½ cups bean sprouts
- 2 tablespoons soy sauce

Prepare steamed rice. Meanwhile, place a wok over medium heat; when wok is hot, add sesame seeds and stir until golden (about 2 minutes). Pour seeds out of wok; crush coarsely with a mortar and pestle or whirl very briefly in a blender. Set aside.

Measure out 2 cups of the cooked rice; keep warm. (Reserve remaining rice for other uses.)

Return wok to medium heat; when wok is hot, add oil. When oil is hot, add sesame seeds, onions, and garlic; stir-fry until onions are soft. Add bean sprouts and stir until heated through.

Add rice and soy to wok; mix gently, being careful not to mash rice grains. Makes about 4 servings.

Steamed Short-grain Rice. Place 1 cup **short-grain rice** (such as pearl) in a heavy 1½- to 2-quart pan. Cover with **cold water,** stir, and drain; repeat until water is clear. To drained rice, add 1¼ cups **cold water** and, if desired, ½ teaspoon **salt.** Bring to a boil over high heat. Reduce heat to low, cover, and simmer for 20 minutes without lifting lid. Remove from heat and let stand, covered, for 5 to 10 minutes. Uncover; fluff with a fork. Makes about 3½ cups.

Per serving: 297 calories, 7 g protein, 51 g carbohydrates, 7 g total fat, 0 mg cholesterol, 834 mg sodium

Tomato Fried Rice

Preparation time: About 5 minutes

Cooking time: About 10 minutes

Colors remain bright in this quick rice dish. To vary the flavor of the rice, omit the salt and add about a tablespoon of soy sauce with the sherry.

- 2 tablespoons salad oil
- 2 tablespoons butter or margarine
- 1 small onion, finely chopped
- 3 cups cold cooked rice
- ½ teaspoon *each* salt and sugar
  Dash of pepper
- 1 jar (2 oz.) sliced pimentos, drained
  About 2 tablespoons dry sherry, white wine, or water
- 2 medium-size tomatoes, peeled, seeded, and diced
  Chopped parsley or sliced green onion tops

Place a wok over medium-high heat; when wok is hot, add oil and butter. When butter is melted, add onion and stir-fry until tender-crisp to bite (about 2 minutes).

Add rice and stir-fry until rice is golden (about 7 minutes). Stir in salt, sugar, pepper, pimentos, and 2 tablespoons of the sherry. Continue to stir, adding a little more sherry if needed, for about 1 more minute. Stir in tomatoes and cook for 1 to 2 more minutes.

Spoon into a serving dish and sprinkle with parsley. Makes 4 to 6 servings.

Per serving: 169 calories, 2 g protein, 21 g carbohydrates, 9 g total fat, 10 mg cholesterol, 227 mg sodium

(Pictured on facing page)

Fried Rice with Ham & Peanuts

Preparation time: About 10 minutes

Cooking time: About 10 minutes

Fried rice is a classic quick meal, easily embellished with leftover meat and your favorite vegetables. For best success, start with *cold* cooked rice; if it's warm or hot, the grains will stick together.

- 2 cups cold cooked long-grain white rice
- 2 eggs
- ¼ teaspoon salt
- ¼ cup salad oil
- 1 small onion, chopped
- 1 clove garlic, minced or pressed
- 1 medium-size green bell pepper, seeded and diced
- ¼ pound mushrooms, chopped
- ½ pound cold cooked ham, chicken, turkey, or pork, diced (about 1½ cups)
- ½ cup salted roasted peanuts
- 2 tablespoons soy sauce
  Tomato wedges and cucumber slices

Rub cooked rice with wet hands so all grains are separated; set aside. In a small bowl, lightly beat together eggs and salt.

  Place a wok over medium heat; when wok is hot, add 1 tablespoon of the oil. When oil is hot, add eggs and cook, stirring occasionally, until soft curds form; remove from wok and set aside.

  Increase heat to medium-high; add 1 tablespoon more oil to wok. When oil is hot, add onion and garlic. Stir-fry until onion is soft; then add bell pepper, mushrooms, ham, and peanuts. Stir-fry until heated through (about 2 minutes). Remove from wok and set aside.

  Pour remaining 2 tablespoons oil into wok. When oil is hot, add rice and stir-fry until heated through (about 2 minutes); stir in ham mixture and soy. Add eggs; stir mixture gently until eggs are in small pieces. Garnish with tomato and cucumber. Makes 4 servings.

Per serving: 467 calories, 24 g protein, 25 g carbohydrates, 31 g total fat, 170 mg cholesterol, 1,616 mg sodium

Cajun Dirty Rice

Preparation time: About 10 minutes

Cooking time: About 15 minutes

This rice may be "dirty," but it's delicious! It's one of the most popular dishes in Louisiana. Vary the spiciness by adding cayenne to taste; real Cajuns like it fiery.

- ¼ pound chicken giblets, including liver
- ¼ cup salad oil
- ½ pound lean ground beef
- 2 stalks celery, chopped
- 1 red bell pepper, seeded and chopped
- 1 medium-size onion, chopped
- 2 teaspoons all-purpose flour
- ½ to 2 teaspoons ground red pepper (cayenne)
- 2 teaspoons paprika
- 1½ teaspoons dry oregano leaves
- 1 cup regular-strength chicken broth
- 3 cups cold cooked white rice
- 2 green onions (including tops), thinly sliced
  Salt and black pepper

Using a sharp knife, trim giblets of any hard membranes or connective tissue. Finely chop giblets or grind them in a food processor.

  Place a wok over high heat; when wok is hot, add 2 tablespoons of the oil. When oil is hot, add giblets and beef and cook, stirring, until no longer pink (about 4 minutes). Using a slotted spoon, transfer to a small bowl and set aside.

  Pour remaining 2 tablespoons oil into wok; when oil is hot, add celery, bell pepper, and chopped onion. Stir-fry until vegetables are soft (about 7 minutes). Sprinkle in flour, red pepper, paprika, and oregano; cook until flour is browned (about 1 minute). Pour in broth, bring to a boil, and stir in giblets and beef. Add rice and stir-fry until heated through (about 3 minutes); stir in green onions. Season to taste with salt and black pepper. Makes 6 servings.

Per serving: 315 calories, 13 g protein, 23 g carbohydrates, 19 g total fat, 78 mg cholesterol, 221 mg sodium

Vegetarian Dirty Rice

Follow directions for **Cajun Dirty Rice,** using ½ cup **peanuts** in place of the giblets and ground beef, and stir-frying until golden (about 2 minutes). Replace broth with 1 cup **water** and white rice with 3 cups cold cooked **brown rice.**

In China, fried rice in countless variations is a standard vehicle
for leftovers. Try Fried Rice with Ham & Peanuts (recipe on facing page)
and you'll understand its popularity, whether you
use leftovers or not.

Tofu & Vegetable Stir-fry

Preparation time: about 15 minutes

Cooking time: 6 minutes

For a speedy vegetarian meal, try Vietnamese *rau xao*. The dish is made in countless variations; this one features vegetables readily available in North American markets.

- ½ **pound medium-firm tofu (bean curd), cut into ½-inch cubes**
- 3 **tablespoons soy sauce**
- 1 **teaspoon rice wine vinegar or white vinegar**
- ¼ **teaspoon ground cumin**
- 2 **cloves garlic, minced or pressed**
- ½ **teaspoon grated fresh ginger or ⅛ teaspoon ground ginger**
- 3 **tablespoons peanut oil or salad oil**
- 1 **large carrot, chopped**
- 2 **cups thinly sliced broccoli stems and bite-size flowerets**
- 1 **cup *each* bean sprouts and sliced mushrooms**
- ½ **cup thinly sliced green onions (including tops)**
- 3 **tablespoons minced fresh cilantro (coriander)**

Place tofu in a shallow bowl. In another bowl, mix soy, vinegar, cumin, garlic, and ginger; drizzle over tofu. Set aside.

Place a wok over high heat. When wok is hot, add oil. When oil is hot, add carrot and stir-fry for 1 minute; add broccoli and stir-fry for 2 more minutes. Then mix in bean sprouts, mushrooms, and onions; stir-fry for 30 more seconds.

Reduce heat to medium-high. Add tofu mixture and stir gently just until tofu is heated through but vegetables are still crisp (1 to 2 minutes). Garnish with cilantro. Makes 4 servings.

Per serving: 181 calories, 7 g protein, 11 g carbohydrates, 13 g total fat, 0 mg cholesterol, 800 mg sodium

Greens & Tofu in Peanut Sauce

Preparation time: 10 minutes

Cooking time: 15 minutes

Tofu, cabbage, spinach, and bean sprouts dressed with a delicious peanut-coconut sauce are served over rice noodles in this Thai specialty. If you like, top servings with crisp onion flakes; they're sold in Asian grocery stores.

- ⅓ **cup crunchy peanut butter**
- 1 **small can (7¾ oz.) sweetened coconut milk**
- 2 **cloves garlic, minced or pressed**
- 1½ **tablespoons *each* white vinegar and soy sauce**
- 1 **teaspoon grated fresh ginger or ¼ teaspoon ground ginger**
- ⅛ **to ¼ teaspoon ground red pepper (cayenne)**
- 1 **tablespoon peanut oil or salad oil**
- 2 **cups *each* thinly shredded cabbage and spinach**
- ½ **cup thinly sliced green onions (including tops)**
- 2 **cups bean sprouts**
- ½ **pound firm tofu (bean curd), cut into ½-inch cubes**
- 8 **ounces dried thin rice noodles (rice sticks) or Chinese wheat flour noodles, cooked; or 4 to 5 cups hot cooked rice**
- ½ **cup crisp onion flakes (optional)**

In a small pan, combine peanut butter, coconut milk, garlic, vinegar, and soy. Stir over medium heat until well combined; then continue to cook, uncovered, for 3 minutes. Remove from heat and stir in ginger and red pepper.

Place a wok over medium heat; when wok is hot, add oil. When oil is hot, add cabbage and spinach and stir-fry until greens are slightly wilted (about 2 minutes). Stir in onions and bean sprouts, then add tofu and peanut sauce; stir gently to mix well. Cover and cook just until heated through.

Serve over noodles and, if desired, sprinkle with onion flakes. Makes 4 to 6 servings.

Note: To cook rice noodles, in a 5- to 6-quart pan, bring 4 quarts of salted water to a boil. Add noodles and return to a boil; then boil, uncovered, until noodles are barely tender to bite (2 to 4 minutes). Drain; rinse with hot water, drain again, and serve immediately.

Per serving: 366 calories, 12 g protein, 40 g carbohydrates, 19 g total fat, 0 mg cholesterol, 348 mg sodium

Glossary of Asian Ingredients

Because many wok recipes have Asian origins, some of the ingredients called for in this book may be unfamiliar to you. We describe a few of these ingredients here. All are sold in Asian markets, and several—dried mushrooms and five-spice—are stocked in most grocery stores.

Bean sauce. A thick brown sauce made from fermented soybeans, salt, flour, and sugar. Packaged in cans or jars, it's available in two forms: regular, which contains whole beans, and ground, which has a fairly smooth texture. Refrigerate in a tightly closed jar after opening.

Sweet bean sauce, sweeter than the standard product, can be replaced with hoisin sauce; *hot bean sauce* can be replaced with crushed dried hot red chiles or liquid hot pepper seasoning.

Bean threads. Thin, near-transparent strands made from ground mung beans, also sold as *harusame* and as cellophane, translucent, and shining noodles. Uncooked bean threads will keep indefinitely if stored in a cool, dry place. Before using, soak in warm water until pliable (about 30 minutes) or deep-fry (see page 107).

Black beans. Small fermented black beans, preserved in salt and sold in small jars or plastic bags, are often used to flavor Chinese sauces. Store them in a tightly covered jar in a cool, dry place; rinse thoroughly before using.

Chinese five-spice. Widely available five-spice is a fragrant blend of ground cloves, fennel, licorice root, cinnamon, and star anise.

Chinese wheat flour noodles. Sometimes labeled *mein;* available fresh or dried. Use fresh noodles within a day or two, or freeze for longer storage; dried noodles will keep indefinitely in a cool, dry place. Any fresh or dried thin noodles or spaghetti can substitute for mein.

Coconut milk. Prepared coconut milk is available canned or frozen. If it's very thick, dilute it with water.

Dried mushrooms. Shiitake mushrooms are the most commonly sold type of dried Oriental mushrooms. Before using them, you'll need to soak them in warm water, then discard the woody stems.

Black fungus, also called cloud or tree ears, are small and crinkly—but when soaked, the "ears" expand dramatically. Before using the soaked fungus, pinch out the hard, knobby centers.

Stored in a cool, dry place, both dried mushrooms and black fungus will keep indefinitely.

Fish sauce. The Thai version (*nam pla*) of this thin, salty sauce is recommended for use in our recipes; it's much milder than the Vietnamese *nuoc mam*, which has an extremely strong odor and flavor. Store airtight in the refrigerator for up to several months.

Gyoza. Round pot sticker wrappers made from flour and water. Unopened, they'll keep in the refrigerator for up to 3 weeks; once opened, they should be used within a few days. Won ton skins can take the place of gyoza.

Hoisin sauce. Made from soybeans blended with flour, sugar, vinegar, and spices, brownish-red hoisin sauce is used both as a cooking sauce and a condiment. It's available in cans or jars; the canned sauce should be transferred to an airtight jar after opening. Hoisin sauce will keep for several months in the refrigerator.

Oyster sauce. This thick brown sauce, available in most supermarkets, has a subtle oyster flavor. Refrigerate after opening (it will keep for several months).

Rice. *Long-grain rice* is preferred for Chinese and many Southeast Asian dishes; *short-grain rice,* slightly sticky when cooked, is favored by Japanese and Korean cooks. *Sticky (glutinous) rice* requires special preparation (see page 148). It's a popular base for desserts in China and Japan; in Laos and northern Thailand, it's the favorite for every use.

Rice noodles. Also called rice sticks and *mai fun,* these slender strands are made from rice flour. Uncooked noodles will keep indefinitely if stored in a cool, dry place. Before using, boil (see page 80) or deep-fry (see page 121).

Rice paper rounds. Translucent, papery sheets made from rice flour and water. When used as wrappers for deep-fried foods such as Imperial Rolls (see page 110), they become delicately crisp. Choose the thinnest ones you can find. Store unopened packages in a cool, dry place.

Szechwan peppercorns. Unrelated to familiar black pepper, these tiny pods have a mildly hot taste. To bring out the flavor, dry-roast them before using (see Dry-fried Beef, page 112). Store them as you would any other spice.

Tamarind. The fruit of a Southeast Asian legume, tamarind is sold as whole pods, bottled pulp, and in powder and brick form. Pods and pulp are soaked in warm water to make a sour liquid used in sauces.

Unopened packaged pods, powder, and pulp will keep indefinitely; once opened, they'll stay fresh for weeks in the refrigerator, for months in the freezer.

Start this extraordinary main dish by stir-frying strips of marinated beef.
Then spoon the sizzling meat over cool, crisp watercress and onions
to create Hot Beef & Watercress Salad (recipe on facing page).
Add fresh tangerines for dessert.

Salads

(Pictured on facing page)

Hot Beef & Watercress Salad

Preparation time: About 10 minutes

Marinating time: 30 minutes

Cooking time: About 3 minutes

Hot, garlicky stir-fried beef strips top chilled watercress dressed with a light vinaigrette in this unusual salad. Marinate the meat for about half an hour before cooking or, if you like, marinate it overnight in the refrigerator.

- ½ pound lean boneless beef steak (such as top round, flank, or sirloin), cut about 1 inch thick
- 4 cloves garlic, minced or pressed
- 2 teaspoons soy sauce
- 1 teaspoon sugar
- 1 tablespoon salad oil
- 2 tablespoons white wine vinegar
- ¼ teaspoon pepper
- 1 small white onion, thinly sliced and separated into rings
- About ½ pound watercress

Cut beef with the grain into 3-inch-wide strips; then cut each strip across the grain into ⅛-inch-thick slanting slices. In a bowl, stir together garlic, soy, ½ teaspoon of the sugar, and 1 teaspoon of the oil. Add beef; stir to coat. Cover and refrigerate for at least 30 minutes or until next day.

In another bowl, stir together remaining ½ teaspoon sugar, remaining 2 teaspoons oil, vinegar, and pepper. Add onion and mix lightly. Cover and refrigerate for at least 30 minutes or until next day.

Remove and discard tough watercress stems; rinse sprigs thoroughly and pat dry. Then measure 3 cups sprigs, lightly packed. Shortly before serving, add watercress to onion mixture, mixing lightly to coat. Arrange on 2 dinner plates.

Place a wok over high heat. When wok is hot, add beef mixture and stir-fry until meat is browned (1½ to 2 minutes). Arrange meat evenly atop watercress salads. Makes 2 servings.

Per serving: 258 calories, 29 g protein, 8 g carbohydrates, 12 g total fat, 65 mg cholesterol, 449 mg sodium

Hot Chicken & Fruit Salad Platter

Preparation time: 30 minutes

Cooking time: 7 minutes

Here's an extra-pretty whole-meal salad: cantaloupe chunks and warm stir-fried chicken tumbled in a sweet-sour lime sauce, then mounded atop hot rice and ringed with golden pineapple wheels.

- **Sweet Lime Sauce (recipe follows)**
- 1 **small cantaloupe (about 1½ lbs.)**
- 2 **whole chicken breasts (about 1 lb. *each*), skinned and boned**
- 1 **small pineapple (about 3 lbs.)**
- 8 **to 10 large romaine lettuce leaves**
  About 1 tablespoon salad oil
- ¼ **cup lightly packed chopped fresh mint leaves**
- 4 **cups hot cooked rice**
  Fresh mint sprigs (optional)

Prepare Sweet Lime Sauce; set aside.

Seed and peel cantaloupe. Cut fruit into bite-size chunks; set aside. Cut chicken breasts across the grain into ¼-inch-thick strips; set aside.

Peel pineapple. Cut fruit crosswise into 8 equal slices; trim core from each slice, if desired. On a large platter (at least 12 inches in diameter), arrange romaine leaves with tips extending beyond rim of platter. Arrange pineapple on leaves around edge of platter. (At this point, you may cover and refrigerate sauce, cantaloupe, chicken, and salad platter separately for up to 4 hours.)

Place a wok over high heat; when wok is hot, add 1 tablespoon of the oil. When oil is hot, add half the chicken. Stir-fry until meat is no longer pink in center; cut to test (about 3 minutes). Lift out chicken with a slotted spoon and set aside. Repeat to cook remaining chicken, adding more oil as needed.

Stir sauce and pour into wok; bring to a boil, stirring. Remove wok from heat. Add chicken, cantaloupe, and chopped mint; gently turn meat and melon in sauce to coat.

Mound rice on platter atop lettuce. Spoon chicken mixture over rice; garnish with mint sprigs, if desired. Serve hot. Makes 6 servings.

Sweet Lime Sauce. Stir together ½ cup **white wine vinegar**, ¼ cup **sugar**, 1 teaspoon grated **lime peel**, 3 tablespoons **lime juice**, 2 tablespoons **soy sauce**, 1 tablespoon **cornstarch**, and ¼ teaspoon **ground red pepper** (cayenne).

Per serving: 379 calories, 21 g protein, 64 g carbohydrates, 4 g total fat, 42 mg cholesterol, 400 mg sodium

Hot, Wilted Salads

Usually crisp and cool, a salad takes on a completely different character when its greens are briefly touched by a hot, robustly seasoned, meaty dressing. For a light yet satisfying main dish, choose one of these six versions of the old-fashioned wilted salad. You can put each together right at the table, using an electric wok or a regular wok with a portable heat source. Or, if it's more convenient for you, you can make the salad in the kitchen, then transfer it to individual salad plates or a large salad bowl.

Wilted Romaine with Hot Sausage Dressing

Lime Dressing (recipe follows)
3 **quarts bite-size pieces romaine lettuce (about 1 large head)**
1 **small cucumber, thinly sliced**
1 **large tomato, cut into wedges**
1 **small red onion, thinly sliced**
½ **cup fresh cilantro (coriander) leaves**
About ⅓ **pound (4 or 5) Chinese sausages (lop cheong), cut into ¼-inch-thick slanting slices; or ⅓ pound dry salami, thinly sliced**
2 **tablespoons salad oil**
4 **cloves garlic, minced or pressed**

Prepare Lime Dressing and set aside. In a large bowl, combine lettuce, cucumber, tomato, onion, and cilantro. Set aside.

Place sausages and oil in a wok over low heat; cook, stirring occasionally, until meat is lightly browned. Add garlic and stir just until golden. Add Lime Dressing;

stir just until heated through. Pour sausage mixture over lettuce mixture and toss lightly. Serve immediately. Makes 4 first-course servings, 2 entrée servings.

Lime Dressing. Stir together ⅓ cup **lime juice,** 2½ tablespoons **sugar,** 1 tablespoon **fish sauce** (*nam pla*) or soy sauce, and ½ to ¾ teaspoon **crushed red pepper.**

Per first-course serving: 299 calories, 13 g protein, 19 g carbohydrates, 20 g total fat, 0 mg cholesterol, 1126 mg sodium

Wilted Greens

¼ **cup each salad oil and wine vinegar**
2 **teaspoons Dijon mustard**
4 **small thin-skinned potatoes, cooked, peeled, and sliced**
Garlic Croutons (recipe follows)
8 **slices bacon, cut into ½-inch pieces**
5 **cups bite-size pieces mustard or turnip greens**
Salt and pepper

Stir together oil, vinegar, and mustard. Mix half the dressing with potatoes; cover and refrigerate for 2 to 4 hours. Meanwhile, prepare croutons; set aside.

Shortly before serving, place a wok over medium heat; when wok is hot, add bacon and stir-fry until crisp. While bacon is cooking, combine greens and potatoes in a salad bowl. Remove bacon from wok; add to salad. Spoon off and discard all but 3 tablespoons of the drippings; add remaining dressing to drippings and bring to a boil. Pour hot dressing over salad;

invert wok over salad for a few seconds to wilt greens. Season to taste with salt and pepper; add croutons and mix well. Serve immediately. Makes 4 servings.

Garlic Croutons. In a wok or wide frying pan, combine 2 tablespoons **olive oil,** 2 cloves **garlic** (minced or pressed), and 1½ cups **French bread cubes.** Cook over medium-low to medium heat, stirring often, until bread is toasted (about 10 minutes).

Per serving: 431 calories, 8 g protein, 22 g carbohydrates, 35 g total fat, 18 mg cholesterol, 425 mg sodium

Tri-color Salami Salad

1 **pound curly endive (about 2 heads)**
2 **tablespoons salad oil**
6 **ounces thinly sliced dry salami, cut into ¼-inch strips**
3 **tablespoons lemon juice**
2 **cloves garlic, minced or pressed**
1 **teaspoon dry basil**
½ **teaspoon sugar**
2 **cups thinly sliced cauliflowerets**
2 **red bell peppers, seeded and cut into ¼-inch strips**

Wash endive well and shake dry, then tear into bite-size pieces. Set aside.

Place a wok over medium-high heat; when wok is hot, add oil. When oil is hot, add salami and stir-fry until edges are lightly browned. Add lemon juice, garlic, basil, and sugar; stir to blend. (At this point, you may cover mixture and let stand at room temperature for 3 to 4 hours or refrigerate until next day; transfer to another container if wok is not resistant to acid.)

Increase heat under wok to high and bring salami mixture to a boil. Add cauliflower and bell peppers and stir-fry for 1 minute. Add endive and turn off heat. Lift and turn greens and vegetables with 2 forks or spoons until endive is coated with dressing. Immediately spoon onto individual plates and serve. Makes 6 servings.

Per serving: 188 calories, 8 g protein, 7 g carbohydrates, 14 g total fat, 0 mg cholesterol, 665 mg sodium

Red Cabbage & White Sausage Salad

¼ cup salad oil
1 to 1¼ pounds white veal sausages such as bratwurst, bockwurst, or weisswurst, cut into ¼-inch slices
3 tablespoons white wine vinegar
2 tablespoons sugar
1½ teaspoons *each* Dijon mustard, celery seeds, and Worcestershire
1 clove garlic, minced or pressed
1 cup thinly sliced green onions (including tops)
6 cups finely shredded red cabbage (about 1½ lbs.)
   Salt and pepper

Place a wok over medium-high heat; when wok is hot, add oil. When oil is hot, add sausages and cook, turning frequently, until browned. Add vinegar, sugar, mustard, celery seeds, Worcestershire, and garlic. (At this point, you may let mixture stand for 3 to 4 hours at room temperature or cover and refrigerate until next day; transfer to another container if wok is not resistant to acid.)

Increase heat under wok to high and bring sausage mixture to a boil; mix in onions and cabbage.

Turn off heat; lift and turn cabbage with 2 forks or spoons until coated with dressing. Season to taste with salt and pepper; immediately spoon onto individual plates and serve. Makes 6 servings.

Per serving: 422 calories, 15 g protein, 15 g carbohydrates, 34 g total fat, 57 mg cholesterol, 592 mg sodium

Hot Spinach, Apple & Sausage Salad

1 to 1¼ pounds spinach
1¼ to 1½ pounds mild Italian sausages, casings removed
¼ cup *each* red wine vinegar and sugar
¼ teaspoon *each* ground nutmeg and dry mustard
1 large red onion, thinly sliced and separated into rings
2 large red-skinned apples, cored and thinly sliced
   Salt

Remove and discard tough spinach stems and any yellow or wilted leaves. Rinse remaining leaves well, pat dry, and set aside.

Slice or break sausages into ½-inch pieces. Place a wok over medium heat; when wok is hot, add sausages. Cook, stirring occasionally, until well browned; pour off and discard all but ¼ cup of the fat.

Add vinegar, sugar, nutmeg, and mustard to sausages and fat in wok; stir to blend. (At this point, you may let mixture stand for 3 to 4 hours at room temperature or cover and refrigerate until next day; transfer to another container if wok is not resistant to acid.)

Increase heat under wok to high and bring sausage mixture to a boil. Then add onion and apples; cook, stirring, for 1 minute. Add spinach, then turn off heat.

Lift and turn greens with 2 forks

or spoons until coated with dressing. Season to taste with salt, then serve immediately. Makes 6 servings.

Per serving: 437 calories, 19 g protein, 23 g carbohydrates, 30 g total fat, 73 mg cholesterol, 819 mg sodium

Wilted Chinese Cabbage

¼ cup sesame seeds
¼ cup salad oil
½ cup thinly sliced green onions, including tops
½ pound lean ground pork
¼ cup sugar
1 teaspoon sesame oil
6 tablespoons rice wine vinegar
1 tablespoon soy sauce
½ teaspoon pepper
1 large head napa cabbage (about 3 lbs.), finely shredded
   Fresh cilantro (coriander) sprigs

Place a wok over medium-high heat; when hot, add sesame seeds and stir-fry until golden (about 2 minutes). Pour out of wok and set aside.

Add 2 tablespoons salad oil to wok; when oil is hot, add onions and stir-fry for 1 minute. Add pork and stir-fry until meat is lightly browned (about 3 minutes).

Add remaining 2 tablespoons oil, sugar, sesame oil, vinegar, soy and pepper to wok; stir to blend. Increase heat under wok to high and bring pork mixture to a boil. Add cabbage and sesame seeds and turn off heat. Lift and turn cabbage with 2 forks or spoons until coated with dressing. Immediately spoon onto individual plates, garnish with cilantro, and serve. Makes 8 servings.

Per serving: 226 calories, 8 protein, 14 carbohydrates, 17 total fat, 21 mg cholestrol, 163 mg sodium

Hot & Cold Ginger Chicken Salad

Preparation time: About 25 minutes

Marinating time: 30 minutes

Cooking time: About 10 minutes

Hot, gingery chicken strips contrast with cold, crisp watercress; buttery avocado slices provide a pleasant foil to the peppery flavors of meat and greens.

> **Ginger Marinade (recipe follows)**
> 3 **whole chicken breasts (about 1 lb. *each*), skinned, boned, and cut into ½- by 2-inch strips**
> 3 **tablespoons olive oil or salad oil**
> ¼ **cup lemon juice**
> 6 **cups lightly packed watercress sprigs (about 1 lb.), washed and crisped**
> **Salt and pepper**
> 2 **large ripe avocados**
> 1 **lemon, cut into 6 wedges**
> **About 6 tablespoons salad oil**

Prepare Ginger Marinade; add chicken and mix until well coated. Let marinate at room temperature for 30 minutes, or cover and refrigerate until next day.

In a large bowl, combine olive oil and 3 table-spoons of the lemon juice; mix until well blended. Add watercress and season to taste with salt and pepper; mix lightly until well coated. Pit and peel avocados; cut lengthwise into thin wedges. Moisten with remaining 1 tablespoon lemon juice. Arrange watercress, avocado, and lemon wedges on individual dinner plates or on a platter.

Lift chicken from marinade; discard marinade. Place a wok over high heat; when wok is hot, add 2 tablespoons of the salad oil. When oil is hot, add about a third of the chicken (do not crowd wok). Stir-fry until lightly browned on outside and no longer pink in center; cut to test (about 3 minutes). Remove from wok and set aside. Repeat to cook remaining chicken, adding remaining salad oil as needed.

Spoon hot chicken over watercress and serve immediately. Makes 6 servings.

Ginger Marinade. In a large bowl, stir together 2 tablespoons **cornstarch** and ¼ cup **soy sauce** until smooth. Add ⅓ cup *each* **sesame oil** and minced **fresh ginger,** ¼ cup **lemon juice,** 1 tablespoon **salad oil,** ⅛ teaspoon **chili oil** or liquid hot pepper seasoning, and 1 clove **garlic,** minced or pressed. Mix until well blended.

Per serving: 596 calories, 44 g protein, 12 g carbohydrates, 43 g total fat, 100 mg cholesterol, 639 mg sodium

(Pictured on facing page)
Shrimp & Vegetable Salad

Preparation time: 20 minutes

Cooking time: 6 minutes

Chilling time: At least 4 hours

Crisp vegetables and small shrimp are chilled in a soy-flavored marinade and topped with crunchy cashews to make a satisfying one-dish lunch.

> ½ **pound broccoli**
> 2 **tablespoons salad oil**
> 2 **cloves garlic, minced or pressed**
> ¾ **teaspoon minced fresh ginger**
> ½ **pound mushrooms, thinly sliced**
> ½ **pound Chinese pea pods (also called snow or sugar peas) or sugar snap peas, ends and strings removed; or 1 package (6 oz.) frozen Chinese pea pods, thawed and drained**
> ⅓ **cup regular-strength chicken broth**
> 1 **tablespoon soy sauce**
> ½ **teaspoon sugar**
> 1 **tablespoon oyster sauce (optional)**
> 1 **can (4½ oz.) small shrimp, drained**
> ½ **cup mayonnaise (optional)**
> **Salad greens, such as butter lettuce leaves, endive spears, and dandelion greens**
> ¼ **cup salted roasted cashews or slivered almonds**
> 1 **jar (2 oz.) sliced pimentos, drained**

Cut off and discard tough ends of broccoli stalks. Cut flowerets off broccoli stalks; then cut flowerets into ¼-inch-thick slices. Peel stalks and cut crosswise into ⅛-inch-thick slices. Set aside.

Place a wok over high heat; when wok is hot, add oil. When oil begins to heat, add garlic and ginger and stir-fry for 1 minute. Add broccoli, mushrooms, and fresh pea pods; stir-fry just until broccoli and pea pods are tender-crisp to bite (3 to 4 minutes; if using frozen pea pods, add for last 30 seconds). Pour into a bowl.

In a cup, stir together broth, soy, sugar, and, if desired, oyster sauce. Pour over vegetables; then stir in shrimp. Let cool, then cover and refrigerate for at least 4 hours. Drain vegetable mixture, discarding liquid. If desired, stir in mayonnaise. Spoon over greens, sprinkle with cashews, and garnish with pimentos. Makes 4 servings.

Per serving: 206 calories, 14 g protein, 14 g carbohydrates, 12 g total fat, 48 mg cholesterol, 454 mg sodium

You'll want to linger over lunch when the main course is
Shrimp & Vegetable Salad (recipe on facing page). Soy-seasoned
broccoli, mushrooms, and delicate shrimp cascade over flavorful greens;
cashews add crunch.

Chile Shrimp & Corn Salad

Preparation time: About 20 minutes

Cooking time: 11 minutes

Chilling time: 1 to 4 hours

The salad is cold, but its flavor is *hot:* corn, bell peppers, and juicy shrimp are stir-fried in a zippy chile-infused oil. Before serving, you toss the chilled stir-fry with fresh spinach and leaf lettuce.

- ¼ **cup olive oil or salad oil**
- 3 **small dried hot red chiles**
- ½ **teaspoon pepper**
- 2 **cups fresh corn kernels, cut from about 3 large ears of corn; or 1 package (10 oz.) frozen whole-kernel corn, thawed and drained**
- 1 **medium-size red bell pepper, seeded and diced**
- 1 **pound medium-size raw shrimp, shelled and deveined**
- 1 **tablespoon soy sauce**
- ⅔ **cup cider vinegar**
- 1 **pound spinach, stems and any tough or wilted leaves removed, green leaves washed and crisped**
- 1 **pound green leaf lettuce, washed and crisped**

Place a wok over medium heat; when wok is hot, add oil. When oil is hot, add chiles and stir until lightly browned (about 4 minutes). Add pepper, corn, and bell pepper. Increase heat to high; stir-fry until bell pepper is tender to bite (about 3 minutes). Add shrimp; stir-fry just until shrimp turn pink (about 3 minutes).

Remove wok from heat. Stir in soy and vinegar, then spoon shrimp mixture into a small bowl. Let cool, then cover and refrigerate until shrimp are cold (at least 1 hour) or for up to 4 hours.

Meanwhile, tear spinach and lettuce into bite-size pieces; you should have about 4 quarts, lightly packed. Place torn greens in a large salad bowl;

spoon shrimp mixture over greens. Use chiles as garnish or remove and discard. Toss salad and serve. Makes 6 to 8 servings.

Per serving: 172 calories, 13 g protein, 14 g carbohydrates, 9 g total fat, 65 mg cholesterol, 269 mg sodium

Calamari Salad al Pesto

Preparation time: About 15 minutes

Cooking time: 7 minutes

Chilling time: At least 3 hours

Julienne strips of squid and crunchy toasted walnuts go into this delicious and attractive salad. The dressing's a homemade pesto sauce you whirl together in your blender.

- **Fresh Pesto (recipe follows)**
- ¼ **cup olive oil**
- 1 **small onion, finely diced**
- 2 **cloves garlic, minced or pressed**
- 3 **tablespoons chopped walnuts**
- 1 **pound tenderized giant squid (calamari) steaks, cut into ¼-inch-wide strips**
- 2 **tablespoons dry sherry**
- 1 **medium-size red bell pepper, seeded and diced**
- ¼ **cup diced celery**
- 1 **tablespoon chopped parsley**
- ¼ **cup cider vinegar**
- 1 **tablespoon lemon or lime juice**
  Salt and pepper
  About 4 cups shredded iceberg lettuce

Prepare Fresh Pesto and set aside.

Place a wok over medium heat; when wok is hot, add oil. When oil is hot, add onion, garlic, and walnuts. Stir-fry until onion is soft and walnuts are toasted (about 5 minutes). Add squid and sherry and stir-fry just until squid turns an opaque chalky white (about 1 minute); do not overcook. With a slotted spoon, transfer contents of wok to a bowl.

To squid mixture, add bell pepper, celery, parsley, Fresh Pesto, vinegar, and lemon juice; mix well. Season to taste with salt and pepper. Cover and refrigerate for at least 3 hours or until next day. Serve over lettuce. Makes 4 to 6 servings.

Fresh Pesto. In a blender or food processor, whirl until smoothly puréed ¼ cup **olive oil,** ¼ cup lightly packed **fresh basil leaves,** 2 tablespoons **pine nuts,** 1 clove **garlic,** and 1 teaspoon **dry white wine** (optional).

Per serving: 284 calories, 15 g protein, 7 g carbohydrates, 23 g total fat, 42 mg cholesterol, 67 mg sodium

Sesame Noodle Salad

Preparation time: About 10 minutes, plus 30 minutes to soak dried mushrooms

Cooking time: 5 minutes

Chilling time: At least 2 hours

Al dente vermicelli combined with tender-crisp vegetables and a light, sweet-tart dressing makes a delightful chilled salad. For a perfect summer meal, serve it with cold roast chicken and fresh fruit in season.

> **Sesame Dressing (recipe follows)**
> 8   **medium-size fresh shiitake or dried Oriental mushrooms; or 8 large button mushrooms**
> 8   **ounces dried vermicelli**
>   **Boiling salted water**
>   **About 3 tablespoons salad oil**
> 2   **teaspoons minced fresh ginger**
> ¼   **pound green beans (ends removed), cut into ¼-inch slanting slices**
> 2   **medium-size carrots, peeled and cut into julienne strips**
> 2   **medium-size crookneck squash, cut into julienne strips**
> 1   **tablespoon** *each* **soy sauce and dry sherry**
>   **Salt**

Prepare Sesame Dressing; set aside.

If using dried mushrooms, soak in warm water to cover for 30 minutes, then drain. Cut off and discard stems; squeeze caps dry. If using fresh mushrooms, trim any tough stems from shiitake mushrooms. Then set shiitake or button mushroom caps aside; cut stems into julienne strips.

Meanwhile, following package directions, cook vermicelli in boiling salted water until barely tender to bite. Drain, rinse with cold water, and drain again. Place in a large bowl and set aside.

Place a wok over high heat; when wok is hot, add 2 tablespoons of the oil. When oil is hot, add ginger, beans, carrots, squash, and julienned mushroom stems. Stir-fry just until vegetables are barely tender-crisp to bite (about 1½ minutes). Remove from wok; add to noodles.

To wok, add remaining 1 tablespoon oil, soy, sherry, and mushroom caps. Reduce heat to medium; cover wok if using dried mushrooms (leave uncovered if using fresh mushrooms). Cook, turning occasionally, until mushrooms have absorbed all liquid (about 2 minutes). Pour into a small bowl, cover, and refrigerate.

Mix dressing with noodles and vegetables. Season to taste with salt. Cover and refrigerate, stirring occasionally, for at least 2 hours or until next day.

To serve, garnish salad with mushroom caps. Makes 4 to 6 servings.

Sesame Dressing. In a wok, combine ¼ cup **salad oil** and 3 tablespoons **sesame seeds.** Stir over medium-low heat until seeds are golden (2 to 3 minutes). Remove from heat and let cool. Stir together ⅓ cup **sugar,** ½ cup **distilled white vinegar,** and 2 tablespoons **dry sherry** until sugar is dissolved. Mix in cooled sesame seed mixture.

Per serving: 402 calories, 7 g protein, 52 g carbohydrates, 19 g total fat, 0 mg cholesterol, 185 mg sodium

Soy-braised Eggplant Salad

Preparation time: 20 minutes

Cooking time: About 30 minutes

Flavored with vinegar, ginger, chiles, and soy, tender braised eggplant is equally good as an appetizer or an accompaniment to barbecued meats.

> 1   **medium-size eggplant (¾ to 1 lb.)**
> 3   **tablespoons salad oil**
> 1   **cup water**
> ¼   **cup soy sauce**
> 5   **thin, quarter-size slices fresh ginger**
> 2   **cloves garlic, minced or pressed**
> 1   **teaspoon sugar**
> 3   **tablespoons red wine vinegar**
> ⅓   **cup coarsely chopped fresh cilantro (coriander)**
> 2   **teaspoons minced fresh ginger**
> ¼   **to ½ teaspoon crushed dried hot red chiles**

Remove stem from eggplant, then peel eggplant and cut lengthwise into 1-inch-thick slices. Cut slices into 1-inch strips.

Place a wok over medium-high heat; when wok is hot, add oil. When oil is hot, add eggplant and stir-fry for 3 minutes. (Eggplant will soak up oil immediately; stir constantly to prevent burning.)

Add water, soy, ginger slices, garlic, and sugar. Reduce heat to low, cover, and simmer, stirring occasionally, until eggplant is tender when pierced (about 15 minutes). Add vinegar. Let cool, turning eggplant occasionally. (At this point, you may cover and refrigerate until next day.)

Transfer eggplant and sauce to a serving dish, then sprinkle with cilantro, minced ginger, and chiles. Serve cold or at room temperature. Makes 4 servings.

Per serving: 232 calories, 3 g protein, 11 g carbohydrates, 21 g total fat, 0 mg cholesterol, 1035 mg sodium

Bright carrot and cucumber slivers, cauliflowerets, and sweet-sour flavorings
come together in these Sesame-topped Vegetables from Malaysia
(recipe on facing page). Garnish with arugula leaves and a delicate fan
of paper-thin cucumber slices.

Vegetables

Cantonese Vegetable Medley

Preparation time: About 10 minutes, plus 30 minutes to soak fungus

Cooking time: 5 minutes

Meaty "cloud ears" combine with crisp carrots, broccoli, and water chestnuts in this colorful Cantonese dish. Be sure to allow an extra half hour or so to soak the black fungus.

- ½ **cup dried black fungus (also called cloud or tree ears)**
- 1 **tablespoon** *each* **cornstarch, water, and soy sauce**
- 1 **cup regular-strength chicken broth**
- 2 **tablespoons salad oil**
- ½ **teaspoon minced fresh ginger**
- 1 **small clove garlic, minced or pressed**
- 1½ **cups** *each* **broccoli flowerets and thinly sliced carrots**
- ⅓ **cup sliced water chestnuts**

Soak fungus in warm water to cover for 30 minutes; drain. Pinch out and discard hard, knobby centers; cut remaining fungus into bite-size pieces.

In a small bowl, stir together cornstarch, water, and soy; stir in broth and set aside.

Place a wok over high heat; when wok is hot, add oil. When oil is hot, add ginger, garlic, broccoli, carrots, and fungus. Stir-fry for 1 minute. Stir cornstarch mixture; add to vegetables along with water chestnuts. Stir until sauce boils and thickens. Makes 4 to 6 servings.

Per serving: 93 calories, 2 g protein, 11 g carbohydrates, 5 g total fat, 0 mg cholesterol, 190 mg sodium

(Pictured on facing page)

Sesame-topped Vegetables

Preparation time: 10 minutes

Cooking time: 8 minutes

Malaysian *achar*, a colorful tumble of sweet-and-sour vegetables, provides a cooling contrast to any spicy entrée. Serve warm or at room temperature.

- ½ **English or European cucumber**
- 3 **large carrots**
- 3 **cups cauliflowerets**
- ½ **cup sesame seeds**
- ⅓ **cup salad oil**
- 2 **cloves garlic, minced or pressed**
- ½ **cup minced shallots**
- ½ **cup distilled white vinegar**
- ¼ **cup sugar**
  Soy sauce
  Arugula leaves (optional)

Cut cucumber and carrots into thin, about 6-inch-long slivers. Break cauliflowerets into smaller flowerets. Set vegetables aside.

Place a wok over medium heat. When wok is hot, add sesame seeds and stir until golden (2 to 3 minutes). Pour out of wok and set aside.

Pour oil into wok. When oil is hot, add garlic and shallots; stir-fry until shallots are soft. Increase heat to high and add vinegar, sugar, cauliflowerets, and carrots. Stir-fry until vegetables are tender-crisp to bite; add cucumber and stir-fry until hot. Season to taste with soy. Transfer to a serving plate; sprinkle with sesame seeds. Garnish with arugula, if desired. Makes 6 to 8 servings.

Per serving: 192 calories, 3 g protein, 17 g carbohydrates, 14 g total fat, 0 mg cholesterol, 22 mg sodium

Chinese Ginger-Garlic Asparagus

Preparation time: About 10 minutes

Cooking time: About 5 minutes

Crisp stir-fried asparagus is especially tasty when accented with garlic and fresh ginger; broccoli benefits from the same treatment.

- 1 **pound asparagus**
- 2 **tablespoons salad oil**
- 1 **large clove garlic, minced or pressed**
- ½ **to 1 teaspoon grated fresh ginger**
- 2 **tablespoons water**

Snap off and discard tough ends of asparagus, then cut spears into ¼-inch slanting slices.

Place a wok over high heat; when wok is hot, add oil. When oil begins to heat, add garlic and ginger and stir once; then add asparagus and stir-fry for 1 minute. Add water; cover and cook until asparagus is tender-crisp to bite (2 to 3 minutes). Makes 4 servings.

Per serving: 75 calories, 2 g protein, 3 g carbohydrates, 7 g total fat, 0 mg cholesterol, 1 mg sodium

A Light Technique

Stir-frying is widely appreciated for its bright, fresh-tasting results. But not everyone realizes that those rich colors and peak flavors can be enjoyed for a surprisingly small investment of calories. The following hearty entrées, for example, weigh in at just 226 to 274 calories per serving.

If it's salt that you wish to reduce, use a low-sodium soy sauce. We also recommend using your own homemade unsalted chicken broth in these and other stir-fries; you and your guests can add salt to taste at the table.

Lamb with Spring Onions

1   **pound boneless leg of lamb**
½   **teaspoon Chinese five-spice**
1   **egg white**
2   **cloves garlic, slivered**
4   **thin, quarter-size slices fresh ginger or ⅛ teaspoon ground ginger**
1   **tablespoon cornstarch**
5   **teaspoons soy sauce**
6   **tablespoons dry sherry**
2   **tablespoons water**
10 **green onions (including tops)**
2   **tablespoons salad oil**

Trim and discard fat from lamb; cut meat into bite-size strips ⅛ inch thick. In a bowl, mix lamb, five-spice, egg white, garlic, ginger, 1 teaspoon of the cornstarch, and 1 teaspoon of the soy. Let stand for 10 minutes.

Meanwhile, blend sherry, water, remaining 2 teaspoons cornstarch, and remaining 4 teaspoons soy in a small bowl. Cut off white part of each onion, then cut each of these pieces in half. Cut two 1½-inch-long sections from each green top; discard remainder of green tops.

Place a wok over high heat; when wok is hot, add oil. When oil is hot, add meat mixture and stir-fry until lightly browned (2 to 3 minutes). Return to bowl.

To wok, add sherry mixture and white part of onions. Cook, stirring, until mixture is thickened. Add meat mixture and onion tops and cook, stirring, just until heated through (1 to 2 minutes). Makes 4 servings.

Per serving: 226 calories, 21 g protein, 8 g carbohydrates, 12 g total fat, 66 mg cholesterol, 511 mg sodium

Beef & Vegetable Sauté

⅓   **cup firmly packed brown sugar**
2   **tablespoons cornstarch**
¼   **cup cider vinegar**
3   **tablespoons soy sauce**
1½ **pounds top round or flank steak, cut ½ to ¾ inch thick**
2   **tablespoons butter or margarine**
1   **large onion, thinly sliced**
1½ **cups thinly sliced carrots**
1   **cup green beans, in 1-inch lengths**
1   **cup water**
1½ **cups thinly sliced zucchini**

In a small bowl, stir together sugar, cornstarch, vinegar, and soy until cornstarch is dissolved. Set aside.

Trim and discard fat from meat. Cut meat into slanting slices ⅛ to ¼ inch thick.

Place a wok over medium heat; when wok is hot, add 1 tablespoon of the butter. When butter is melted, add meat strips, a few at a time, and stir-fry until well browned, adding remaining 1 tablespoon butter as needed. As meat is browned, lift out and set aside.

When all meat has been cooked, add onion, carrots, beans, and ½ cup of the water to wok; stir well, cover, and cook, stirring often, for 8 minutes. Stir in zucchini and remaining ½ cup water; cook, uncovered, just until all vegetables are tender to bite (about 2 more minutes).

Stir cornstarch mixture and add to vegetables along with meat; stir until sauce boils and thickens. Serve immediately. Makes 6 servings.

Per serving: 274 calories, 26 g protein, 23 g carbohydrates, 9 g total fat, 71 mg cholesterol, 628 mg sodium

Shrimp with Peking Sauce

   Peking Stir-fry Sauce (recipe follows)
2   **tablespoons salad oil**
1   **pound medium-size raw shrimp, shelled and deveined**

1 large red onion, slivered

2 cups broccoli flowerets

1 red bell pepper, seeded and cut into long strips

1 green or yellow bell pepper, seeded and cut into long strips

2 to 4 tablespoons water

2 teaspoons cornstarch

Prepare Peking Stir-fry Sauce; set aside.

Place a wok over high heat; when wok is hot, add 1 tablespoon of the oil. When oil is hot, add shrimp. Stir-fry just until shrimp turn pink (about 2 minutes). Remove shrimp from wok.

Add remaining 1 tablespoon oil, onion, broccoli, all bell peppers, and 1 tablespoon of the water. Stir-fry, adding more water as needed, until broccoli is barely tender to bite (2 to 4 minutes).

Blend cornstarch into prepared sauce. Add to wok and stir just until sauce is thickened and clear. Add shrimp; stir just until heated through. Serve immediately. Makes 4 servings.

Peking Stir-fry Sauce. Stir together 2 cloves **garlic,** minced or pressed; 2 tablespoons minced **fresh ginger** or 1 teaspoon ground ginger; ½ cup **water;** ¼ cup **hoisin sauce;** 2 tablespoons **soy sauce;** 1 tablespoon **rice wine vinegar;** and 2 teaspoons **sugar.**

Per serving: 246 calories, 23 g protein, 19 g carbohydrates, 9 g total fat, 140 mg cholesterol, 1179 mg sodium

Asparagus Chicken Stir-fry

½ cup Homemade Chicken Broth (recipe follows) or regular-strength chicken broth

8 green onions (including tops)

1 pound asparagus

½ pound mushrooms

1 tablespoon *each* cornstarch, dry sherry, and soy sauce

3 tablespoons sesame oil or salad oil

1 tablespoon minced fresh ginger or ½ teaspoon ground ginger

2 cloves garlic, minced or pressed

1½ pounds chicken breasts, skinned, boned, and cut into ½- by 1-inch strips

Prepare Homemade Chicken Broth and set aside.

Cut onions diagonally into 1-inch pieces. Snap off and discard tough ends of asparagus; cut spears into 1-inch slanting slices. Thinly slice mushrooms. Combine cornstarch, sherry, soy, and broth; stir until cornstarch is dissolved.

Place a wok over high heat; when wok is hot, add oil. When oil is hot, add ginger, garlic, and chicken. Stir-fry until chicken is no longer pink in center; cut to test (about 2 minutes). Lift chicken from wok and set aside.

To wok, add onions, asparagus, and mushrooms; stir-fry for 1 minute. Add chicken; stir broth mixture and add. Bring to a boil, stirring; stir for 1 more minute. Makes 4 servings.

Per serving: 268 calories, 30 g protein, 10 g carbohydrates, 12 g total fat, 65 mg cholesterol, 343 mg sodium

Homemade Chicken Broth. Rinse 5 pounds **bony chicken pieces** (wings, backs, necks, carcasses); place in a 6- to 8-quart pan. Add 2 large **onions,** cut into chunks; 2 large **carrots,** cut into chunks; 6 to 8 **parsley sprigs;** ½ teaspoon **whole black peppercorns;** and 3½ quarts **water.** Bring to a boil; then reduce heat, cover, and simmer for 3 hours. Let cool.

Strain broth into a bowl. Discard scraps. Cover broth and refrigerate until fat solidifies (at least 4 hours)

or for up to 2 days. Lift off and discard fat. To store, freeze in 1-cup to 4-cup portions. Makes about 10 cups.

Vegetable & Bulgur Stir-fry

2 tablespoons salad oil

1 cup bulgur

1 tablespoon sesame seeds

2 medium-size carrots, thinly sliced

1 *each* medium-size zucchini and crookneck squash, thinly sliced

¼ pound mushrooms, thinly sliced

1 clove garlic, minced or pressed

½ teaspoon *each* dry basil, dry marjoram leaves, and dry oregano leaves

⅛ teaspoon pepper

1¾ cups water

2 cups broccoli flowerets

½ cup shredded jack cheese

½ cup sliced green onions (including tops)

3 pocket breads, halved and warmed (optional)

Lemon wedges

Place a wok over medium-high heat; when wok is hot, add 1 tablespoon of the oil. When oil is hot, add bulgur, sesame seeds, and carrots; stir-fry for 2 minutes. Add remaining 1 tablespoon oil, zucchini, crookneck squash, mushrooms, and garlic; stir-fry for 2 more minutes. Add herbs, pepper, and water; reduce heat, cover, and simmer until liquid is absorbed (about 10 minutes).

Add broccoli; cover and cook for 2 minutes. Stir in cheese. Sprinkle with onions and spoon into pocket bread, if desired. Serve with lemon wedges. Makes 6 servings.

Per serving: 231 calories, 8 g protein, 32 g carbohydrates, 9 g total fat, 9 mg cholesterol, 78 mg sodium

Broccoli with Gorgonzola & Walnuts

Preparation time: About 10 minutes

Cooking time: About 15 minutes

Gorgonzola is a creamy blue-veined cheese from a small Italian town of the same name; if you can't find the Italian product, use one of the delicious American Gorgonzolas or any other blue-veined cheese.

- 1¼ **pounds broccoli**
- ¼ **cup butter or margarine**
- ¾ **cup walnut pieces**
- ½ **cup regular-strength chicken broth**
- 1 **small onion, finely chopped**
- 1 **teaspoon cornstarch**
- 1 **tablespoon white wine vinegar**
- ½ **teaspoon pepper**
- 1 **cup (about 4 oz.) crumbled Gorgonzola or other blue-veined cheese**

Cut off broccoli flowerets and slash their stems; discard broccoli stalks or reserve for another use. You should have about 4½ cups flowerets.

Place a wok over medium-high heat; when wok is hot, add 1 tablespoon of the butter. When butter is melted, add walnuts and stir-fry until browned (about 1½ minutes). Transfer to a bowl; set aside.

Wipe wok clean and add 2 tablespoons more butter; when butter is melted, add broccoli and stir-fry for 3 minutes. Add ¼ cup of the broth, cover, and cook until tender-crisp to bite (about 5 more minutes). Transfer broccoli to bowl with walnuts.

Wipe wok clean again and add remaining 1 tablespoon butter; when butter is melted, add onion and stir-fry until golden brown (about 3 minutes). Mix cornstarch with remaining ¼ cup broth, add to wok, bring to a boil, and boil for 30 seconds. Reduce heat to low; stir in vinegar, pepper, broccoli, and walnuts and cook until heated through (about 2 minutes). Add cheese and stir until partially melted. Makes 2 or 3 servings.

Per serving: 536 calories, 20 g protein, 20 g carbohydrates, 46 g total fat, 70 mg cholesterol, 901 mg sodium

Spicy Napa Cabbage

Preparation time: About 5 minutes

Cooking time: 4 minutes

Spiced with ground red pepper, mild-flavored napa cabbage turns zesty—and makes a good companion dish for roast pork or ham.

- 2 **tablespoons white wine vinegar**
- 2 **tablespoons sugar**
- 1 **tablespoon soy sauce**
- ¼ **teaspoon ground red pepper (cayenne)**
- 3 **tablespoons salad oil**
- 1 **small head napa cabbage (1¼ to 1½ lbs.), cut into 2-inch pieces**

In a small bowl, stir together vinegar, sugar, soy, and red pepper; set aside.

Place a wok over high heat; when wok is hot, add oil. When oil is hot, add cabbage and stir-fry until cabbage begins to wilt (2 to 3 minutes). Add vinegar mixture and mix well. Serve warm or at room temperature. Makes 4 to 6 servings.

Per serving: 137 calories, 2 g protein, 11 g carbohydrates, 10 g total fat, 0 mg cholesterol, 362 mg sodium

(Pictured on facing page)

Sweet & Sour Carrots

Preparation time: About 10 minutes

Cooking time: 8 minutes

A simple, not-too-sweet sauce intensifies the natural sweetness of carrots. The sauce enhances cauliflower and green beans, too.

- ¼ **cup regular-strength chicken broth**
- 2 **tablespoons *each* vinegar and firmly packed brown sugar**
- 1 **tablespoon cornstarch**
- 1 **tablespoon salad oil**
- 1 **pound carrots (about 4 medium-size), cut into ¼-inch-thick slanting slices**
- 1 **small onion, cut in half, then cut crosswise into ¼-inch-thick slices**
- 3 **tablespoons regular-strength chicken broth**
  Salt
  Minced parsley (optional)

In a bowl, stir together the ¼ cup broth, vinegar, sugar, and cornstarch. Set aside.

Place a wok over high heat; when wok is hot, add oil. When oil is hot, add carrots and onion and stir-fry for 1 minute. Add the 3 tablespoons broth and reduce heat to medium; cover and cook until carrots are tender-crisp to bite. Increase heat to high. Stir cornstarch mixture, pour into wok, and stir until sauce boils and thickens. Season to taste with salt. Sprinkle with parsley, if desired. Makes 4 servings.

Per serving: 114 calories, 1 g protein, 20 g carbohydrates, 4 g total fat, 0 mg cholesterol, 147 mg sodium

In all their golden glory, Sweet & Sour Carrots (recipe on facing page)
show off the Chinese cook's artistry with humble ingredients.
Covered cooking in a wok preserves the vegetable's intense color
and sweet flavor.

Sesame-blacked Carrots

Preparation time: About 10 minutes

Cooking time: About 10 minutes

Sold in Asian markets, black sesame seeds cost and taste the same as the familiar yellow or white seeds—but they look a lot more dramatic. Here, they're toasted and blended with gingery stir-fried carrots.

- ¼ **cup black sesame seeds**
- 1 **tablespoon olive oil or salad oil**
- 1 **small onion, thinly sliced**
- 2 **tablespoons butter or margarine**
- 1½ **pounds carrots (about 6 medium-size), peeled and shredded**
- 1 **tablespoon minced crystallized ginger**
  Salt and pepper

Place a wok over medium heat; when wok is hot, add sesame seeds and stir often until seeds taste toasted and the few light-colored seeds among the black turn golden (about 2 minutes). Pour seeds out of wok and set aside.

Add oil to wok and increase heat to medium-high. When oil is hot, add onion and stir-fry until soft (about 4 minutes). Add butter, carrots, and ginger; stir-fry until carrots are tender-crisp to bite (about 3 minutes). Stir in sesame seeds and season to taste with salt and pepper. Makes 4 to 6 servings.

Per serving: 143 calories, 2 g protein, 14 g carbohydrates, 9 g total fat, 10 mg cholesterol, 77 mg sodium

Acapulco Corn Medley

Preparation time: About 15 minutes

Cooking time: About 10 minutes

Enjoy this red, green, and yellow side dish in any season—you can use either fresh or frozen corn, and the other ingredients are available year round. If you'd like to tone down the snappy flavor, cut back on the hot pepper seasoning and chili powder.

- 2 **tablespoons butter or margarine**
- 1 **medium-size onion, chopped**
- 1 **red or green bell pepper, seeded and chopped**
- 1 **pound zucchini, cut into ½-inch cubes**
- 1 **canned whole green chile, seeded and chopped**
- 1½ **cups fresh corn kernels, cut from about 2 large ears of corn; or 1½ cups frozen whole-kernel corn, thawed and drained**

- 1 **can (about 14 oz.) pear-shaped tomatoes**
- ¼ **teaspoon liquid hot pepper seasoning**
- 1 **teaspoon paprika**
- ½ **teaspoon chili powder**

Place a wok over medium heat; when wok is hot, add butter. When butter is melted, add onion and bell pepper; stir-fry until vegetables are soft (about 5 minutes).

Stir in zucchini, chile, corn, tomatoes (break up with a spoon) and their liquid, hot pepper seasoning, paprika, and chili powder. Increase heat to high; stir often until almost all liquid has evaporated and zucchini is tender to bite (about 5 minutes). Makes 4 to 6 servings.

Per serving: 102 calories, 3 g protein, 15 g carbohydrates, 7 g total fat, 10 mg cholesterol, 209 mg sodium

Szechwan Eggplant

Preparation time: About 10 minutes

Cooking time: 15 minutes

Braised in broth that's richly flavored with pork and chiles, eggplant turns out savory and tender. Use either regular eggplant or the smaller, slimmer Japanese eggplant.

- ½ **cup regular-strength chicken broth**
- 1 **teaspoon *each* sugar and vinegar**
- 1 **tablespoon soy sauce**
- ½ **teaspoon salt**
  Dash of pepper
- 1 **large eggplant or about 3 Japanese eggplants (about 1¼ lbs. *total*)**
- 5 **tablespoons salad oil**
- ¼ **pound lean ground pork**
- 2 **green onions (including tops), finely chopped**
- 1 **teaspoon minced fresh ginger**
- 2 **teaspoons minced garlic**
- 2 **teaspoons hot bean sauce; or 2 small dried hot red chiles, crumbled and seeded**
- 1 **teaspoon cornstarch and 1 tablespoon water, stirred together**
- 1 **teaspoon sesame oil**

In a bowl, stir together broth, sugar, vinegar, soy, salt, and pepper; set aside. Peel eggplant, if desired (don't peel Japanese eggplant); cut into strips 2 inches long and ½ inch thick.

Place a wok over medium-high heat. When wok is hot, add 3 tablespoons of the salad oil. When oil is hot, add eggplant and stir-fry for 3 minutes. (Eggplant will soak up oil immediately; stir constantly to prevent burning.) Remove from wok and set aside.

Pour remaining 2 tablespoons salad oil into wok. When oil is hot, crumble in pork and add onions, ginger, garlic, and bean sauce. Stir-fry until meat is no longer pink (about 2 minutes). Return eggplant to wok and pour in broth mixture; cover and cook over medium-low heat until eggplant is tender when pierced (about 6 minutes).

Stir cornstarch-water mixture; pour into wok and stir until sauce boils and thickens. Stir in sesame oil. Makes 4 servings.

Per serving: 264 calories, 8 g protein, 12 g carbohydrates, 22 g total fat, 19 mg cholesterol, 682 mg sodium

Quick-fried Gobo

Preparation time: 10 to 15 minutes

Cooking time: 10 minutes

Brown-skinned gobo is known in the United States as burdock—a common weed. In Japan, though, this root is a cultivated crop; its crunchy white flesh has a delicious flavor that's compatible with typical Japanese seasonings. When choosing fresh gobo in an Asian market, look for young, tender roots less than an inch in diameter.

- 1 tablespoon sesame seeds
- 4 cups water
- 1 tablespoon vinegar
  About 1 pound gobo (also called burdock)
- 2 tablespoons soy sauce
- 2 tablespoons mirin (sweet sake) or cream sherry
- 1 teaspoon sugar
  Few drops of liquid hot pepper seasoning
- 2 tablespoons salad oil
  Sliced green onions (including tops)

Place a wok over medium heat; when wok is hot, add sesame seeds and stir until golden (about 2 minutes). Pour out of wok and set aside.

In a bowl, combine water and vinegar. Scrub gobo with a brush, then scrape off and discard brown skin. Rinse well. With a small knife, slice down sides of gobo the way you'd sharpen a pencil, cutting root into shavings. Drop cut pieces immediately into vinegar-water mixture.

In a small bowl, combine soy, mirin, sugar, and hot pepper seasoning; set aside.

Return wok to medium heat. When wok is hot, add oil. When oil is hot, lift gobo from vinegar-water mixture and drain briefly; then add to wok. Stir-fry for 1 minute. Add soy mixture and stir-fry until gobo is glazed and tender-crisp to bite (5 to 6 minutes). Sprinkle with sesame seeds and onions. Makes 4 to 6 servings.

Per serving: 110 calories, 2 g protein, 13 g carbohydrates, 5 g total fat, 0 mg cholesterol, 347 mg sodium

Green Beans with Garlic

Preparation time: About 10 minutes

Cooking time: About 15 minutes

Those familiar Asian seasonings of soy, sherry, ginger, and garlic enhance just about any food; here, they accent tender-crisp green beans. Sesame seeds add extra crunch.

- 4 teaspoons soy sauce
- 1 teaspoon sugar
- 1 tablespoon dry sherry or water
- 1 tablespoon sesame seeds
- 1½ tablespoons salad oil
- 3 cloves garlic, minced or pressed
- 1 tablespoon minced fresh ginger
- 1 pound green beans (ends removed), cut diagonally into 2-inch lengths

In a small bowl, stir together soy, sugar, and sherry; set aside.

Place a wok over medium heat; when wok is hot, add sesame seeds and stir until golden (about 2 minutes). Pour out of wok and set aside.

Increase heat to medium-high and pour oil into wok. When oil is hot, add garlic, ginger, and beans; stir-fry for 1½ minutes. Stir in soy mixture; reduce heat to medium, cover, and cook until beans are tender-crisp to bite (4 to 7 more minutes).

Uncover, increase heat to high, and boil, stirring, until almost all liquid has evaporated (1 to 3 minutes). Pour onto a warmed platter and sprinkle with sesame seeds. Makes 4 servings.

Per serving: 105 calories, 3 g protein, 11 g carbohydrates, 6 g total fat, 0 mg cholesterol, 448 mg sodium

Elegantly garnished with enoki mushrooms and
red bell pepper, a light side dish of briefly cooked Zucchini Sticks
(recipe on facing page) looks almost too good to eat—
but it's too delicious to pass up.

Hominy Fry Delight

Preparation time: About 10 minutes

Cooking time: 4 minutes

Plump grains of white or yellow hominy look like tiny dumplings among the vegetables in this dish. Lemon pepper adds a pleasantly tangy accent.

- 2 tablespoons salad oil
- 1 medium-size carrot, thinly sliced
- 1 medium-size red or green bell pepper, seeded and cut into thin, short strips
- 1 medium-size zucchini, thinly sliced
- 1 can (about 1 lb.) white or yellow hominy, drained
- ½ teaspoon lemon pepper
- 3 green onions (including tops), sliced
- 1 tablespoon Worcestershire

Place a wok over high heat; when wok is hot, add oil. When oil is hot, add carrot, bell pepper, zucchini, hominy, and lemon pepper. Stir-fry until vegetables are tender-crisp to bite (about 3 minutes). Stir in onions and Worcestershire; serve. Makes about 4 servings.

Per serving: 148 calories, 2 g protein, 20 g carbohydrates, 7 g total fat, 0 mg cholesterol, 467 mg sodium

Parsnip & Carrot Sauté with Tarragon

Preparation time: About 10 minutes

Cooking time: About 5 minutes

A sprinkling of tarragon is a perfect accent for sweet, tender carrots and parsnips in this easy side dish.

- 3 *each* medium-size parsnips and carrots (about 1½ lbs. *total*)
- 5 tablespoons butter or margarine
- 1 tablespoon minced shallot or onion
- ⅓ cup regular-strength chicken broth
- 1 tablespoon fresh tarragon leaves, chopped, or 1½ teaspoons dry tarragon
- 2 tablespoons minced parsley

Peel parsnips and carrots and cut into matchstick pieces. Set aside.

Place a wok over medium-high heat; when wok is hot, add butter. When butter is melted, add shallot and stir once. Add carrots and parsnips; stir-fry just until tender-crisp to bite (about 2 minutes). Add broth, cover, and cook until tender to bite (2 to 3

more minutes). Stir in tarragon and parsley; serve. Makes 4 servings.

Per serving: 223 calories, 2 g protein, 22 g carbohydrates, 15 g total fat, 39 mg cholesterol, 262 mg sodium

(Pictured on facing page)

Zucchini Sticks

Preparation time: About 10 minutes

Cooking time: 4 minutes

For a simple side dish that's also light on calories, cut zucchini into strips, then stir-fry in a bit of oil. Season simply with garlic and pepper—or add a sprinkle of Parmesan cheese.

- 4 medium-size zucchini (about 1½ lbs. *total*)
- 1 tablespoon olive oil or salad oil
- 2 cloves garlic, minced or pressed
  Pepper
  Enoki mushrooms and red bell pepper (optional)
  Grated Parmesan cheese (optional)

Cut zucchini in half lengthwise. Then cut each half lengthwise into thirds.

Place a wok over medium heat; when wok is hot, add oil. When oil is hot, add zucchini and garlic and stir-fry gently until zucchini is tender-crisp to bite (about 3 minutes). Season to taste with pepper and serve immediately. If desired, garnish with mushrooms and bell pepper and offer cheese to sprinkle atop individual servings. Makes 4 servings.

Per serving: 61 calories, 2 g protein, 7 g carbohydrates, 4 g total fat, 0 mg cholesterol, 2 mg sodium

Matchstick Zucchini with Marinara Sauce

Place a wok over medium-high heat; when hot, add 2 tablespoons **olive oil.** When oil is hot, add 1 clove **garlic,** minced or pressed, and 1 **onion,** finely chopped; stir-fry until golden (about 3 minutes). Add ¼ cup **fresh basil leaves,** finely chopped, and 1½ pounds **tomatoes,** peeled, cored, and finely chopped. Cook, stirring occasionally, for 15 minutes. Add ½ teaspoon **sugar** and season to taste with **salt** and **pepper.** Keep warm while preparing zucchini. Follow directions for **Zucchini Sticks,** but cut zucchini lengthwise into thin slices; then cut slices into 4 or 5-inch long julienne strips and reduce cooking time to 2 minutes. Omit mushrooms and red bell pepper; serve with sauce and cheese.

An Asian Brunch

The breakfast (or brunch) pancake is a universal preference. In Sri Lanka, it is made of rice flour and coconut milk, shaped like a bowl, and called a "hopper." Traditionally, the lacy-edged creation is served cradling a softly fried egg.

Authentic hoppers take their rounded shape from a small, round-bottomed pan, but you'll discover that your wok works just as well. Some of the batter is swirled around the sloping wok sides to form the crisp edges of the hopper; the remaining batter settles in the bottom, creating the pancake's thicker, slightly spongy center.

Use a well-seasoned wok brushed with salad oil or a wok with a nonstick finish. Before using a nonstick wok, it's a good idea to test it with a small amount of batter; if the batter sticks, coat the wok with a vegetable cooking spray.

Serve the warm hoppers topped with fried eggs; accompany with our Coconut Relish and Crisp Ham Ribbons. Or offer sliced tomatoes topped with chopped onions and lime, or tropical fruits such as papaya, mango, or pineapple.

Hoppers

- 1 **teaspoon active dry yeast**
- 2 **teaspoons sugar**
- 1 **cup warm water (about 110°F)**
- 1½ **cups canned or thawed frozen coconut milk**
- 1½ **cups rice flour**
   Coconut Relish (recipe follows)
   Crisp Ham Ribbons (recipe follows)
   Salad oil
- 6 **or 7 hot softly fried eggs**
   Red pepper paste or chopped fresh hot red chiles

In a large bowl, dissolve yeast and sugar in warm water. Let stand until frothy (20 to 25 minutes). Stir in coconut milk and flour until smooth. Cover and let stand at room temperature until foamy (about 2 hours) or cover and refrigerate for up to 12 hours.

Meanwhile, prepare Coconut Relish and Crisp Ham Ribbons. Set aside.

Place a wok over medium heat; when wok is hot, brush bottom and sides with oil. Pour ½ cup of the batter into center of wok all at once. Quickly tilt wok to form a thin pancake about 8 inches wide. Cover wok and cook until sides of pancake are crisp and bottom is golden (5 to 6 minutes).

With a wide spatula, loosen pancake and remove from wok; keep warm. Scrape browned bits free, grease wok, and repeat to cook remaining batter. (If you have problems with sticking, clean wok and spray with vegetable cooking spray, then heat.)

If you make pancakes ahead, place them in a single layer on baking sheets at room temperature for up to 4 hours. To reheat, set in a 350° oven, uncovered, until hot (about 5 minutes).

Serve pancakes hot, topping each with an egg. Offer Coconut Relish, Crisp Ham Ribbons, and pepper paste to add to individual servings. Makes 6 or 7 servings.

Coconut Relish. Pierce eyes of a small **coconut** and drain out liquid; discard liquid or reserve to drink as a beverage. Place coconut in a 350° oven and bake until shell begins to crack (20 to 30 minutes). Let cool. Hit coconut along crack with a hammer to break open. With a blunt knife, pry coconut meat free. Cut into about ½-inch chunks; whirl about ½ cup of the chunks in a food processor or blender to make ½ cup finely grated coconut. Reserve remaining coconut for another use. (As a substitute, you may mix ½ cup dry unsweetened shredded coconut with 2 tablespoons water.)

Mix coconut with 1 teaspoon **paprika,** ¼ teaspoon **ground red pepper** (cayenne), 2 tablespoons finely chopped **onion,** and 2 teaspoons **lime juice.** Season to taste with **salt.** If made ahead, cover and refrigerate for up to 1 day.

Crisp Ham Ribbons. Cut 6 ounces thinly sliced **cooked ham** into ¼-inch-wide strips about 3½ inches long. In a 10- to 12-inch frying pan, combine 2 tablespoons **salad oil** and ham. Stir over medium heat until ham is crisp (7 to 10 minutes). Serve warm or at room temperature.

Per serving: 458 calories, 14 g protein, 31 g carbohydrates, 31 g total fat, 260 mg cholesterol, 518 mg sodium

Eggs

Silver Thread Stirred Eggs

Preparation time: About 10 minutes, plus 30 minutes to soak bean threads and mushrooms

Cooking time: 8 minutes

Thin, near-transparent bean threads, also sold as cellophane or shining noodles, are made from ground mung beans. They have a neutral flavor and a slippery texture; here, they add a bouncy lightness to scrambled eggs, meat, and vegetables.

- 2 ounces dried bean threads
- 4 dried Oriental mushrooms
- 2 teaspoons soy sauce
- 6 eggs
- ½ teaspoon salt
- ⅛ teaspoon white pepper
- 2 tablespoons salad oil
- 1 clove garlic, minced
- ¼ pound cooked ham, cut into match-stick pieces
- 1 stalk celery, thinly sliced
- ¼ cup sliced bamboo shoots
- 2 green onions (including tops), thinly sliced

Soak bean threads in warm water to cover for 30 minutes, then drain and cut into 4-inch lengths. Also soak mushrooms in ¾ cup warm water for 30 minutes. Remove mushrooms from water. Pour ½ cup of the soaking water into a bowl; stir in soy. Cut off and discard mushroom stems; squeeze caps dry and thinly slice. Set mushrooms and bean threads aside.

In a bowl, beat eggs with salt and white pepper; set aside.

Place a wok over high heat; when wok is hot, add oil. When oil begins to heat, add garlic and stir once; then add ham and mushrooms and stir-fry for 1 minute. Add celery and bamboo shoots and stir-fry for 2 minutes. Add bean threads and mushroom water and cook until liquid is absorbed. Add onions and cook for 30 seconds.

Reduce heat to medium. Pour eggs into wok. Cook, turning eggs occasionally with a wide spatula, until eggs are set but still soft and creamy. Makes 4 servings.

Per serving: 297 calories, 17 g protein, 17 g carbohydrates, 18 g total fat, 428 mg cholesterol, 984 mg sodium

Sausage & Greens with Eggs

Preparation time: About 15 minutes

Cooking time: About 15 minutes

Developed at a popular San Francisco restaurant, this hearty dish was originally made with spinach. Other greens taste just as good with the sausage and eggs, though; we suggest chard or kale.

- 1 pound red or green Swiss chard; or 1 pound green or red kale
- 2 tablespoons salad oil
- 1 pound mild or hot Italian sausages, casings removed
- 2 large onions, finely chopped
- 2 cloves garlic, minced or pressed
- ½ pound mushrooms, sliced
- ¼ teaspoon *each* ground nutmeg, pepper, and dry oregano leaves
- 8 eggs, lightly beaten
  Salt
- 1 cup (4 oz.) shredded jack cheese

Rinse greens well. Cut chard leaves into thin shreds; thinly slice stems. (Or cut off and discard tough stems from kale; cut leaves into thin shreds.) You should have about 8 cups, lightly packed. Set greens aside.

Place a wok over high heat; when wok is hot, add oil. When oil is hot, crumble sausage into wok; stir-fry until meat is well browned. Spoon off and discard all but 2 tablespoons of the fat. Add onions, garlic, mushrooms, nutmeg, pepper, and oregano; stir-fry until all liquid has evaporated and onions are soft. Stir in greens—a portion at a time, starting with stems—until all greens are in wok and just wilted (3 to 4 minutes). Pour eggs into wok. Stir gently over low heat just until softly set. Season to taste with salt. Transfer to a serving dish and sprinkle with cheese. Makes 4 to 6 servings.

Per serving: 522 calories, 26 g protein, 10 g carbohydrates, 42 g total fat, 439 mg cholesterol, 910 mg sodium

Herb Eggs with Yogurt Sauce

Preparation time: 15 minutes

Cooking time: About 5 minutes

It's easy to make perfect scrambled eggs in your wok! Here, the eggs are enlivened with fresh vegetables and served with a minted yogurt sauce.

      Yogurt Sauce (recipe follows)
  8 eggs
  2 tablespoons water
  ¼ teaspoon pepper
  1 tablespoon butter or margarine
  1 tablespoon olive oil
  ½ cup minced parlsey
  2 green onions (including tops), finely
     chopped
  1 medium-size tomato, seeded and
     chopped
     Salt and pepper

Prepare Yogurt Sauce and set aside. Beat eggs, water, and the ¼ teaspoon pepper until blended.

Place a wok over medium heat; when wok is hot, add butter and oil. When butter is melted, add parsley and onions and stir-fry for 1 minute. Add tomato and stir-fry for 30 seconds. Pour in eggs and stir gently until eggs are set but still moist (2 to 3 minutes). Season to taste with salt and pepper. Serve immediately with Yogurt Sauce. Makes 4 servings.

Yogurt Sauce. Stir together 1 cup **plain yogurt,** 2 tablespoons *each* minced **green onion** (including top) and **fresh mint,** 2 teaspoons **lemon juice,** and a dash of **liquid hot pepper seasoning.**

Per serving: 261 calories, 16 g protein, 8 g carbohydrates, 18 g total fat, 559 mg cholesterol, 215 mg sodium

(Pictured on facing page)

Huevos Revueltos Rancheros

Preparation time: About 10 minutes

Cooking time: 25 minutes

A treat to the eye as well as the palate, these scrambled eggs are topped with a spicy tomato-sausage sauce.

  ½ pound chorizo sausage, casings removed
  ½ cup thinly sliced green onions
  1 large firm-ripe tomato, seeded and diced
  ½ cup diced tomatillos
  1 can (4 oz.) diced green chiles
  10 eggs
  3 tablespoons water

  2 tablespoons butter or margarine
     Sliced radishes, sour cream, fresh
     cilantro (coriander) sprigs (optional)
     Salt and pepper

Place a wok over medium heat; when wok is hot, crumble in sausage. Stir-fry until sausage is browned (about 7 minutes); spoon off and discard fat. Stir in onions, tomato, tomatillos, and chiles. Then stir occasionally until almost all liquid in sauce has evaporated and vegetables are soft (about 10 minutes). Pour into a bowl and keep warm; clean and dry wok.

Beat eggs with water until blended. Place wok over medium heat; when wok is hot, add butter. When butter is melted, pour in eggs and stir gently until eggs are set to your liking. Transfer eggs to individual plates, spoon sausage mixture over eggs; garnish with radishes, sour cream, and cilantro, if desired. Season to taste with salt and pepper. Makes 5 servings.

Per serving: 408 calories, 18 g protein, 6 g carbohydrates, 34 g total fat, 591 mg cholesterol, 632 mg sodium

Tortino Italiano

Preparation time: About 10 minutes

Cooking time: About 10 minutes

Red bell pepper and sliced zucchini add flecks of bright color to this *tortino.*

  3 eggs
  1 tablespoon whipping cream or water
  1 tablespoon chopped parsley
  1 tablespoon butter or margarine
  1 tablespoon olive oil or salad oil
  1 small onion, finely chopped
  1 clove garlic, minced or pressed
  1 medium-size zucchini, thinly sliced
  1 small red bell pepper, seeded and diced
     Salt and pepper
  2 tablespoons grated Parmesan cheese

Beat eggs, cream, and parsley until blended.

Place a wok over medium heat. When wok is hot, add butter and oil. When butter is melted, add onion and garlic and stir-fry until onion is soft. Then add zucchini and bell pepper; stir-fry until zucchini is tender-crisp to bite (2 to 3 minutes).

Pour egg mixture over vegetables, season to taste with salt and pepper, and cook, tilting wok and poking holes between vegetables so uncooked egg flows underneath, until eggs are just set. Sprinkle with cheese; remove from heat, cover, and let stand for 1 minute. Makes 2 servings.

Per serving: 302 calories, 13 g protein, 7 g carbohydrates, 25 g total fat, 439 mg cholesterol, 262 mg sodium

Eggs, chorizo, tomatoes, tomatillos, chiles, radishes,
and cilantro contribute zest to Huevos Revueltos Rancheros
(recipe on facing page). Who would expect such a
fiesta from the wok?

Desserts

Apple-Blueberry Delight

Preparation time: About 10 minutes

Cooking time: About 10 minutes

Use crisp, tart apples for this sweet and spicy dessert. For a special treat, cover the hot fruit with cold whipped cream before serving.

- 2 **tablespoons sugar**
- 1 **teaspoon ground cinnamon**
- ¼ **teaspoon ground nutmeg**
  Juice and grated peel of 2 large oranges
- 4 **tart green-skinned apples (such as Granny Smith)**
- 2 **tablespoons butter or margarine**
- 1 **tablespoon orange-flavored liqueur**
- 1 **pint blueberries**
  Whipped cream (optional)

In a small bowl, mix sugar, cinnamon, and nutmeg; set aside.

In a large bowl, mix orange juice and peel. Peel, core, and thinly slice apples; toss with juice.

Place a wok over medium heat; when wok is hot, add butter. When butter is melted, add sugar mixture and cook, stirring constantly, for about 1 minute.

Add apple mixture to wok and stir-fry until apples are soft (about 3 minutes). Add liqueur, bring to a boil, and boil for about 1 minute. Add blueberries and stir-fry until sauce is thickened. Serve hot, topped with whipped cream, if desired. Makes 4 to 6 servings.

Per serving: 157 calories, 1 g protein, 35 g carbohydrates, 5 g total fat, 10 mg cholesterol, 43 mg sodium

Bananas Managua

Preparation time: About 10 minutes

Cooking time: 6 minutes

Here's a tropical delicacy that's decidedly elegant, yet quick and easy to prepare. If you'd like to top it with homemade Mexican Cream, be sure to start a few days ahead; the cream needs plenty of time to thicken and develop its tangy flavor.

- ¾ **cup sour cream or Mexican Cream (recipe follows)**
- 3 **large firm-ripe bananas**
- ⅓ **cup orange juice**
- 6 **tablespoons firmly packed brown sugar**
- 1 **teaspoon ground cinnamon**
- 3 **tablespoons butter or margarine**
- 2 **tablespoons lime or lemon juice**

If using Mexican Cream, prepare 2 days ahead.

Peel bananas and cut into ¼-inch-thick slanting slices. Pour orange juice into a small, shallow bowl. Mix sugar and cinnamon in another bowl.

Place a wok over medium heat; when wok is hot, add 1 tablespoon of the butter. When butter is melted, dip a third of the banana slices into orange juice and then into sugar mixture. Add to wok and cook until lightly browned and glazed on both sides (about 1 minute). Spoon into 2 shallow dessert dishes. Repeat with remaining bananas, using remaining 2 tablespoons butter and filling 4 more dessert dishes.

When all bananas have been cooked, add lime juice and any remaining orange juice and sugar mixture to wok. Cook over medium heat, stirring, until mixture boils and becomes syrupy (this happens quickly). Pour evenly over bananas. Top each serving with a dollop of sour cream or Mexican Cream. Serve immediately. Makes 6 servings.

Mexican Cream. In a small pan, warm 1 cup **whipping cream** to between 90° and 100°F; add 1 tablespoon **buttermilk** or sour cream, mixing well. Cover and let stand at room temperature (68° to 72°F—or put in a yogurt maker) until mixture starts to thicken (12 to 16 hours).

Refrigerate for at least 24 hours before using to allow acid flavor to develop and cream to thicken further; cream should be of almost spreadable consistency. Store in refrigerator for up to 2 weeks or as long as taste is tangy but fresh. Makes 1 cup.

Per serving: 258 calories, 2 g protein, 32 g carbohydrates, 15 g total fat, 49 mg cholesterol, 77 mg sodium

Deep-frying

Crisp golden morsels that disappear almost as soon as you serve them can result from deep-frying in a wok. Success is easy if you understand the technique. Keep the oil continuously at the correct temperature. Don't add too much food at once, because this will lower the temperature. Check the thermometer often, adjusting the heat level as needed. Also, remember that oil and water don't mix and that dangerous spattering can occur when moist foods hit hot oil. Carefully pat dry all meat, fish, poultry, and vegetables before cooking. Make sure that no water clings to utensils before you put them in the wok.

Deep-frying Oriental Chicken Salad *(Recipe on facing page)*

1 To test temperature of oil, drop 1 bean thread into pan—it should expand at once. When oil is ready, drop in bean threads, a handful at a time.

2 As soon as bean threads hit hot oil, they start to expand. To ensure even cooking, push them down into oil with a wire skimmer or slotted spoon; then turn entire mass over and press down into oil.

3 Cook chicken in same pan of oil (test oil temperature with a bean thread before adding chicken). Cook chicken until well browned on all sides; drain.

4 Chicken cuts most easily when still slightly warm. Anchor chicken with fork; then cut meat and skin off bones. Chicken and bean threads can be prepared a day in advance.

5 Accompanied with fresh fruit and tea, Oriental Chicken Salad makes a satisfying meal. Dressing softens crisp bean threads quickly, so serve salad immediately after tossing.

How to deep-fry in a wok

Anything that can be cooked in a deep-fryer can also be done in a wok, and often with less oil. You'll need just a few extra utensils. A deep-frying thermometer is essential for checking the oil temperature; a wire skimmer or slotted spoon is handy for lifting out cooked foods and removing browned bits before they scorch. Another useful accessory is a semi-circular wire draining rack that attaches to the top of the wok. And unless you have an electric or flat-bottomed wok, you'll need to use a ring stand to support the wok over the burner or element and prevent it from tipping.

Almost any kind of salad oil will work well for deep-frying; peanut and safflower oils are particularly good. Avoid olive oil, since it burns at a very low temperature. To reuse oil for frying, let it cool completely; then strain it through several layers of cheesecloth into a wide-mouthed jar and refrigerate it (chilled oil will turn cloudy, then clear again when returned to room temperature). You can generally recycle oil three or four times; discard it when it begins to develop an off odor. Keep in mind that the oil will darken slightly and increase in saturated fat content with each use.

To deep-fry, place your wok over the heat source, pour in oil to the specified depth, and heat it to the temperature indicated in the recipe. Then carefully add the food, remembering that moist foods will spatter. Cook just a few pieces at a time, since crowding the wok will lower the oil temperature and give you greasy, soggy results. As you fry, check your deep-frying thermometer often and adjust the heat as needed to maintain the correct oil temperature.

(Pictured on facing page)

Oriental Chicken Salad

Preparation time: About 35 minutes

Cooking time: About 25 minutes

Start by deep-frying bean threads and chicken; then combine the crisp noodles and sliced meat with salad greens, onions, crunchy peanuts, and a tangy dressing. The process is shown, step by step, on the facing page.

- ¼ **cup all-purpose flour**
- ½ **teaspoon** *each* **Chinese five-spice and salt**
  Dash of pepper
- 1 **whole chicken breast (about 1 lb.), split**
- 2 **chicken thighs (about ½ lb.** *total*)
- 3 **ounces dried bean threads**
  Salad oil
- ½ **cup sesame seeds**
  Soy-Lemon Dressing (recipe follows)
- 4 **cups finely shredded iceberg lettuce**
- 3 **green onions (including tops), thinly sliced**
- 1 **large bunch fresh cilantro (coriander), washed, stemmed, drained, and finely chopped**
- 1 **cup coarsely chopped salted roasted peanuts**

Place flour, five-spice, salt, and pepper on a large plate; stir together. Rinse chicken and pat dry, then dredge in flour mixture until well coated on all sides; shake off excess. Set chicken aside.

Break bean threads into sections. Set a wok in a ring stand. Pour oil into wok to a depth of 1½ inches and heat to 375°F on a deep-frying thermometer (when a bean thread dropped into oil expands immediately, oil is ready).

Drop a handful of bean threads into oil. As they puff and expand, push them down into oil with a wire skimmer or slotted spoon; then turn over entire mass. When bean threads stop crackling (about 30 seconds), remove them with skimmer and drain on paper towels. Repeat until all are cooked. After cooking each batch, skim and discard any bits of bean threads from oil. (At this point, you may let bean threads cool completely, then package airtight and store at room temperature until next day.)

Add chicken to hot oil and cook, turning as needed, until well browned (about 10 minutes for breasts, 12 minutes for thighs); adjust heat as needed to maintain oil temperature at 375°F. Drain on paper towels; set aside and let cool.

Meanwhile, clean and dry wok. Place wok over medium heat; when wok is hot, add sesame seeds and stir until golden (about 2 minutes). Set aside.

Prepare Soy-Lemon Dressing; set aside. Cut cooled chicken and skin off bones, then cut into bite-size pieces.

Place lettuce in a large bowl; top with onions, cilantro, and chicken. Sprinkle with sesame seeds and peanuts. Stir dressing, then drizzle over salad and toss. Add bean threads, lightly crushing some of them with your hands; toss lightly. Serve immediately. Makes 4 servings.

Soy-Lemon Dressing. Stir together ¾ teaspoon **dry mustard**, 1 teaspoon *each* **sugar** and grated **lemon peel**, 1 tablespoon *each* **soy sauce** and **lemon juice**, and ¼ cup **salad oil**.

Per serving: 935 calories, 43 g protein, 40 g carbohydrates, 70 g total fat, 96 mg cholesterol, 796 mg sodium

Appetizers

Chicken Wings with Garlic Sauce

Preparation time: About 25 minutes

Cooking time: About 20 minutes

To make this traditional Thai appetizer, you cut chicken wings apart at the joints, then deep-fry them and serve the crisp results with a sweet-sour garlic sauce. You won't need the wingtips for this recipe; save them for making stock or for other uses, if you like.

> Garlic Sauce (recipe follows)
> 12 chicken wings (about 2¼ lbs. *total*)
> Salad oil
> 2 eggs
> All-purpose flour

Prepare Garlic Sauce; set aside. Rinse chicken and pat very dry. Cut wings apart at joints; reserve wingtips for other uses, if desired.

Set a wok in a ring stand. Pour oil into wok to a depth of 1½ inches; heat to 350°F on a deep-frying thermometer. Meanwhile, in a shallow pan, beat eggs; dip wings in beaten egg, then in flour to coat lightly. Lower chicken into oil, 4 to 6 pieces at a time. Cook, turning, until meat near bone is no longer pink; cut to test (about 5 minutes). Adjust heat as needed to maintain oil temperature at 350°F.

Lift out cooked chicken with tongs and drain on paper towels; keep warm until all chicken has been cooked. Serve with sauce for dipping. Makes 2 dozen pieces (4 to 6 appetizer servings, 2 or 3 entrée servings).

Garlic Sauce. In a 1- to 2-quart pan, stir together ½ cup **sugar,** ¼ cup **water,** ⅓ cup **distilled white vinegar,** ¼ teaspoon **salt,** and 15 cloves **garlic,** minced or pressed. Cover and cook over medium-low heat until garlic is translucent (about 10 minutes). Mix 1½ teaspoons **cornstarch** with 2 teaspoons **water.** Stir into garlic mixture; cook, stirring, until mixture boils.

In a blender or food processor, combine garlic mixture, 8 more cloves **garlic,** and 1 small **fresh hot chile,** cut up; whirl until puréed.

Per appetizer serving: 414 calories, 20 g protein, 25 g carbohydrates, 20 g total fat, 162 mg cholesterol, 183 mg sodium

Meat-filled Fried Rice Balls

Preparation time: About 1 hour

Cooking time: About 1¼ hours

Seedless raisins and pine nuts add texture and a light crunch to the beef filling for these egg-shaped rice balls.

> 6 cups water
> Salt
> 1½ cups long-grain white rice
> ½ teaspoon grated lemon peel
> ½ pound lean ground beef
> 1 small onion, chopped
> 1 clove garlic, minced or pressed
> ½ teaspoon *each* ground cinnamon and allspice
> ¼ teaspoon ground cumin
> ¼ cup *each* raisins and pine nuts
> 2 tablespoons chopped parsley
> Salad oil

In a heavy 3-quart pan, bring water and 1½ teaspoons salt to a boil. Stir in rice. Reduce heat to low, cover, and simmer until water is absorbed (about 40 minutes; rice will be sticky). Uncover, stir in lemon peel, and let cool.

While rice is cooking, place a wok over medium heat. When wok is hot, crumble in beef, then add onion and garlic. Cook, stirring, until meat is no longer pink (about 3 minutes). Stir in cinnamon, allspice, and cumin; mix in raisins, pine nuts, and parsley. Season to taste with salt. Transfer meat mixture to a bowl; clean and dry wok.

To shape each ball, place about ⅓ cup of the cooked rice in your palm and flatten into a thin patty. Top with 1 heaping tablespoon of the meat filling. Cup your hand, then top with additional rice. Press together into an egg shape. If rice is too sticky to handle easily, moisten hands lightly with water.

Set wok in a ring stand. Pour oil into wok to a depth of 2 inches and heat to 375°F on a deep-frying thermometer. With a slotted spoon, lower 1 rice ball at a time into oil. Cook, turning often, until golden brown on all sides (about 5 minutes); adjust heat as needed to maintain oil temperature at 375°F. Lift out and drain on paper towels; keep warm until all rice balls have been cooked.

If made ahead, let cool, then cover and refrigerate until next day. To reheat, place on a baking sheet and heat in a 375° oven until heated through (about 25 minutes). Makes 12 to 14 balls (6 servings).

Per serving: 391 calories, 12 g protein, 46 g carbohydrates, 18 g total fat, 28 mg cholesterol, 30 mg sodium

Chinese Crab Claws

Preparation time: About 20 minutes

Cooking time: About 25 minutes

If you've wondered what to do with the cooked crab claws you see in markets, you might borrow a Chinese idea: turn them into appetizers. You coat the meaty portion of each claw with sole and crab, then brown the claws in hot oil. Each claw's pincers make a convenient handle for out-of-hand eating.

    Lime Sauce (recipe follows)
  1 egg white
  ¼ cup sliced green onions (including tops)
  1 tablespoon *each* dry sherry and minced
    fresh ginger
  2 teaspoons cornstarch
  ¼ teaspoon *each* pepper and sesame oil
  ¼ pound boned and skinned sole fillet
  ¼ pound cooked or canned crabmeat,
    flaked
 12 cooked crab claws, including pincers
    (about ½ lb. *total*), with part of shell
    sawed off (thawed if frozen)
    Salad oil

Prepare Lime Sauce and set aside.

In a food processor or blender, whirl egg white, onions, sherry, ginger, cornstarch, pepper, sesame oil, and sole until smoothly puréed. Scrape into a bowl and mix in crabmeat. With a spoon, spread an equal portion of the purée evenly over meat on each claw, using all purée. Set coated claws slightly apart on wax paper.

Set a wok in a ring stand. Pour salad oil into wok to a depth of 2 inches and heat to 350°F on a deep-frying thermometer. Add 3 claws at a time and cook until fish purée is golden brown (3 to 4 minutes); adjust heat as needed to maintain oil temperature at 350°F. Lift out cooked claws with a slotted spoon and drain on paper towels; keep warm until all claws have been cooked. Serve when pincers are cool enough to touch.

If made ahead, let cool; arrange in a single layer in a 10- by 15-inch baking pan, cover, and refrigerate until next day. To reheat, uncover and bake in a 275° oven until hot (5 to 10 minutes); fish topping will be firmer than for fresh-cooked claws.

Dip hot claws in sauce before eating. Makes 1 dozen appetizers (about 6 servings).

Lime Sauce. Stir together 3 tablespoons *each* **soy sauce** and **lime juice** with 1 small **fresh hot green chile** (such as jalapeño or serrano), seeded and minced.

Per serving: 148 calories, 15 g protein, 3 g carbohydrates, 8 g total fat, 59 mg cholesterol, 680 mg sodium

Crab Pillows

Preparation time: About 20 minutes

Cooking time: About 10 minutes

Meant to be eaten with chopsticks but just as easily picked up with fingers, these tiny open-faced sandwiches make delicious appetizers to pass at a party.

  1 egg white
  1 teaspoon *each* water and dry sherry
  2 teaspoons cornstarch
  ½ teaspoon salt
  1 teaspoon grated fresh ginger
  2 tablespoons chopped fresh cilantro
    (coriander)
  1 cup cooked or canned crabmeat, flaked
  6 sandwich-size slices firm-textured, day-
    old white bread
    Salad oil

In a bowl, beat together egg white, water, and sherry until foamy. Stir in cornstarch, salt, ginger, and cilantro. Squeeze crabmeat lightly to eliminate any moisture, then stir into egg white mixture.

Remove crusts from bread; cut each slice into 4 squares. Mound about 2 teaspoons of the crab mixture on each square, pressing it firmly onto bread and rounding corners. (At this point, you may arrange in a single layer in a baking pan, cover, and refrigerate for up to 8 hours.)

Set a wok in a ring stand. Pour oil into wok to a depth of 1½ inches and heat to 350°F on a deep-frying thermometer. Add 4 squares at a time, crab side down, and cook until edges begin to brown (about 30 seconds); adjust heat as needed to maintain oil temperature at 350°F.

Turn squares over and cook for 10 more seconds; lift out and drain on paper towels. Serve immediately. Makes 2 dozen appetizers (8 servings).

Per serving: 118 calories, 6 g protein, 10 g carbohydrates, 6 g total fat, 20 mg cholesterol, 288 mg sodium

(Pictured on facing page)

Imperial Rolls

Preparation time: About 1½ hours, plus 30 minutes to soak fungus and bean threads

Cooking time: 35 to 40 minutes

With their crackling-crisp wrappers and savory filling, these Vietnamese appetizer treats are much like the familiar Chinese egg rolls. But imperial rolls are enclosed in rice paper (see page 81).

> **Pork & Shrimp Filling (recipe follows)**
> **Dipping Sauce (recipe follows)**
> **About 12 rice paper rounds,** *each* **about 8½ inches in diameter**
> **Beer or water**
> 1 **egg white, lightly beaten**
> **Salad oil**
> **Butter lettuce leaves and fresh mint leaves (optional)**

Prepare filling and sauce; set aside.

With a pastry brush, lightly moisten both sides of rice paper rounds (2 or 3 at a time) with beer or water; place on a wire rack and let stand until pliable (2 to 3 minutes). Keep remaining papers in package until you're ready to use them.

To fill and roll each paper, first place 2 tablespoons of the filling in a 3-inch-long strip across paper about 2 inches above bottom. Fold bottom edge over filling; roll once to enclose. Fold in right and left edges of rolled portion of paper at a 45° angle to the horizontal; brush with egg white. Then fold sides of paper toward center, so folds are vertical; brush folded-in edges and top edge generously with egg white. Roll up, sealing top edge. Brush again with egg white. Continue to moisten, fill, and roll papers until all filling has been used, placing filled rolls in a single layer.

Set a wok in a ring stand. Pour oil into wok to a depth of 2 inches and heat to 325°F on a deep-frying thermometer. Add 2 or 3 rolls and cook, turning occasionally, until crisp and light golden to golden brown (about 6 minutes); adjust heat as needed to maintain oil temperature at 325°F. Lift out and drain on paper towels. Repeat to cook remaining rolls. Serve immediately.

To serve, cut each roll into thirds with a serrated knife. Place on a platter with a bowl of Dipping Sauce; dip rolls into sauce. Or, if desired, surround rolls with lettuce and mint leaves. To eat, place a mint leaf in a lettuce leaf; top with a roll piece, fold up, and dip into sauce. Makes about 3 dozen appetizers (10 to 12 servings).

Pork & Shrimp Filling. Soak 3 or 4 large **dried black fungus** (also called cloud or tree ears) in warm water to cover for 30 minutes. Pinch out and discard hard, knobby centers; cut remaining fungus into thin 1-inch strips. Set aside. Soak 1 ounce **dried bean threads** in warm water to cover for 30 minutes. Drain; cut into 1-inch lengths. Set aside.

Place a wok over high heat; when wok is hot, add 1 tablespoon **salad oil.** When oil is hot, crumble in ½ pound **lean ground pork;** then add ½ cup finely chopped **onion.** Cook, stirring, until pork is lightly browned (about 3 minutes). Add ¼ pound **raw shrimp,** shelled, deveined, and chopped, and 2 cloves **garlic,** minced or pressed. Cook until shrimp turns pink (about 2 more minutes).

Transfer pork mixture to a large bowl and add 1 large **carrot,** shredded; 2½ teaspoons **sugar;** ½ teaspoon *each* **salt** and **pepper;** fungus; bean threads; and ¼ pound **bean sprouts,** cut into 1-inch pieces. Stir until well combined; let cool.

Dipping Sauce. Combine 2 tablespoons **fish sauce** (*nam pla*) or soy sauce, 1 tablespoon **lime juice,** 2 cloves **garlic** minced or pressed, 2 tablespoons **sugar,** ¼ cup **warm water,** and 2 tablespoons finely shredded **carrot.** Stir until sugar is dissolved.

Per serving: 130 calories, 6 g protein, 9 g carbohydrates, 8 g total fat, 24 mg cholesterol, 297 mg sodium

Crisp-fried Onions

Preparation time: About 10 minutes

Cooking time: About 25 minutes

These fragile, crisp-fried onion shreds are good for munching before a meal or alongside the main course.

> 2 **large onions (about 1 lb.** *total***)**
> ½ **cup all-purpose flour**
> **Salad oil**
> **Salt**

Thinly slice onions, then separate into rings. Place flour in a bag, add onions, and shake to coat.

Set a wok in a ring stand. Pour oil into wok to a depth of 1½ inches and heat to 300°F on a deep-frying thermometer. Add onions, about a fourth at a time; cook, stirring often, until golden (about 5 minutes). Adjust heat as needed to maintain oil temperature at 300°F.

Remove onions with a slotted spoon and drain on paper towels; discard any scorched bits. Pile in a napkin-lined basket or on a plate; sprinkle with salt and serve warm. Makes about 6 cups.

Per ½ cup: 92 calories, 98 g protein, 7 g carbohydrates, 7 g total fat, 0 mg cholesterol, 85 mg sodium

Vietnamese cousins of egg rolls, Imperial Rolls (recipe on facing page)
feature a hearty filling enclosed in delicate rice paper. Wrap each bite
in lettuce and mint, if you like, then dunk in the
nippy dipping sauce.

Beef & Pork

Picadillo Turnovers

Preparation time: About 45 minutes

Cooking time: About 25 minutes

Picadillo (page 28) is a satisfying entrée all on its own, but it's also a tasty filling for the flaky fried turnovers called *empanadas*.

  1 teaspoon butter or margarine
  ½ pound *each* lean ground beef and lean ground pork; or 1 pound lean ground beef
  1 large clove garlic, minced or pressed
  ½ cup *each* tomato purée and raisins
  ¼ cup dry sherry
  2 teaspoons ground cinnamon
  ½ teaspoon ground cloves
  2 tablespoons distilled white vinegar
  1 tablespoon sugar
    Salt
  ¾ cup slivered almonds
    Pastry for a double-crust 9-inch pie
    Salad oil

Place a wok over medium heat; when wok is hot, add butter. When butter is melted, crumble in meat and cook, stirring, until meat is no longer pink (3 to 5 minutes). Spoon off and discard fat. Stir in garlic, tomato purée, raisins, sherry, cinnamon, cloves, vinegar, and sugar. Cook, uncovered, until almost all liquid has evaporated (about 10 minutes). Season to taste with salt, then stir in almonds; transfer to a bowl and let cool. Clean and dry wok.

On a floured board, roll out pastry about ⅛ inch thick and cut into 4-inch circles. Spoon filling evenly on 1 side of each pastry circle; moisten edges of pastry, fold over, and seal.

Set wok in a ring stand. Pour oil into wok to a depth of 1½ inches; heat to 375°F on a deep-frying thermometer. Add 4 turnovers at a time and cook until browned on both sides (about 5 minutes); adjust heat as needed to maintain oil temperature at 375°F. Lift out cooked turnovers and drain on paper towels; keep warm until all turnovers have been cooked. Makes about 16 turnovers (about 8 servings).

Per turnover: 264 calories, 7 g protein, 19 g carbohydrates, 18 g total fat, 16 mg cholesterol, 154 mg sodium

Dry-fried Beef

Preparation time: About 15 minutes

Cooking time: About 15 minutes

Shreds of beef—just ⅛ inch thick and ⅛ inch wide—are deep-fried until dark, crisp, and chewy, then combined with stir-fried vegetables and spices. Serve dry-fried beef as an unusual appetizer before an Oriental meal.

  ½ teaspoon Szechwan peppercorns
  ¾ pound lean boneless beef steak (such as top round, flank, or sirloin)
  1 tablespoon hot bean sauce or ¾ teaspoon liquid hot pepper seasoning
  1 tablespoon dry sherry
  ½ teaspoon sugar
  1 or 2 small dried hot red chiles, crumbled (and seeded, if desired)
    Salad oil
  1 large stalk celery, cut into matchstick pieces
  1 medium-size carrot, cut into matchstick pieces
  2 teaspoons minced garlic
  1 teaspoon minced fresh ginger
  2 green onions (including tops), cut into 1½-inch lengths
  1 teaspoon sesame oil

Place peppercorns in a small frying pan; cook over medium-low heat, shaking pan often, until peppercorns are fragrant (about 10 minutes). Let cool; crush coarsely with a mortar and pestle. Set aside.

Cut meat into ⅛-inch-thick slices; then cut into shreds ⅛ inch wide and 2 inches long. Set aside. In a bowl, combine bean sauce, sherry, sugar, and chiles; set aside.

Set a wok in a ring stand and pour in salad oil to a depth of 1½ inches; heat to 360°F on a deep-frying thermometer. Add half the meat and stir to separate shreds. Cook until meat is dark brown, slightly shriveled, and chewy (2½ to 3 minutes). Lift out with a slotted spoon and drain on paper towels. Reheat oil to 360°F and cook remaining meat.

Carefully pour off all but 3 tablespoons of the oil. Increase heat to high. When oil is hot, add celery and carrot and stir-fry for 2 minutes. Add garlic and ginger and stir-fry for 30 seconds. Add onions and stir-fry for 30 seconds. Return meat to pan, add bean sauce mixture, and stir until almost all liquid has evaporated. Stir in sesame oil and crushed peppercorns, then serve. Makes 4 to 6 servings.

Per serving: 181 calories, 13 g protein, 4 g carbohydrates, 12 g total fat, 32 mg cholesterol, 58 mg sodium

Japanese Pork Cutlets

Preparation time: About 50 minutes

Cooking time: About 10 minutes

A popular dish in Japan today, *tonkatsu* appeals to Western diners as well. Both tonkatsu sauce and *pan ko*—the coarse bread crumbs used to coat the meat—are available in many well-stocked markets, but it's easy to make your own.

> 1 to 1½ cups **coarse dry bread crumbs** (*pan ko*), homemade (recipe follows) or purchased
> **Tonkatsu Sauce,** homemade (recipe follows) or purchased
> 1 to 1½ pounds **pork chops or steaks,** cut ½ inch thick
> 1 **egg**
> 1 tablespoon **water**
> **Salt and pepper**
> About 2 tablespoons **all-purpose flour**
> **Salad oil**
> 2 cups finely shredded **cabbage**
> ½ cup shredded **carrot**

Prepare bread crumbs and Tonkatsu Sauce; set aside.

Trim and discard fat and bones from pork. Place meat between sheets of wax paper and pound with a mallet until about ¼ inch thick (overlap any small pieces and pound together into a single piece).

In a shallow bowl, lightly beat egg with water. Spread crumbs on a piece of wax paper. Sprinkle each cutlet lightly with salt and pepper; dust with flour, then shake off excess. Dip cutlets into egg, let drain briefly, and press into crumbs to coat thickly all over. Set aside for 10 minutes to dry slightly.

Set a wok in a ring stand. Pour oil into wok to a depth of 1½ inches and heat to 360°F on a deep-frying thermometer. Add 1 or 2 cutlets at a time and cook, turning as needed, until golden brown on both sides (about 2 minutes); adjust heat as needed to maintain oil temperature at 360°F. Drain briefly on paper towels. Place each cutlet on a dinner plate (if serving with chopsticks, cut each cutlet into 2 or 3 pieces; reassemble on plates). Arrange cabbage and carrot alongside cutlets; offer Tonkatsu Sauce at the table. Makes 3 or 4 servings.

Coarse dry bread crumbs. Trim crusts from 10 slices **firm-textured white or whole wheat bread;** cut bread into cubes. Whirl cubes, a few at a time, in a blender or food processor until evenly coarse crumbs form. Spread crumbs in a shallow rimmed baking pan; bake in a 325° oven, stirring often, until completely dry but not brown (15 to 20 minutes). Makes about 4 cups.

Tonkatsu Sauce. Stir together ½ cup **catsup** and 2 tablespoons *each* **Worcestershire** and **soy sauce.**

Per serving: 512 calories, 34 g protein, 45 g carbohydrates, 22 g total fat, 140 mg cholesterol, 1,331 mg sodium

Sweet & Sour Pork

Preparation time: About 15 minutes

Cooking time: About 25 minutes

Though it's much like the stir-fried Sweet & Sour Pork on page 33, this version of the popular dish features crisp *deep*-fried nuggets of pork. If you like, vary the flavor by using lychees or even mixed sweet pickles in place of the pineapple.

> **Cooking Sauce** (recipe follows)
> 1 **egg yolk**
> 2 teaspoons **water**
> 1 tablespoon *each* **all-purpose flour** and **cornstarch**
> 1 pound lean **boneless pork** (such as shoulder or butt), trimmed of excess fat and cut into 1-inch cubes
> **Salad oil**
> 1 clove **garlic,** minced or pressed
> 1 **green bell pepper,** seeded and cut into 1-inch squares
> 1 medium-size **onion,** cut into wedges, layers separated
> 1 can (13 oz.) **pineapple tidbits,** drained

Prepare Cooking Sauce and set aside. In a bowl, beat egg yolk with water; blend in flour and cornstarch until smooth. Add pork cubes and stir to coat.

Set a wok in a ring stand. Pour oil into wok to a depth of about 1½ inches and heat to 350°F on a deep-frying thermometer. Add pork cubes, a portion at a time. Cook, stirring occasionally, until golden brown on outside and no longer pink in center; cut to test (about 3 minutes). Adjust heat as needed to maintain oil temperature at 350°F. As meat is cooked, lift out with a slotted spoon, drain, and keep warm.

Clean and dry wok, then place over high heat. When wok is hot, add 2 tablespoons oil. When oil begins to heat, add garlic and stir once. Add bell pepper and onion and stir-fry for 1 minute, adding a few drops of water if wok appears dry. Add pineapple and meat. Stir Cooking Sauce and pour into wok; stir until sauce boils and thickens. Makes 4 servings.

Cooking Sauce. Stir together ¾ cup **water;** 1 tablespoon *each* **cornstarch, catsup,** and **soy sauce;** ¼ cup *each* **sugar** and **wine vinegar;** and a few drops of **liquid hot pepper seasoning.**

Per serving: 470 calories, 24 g protein, 37 g carbohydrates, 26 g total fat, 145 mg cholesterol, 387 mg sodium

Spoon savory Green Pepper Beef (recipe on facing page)
into individual-size phoenix nests made from shredded yams
(recipe on facing page). Guests enjoy the filling first, then break apart
and eat its crisp container.

China's Edible Nest

Golden "phoenix nests"— baskets of deep-fried vegetable shreds— make handsome showcases for many stir-fried dishes. After eating the contents, you break the nest apart with your fingers and nibble the crisp pieces.

Making these decorative nests is surprisingly easy. In addition to your wok, the only utensils you'll need are two sieves of the same size: one to act as a form for shaping the shredded vegetable and one to hold the shreds in place as they cook. *To determine how much oil to use,* place an empty sieve in your wok, then pour in enough oil to cover at least three-fourths of the sieve.

Because the nests have an open, meshlike structure, it's best to fill them with lightly sauced stir-fries like the Green Pepper Beef featured here.

Potato Phoenix Nest

Peel 2 medium-size **white thin-skinned potatoes** and shred them lengthwise (you should have 2 cups). Squeeze shreds to remove liquid; then place in a bowl. Sprinkle 1 tablespoon **cornstarch** over potatoes and toss to distribute cornstarch and loosen shreds. Arrange a handful of shreds in a latticework inside a 4-inch-diameter sieve, covering bottom of sieve and extending at least halfway up sides. Fit a second sieve inside first one.

Set a wok in a ring stand. Heat appropriate amount of **salad oil** (see above) to 325°F on a deep-frying thermometer. Place sieve in oil and cook until nest is golden brown (3 to 4 minutes). Remove from oil and lift off top sieve. Loosen edges of nest with tip of a sharp knife, then gently remove nest and drain on paper towels. Repeat, adjusting heat as necessary, to maintain oil temperature at 325°F.

If made ahead, let cool; stack nests, separating them with paper towels, and seal in plastic bags. Store at room temperature for up to 2 days. Makes 4 or 5 nests, each about 4 inches in diameter.

Per nest: 162 calories, .92 g protein, 9 g carbohydrates, 14 g total fat, 0 mg cholesterol, 3 mg sodium

(Pictured on facing page)
Sweet Potato or Yam Nest

Follow directions for **Potato Phoenix Nest,** but substitute 2 cups shredded **sweet potatoes** or yams for potatoes and increase oil temperature to 350°F. Cook sweet potato nests until golden brown (3 to 4 minutes); cook yam nests until a light pumpkin color (4 to 5 minutes).

(Pictured on facing page)
Green Pepper Beef

About ¾ **pound lean boneless beef steak (such as top round, flank, or sirloin)**
1 tablespoon *each* **dry sherry and soy sauce**
2 tablespoons **water**
¼ teaspoon *each* **salt and sugar**
2 teaspoons **cornstarch**
3½ tablespoons **salad oil**
 Cooking Sauce (recipe follows)
1 clove **garlic, minced**
½ teaspoon **minced fresh ginger**
2 small **green bell peppers, seeded and cut into ¼-inch-wide strips**

Cut beef with the grain into 1½-inch-wide strips; then cut each strip across the grain into ⅛-inch-thick slanting slices. In a bowl, combine sherry, soy, 1 tablespoon of the water, salt, sugar, and cornstarch. Add beef and stir to coat, then stir in 1½ teaspoons of the oil and let marinate for 15 minutes.

Meanwhile, prepare Cooking Sauce and set aside.

Place a wok over high heat; when wok is hot, add 2 tablespoons of the oil. When oil begins to heat, add garlic and ginger and stir once. Add beef mixture and stir-fry until meat is browned (about 2 minutes); remove from wok.

Pour remaining 1 tablespoon oil into wok; when oil is hot, add bell peppers and stir-fry for 30 seconds. Add remaining 1 tablespoon water, cover, and cook for 1 minute. Return meat to wok. Stir Cooking Sauce, pour into wok, and stir until sauce boils and thickens. Makes 4 servings.

Cooking Sauce. Stir together 1½ teaspoons *each* **soy sauce** and **cornstarch** and ¼ cup **regular-strength chicken broth** or water. *(If you don't plan to serve the stir-fry in a phoenix nest, double this sauce recipe.)*

Per serving: 249 calories, 21 g protein, 5 g carbohydrates, 16 g total fat, 49 mg cholesterol, 692 mg sodium

Chicken

Seasoned Fried Chicken

Preparation time: About 20 minutes

Marinating time: About 30 minutes

Cooking time: About 30 minutes

Like Chili Chicken Chunks (facing page), these crumb-coated chicken cubes are crusty and crisp— but they're marinated in ginger, soy, and lemon juice before frying. Leftover marinade makes a simple dip.

  ½ **cup soy sauce**
  1 **tablespoon grated or minced fresh ginger**
  1 **tablespoon lemon juice**
  2 **tablespoons sake or dry sherry**
  3 **whole chicken breasts (about 1 lb. *each*), skinned, boned, and cut into 1-inch chunks**
  1½ **cups coarse dry bread crumbs (*pan ko*), purchased or homemade (page 113)**
  6 **tablespoons all-purpose flour**
  2 **tablespoons cornstarch**
  2 **eggs**
     Salad oil

In a bowl, combine soy, ginger, lemon juice, and sake. Add chicken and stir to coat; let marinate for about 30 minutes, stirring occasionally. Drain chicken and pat dry; reserve marinade.

Spread bread crumbs in a pie pan or rimmed plate. In another pie pan, combine flour and corn-starch. In a third pie pan, lightly beat eggs. Dredge chicken in flour mixture; shake off excess. Dip into eggs, then roll in crumbs to coat.

Meanwhile, set a wok in a ring stand. Pour oil into wok to a depth of 2 inches and heat to 375°F on a deep-frying thermometer. Add as many pieces of chicken at a time as will fit without crowding. Cook, turning occasionally, until coating is browned on all sides and meat is no longer pink in center; cut to test (about 2 minutes). Adjust heat as needed to maintain oil temperature at 375°F.

Lift out cooked chicken with a slotted spoon, drain briefly on paper towels, and serve at once; offer reserved marinade in a small bowl for dipping. Makes 4 to 6 servings.

Per serving: 464 calories, 42 g protein, 30 g carbohydrates, 19 g total fat, 178 mg cholesterol, 1,677 mg sodium

Chicken with Plum Sauce

Preparation time: About 20 minutes

Marinating time: 15 minutes

Cooking time: About 15 minutes

A flavorful sweet-sour plum sauce laced with strips of pickled ginger makes this dish distinctive. Another time, try topping the golden squares of chicken with a tangy lemon sauce.

      Plum Sauce or Lemon Sauce (recipes follow)
  1½ **pounds chicken breasts or thighs, skinned, boned, and cut into about 1½-inch-square pieces**
  2 **tablespoons soy sauce**
  1 **tablespoon *each* cornstarch and water, stirred together**
  ¼ **teaspoon sesame oil**
     Dash of white pepper
     Salad oil
  1 **cup all-purpose flour**
  ¼ **cup cornstarch**
  1½ **teaspoons baking powder**
  1 **cup water**

Prepare sauce of your choice and set aside.

Pound chicken lightly with the back of a cleaver or heavy knife so pieces are of uniform thickness. In a bowl, stir together soy, cornstarch-water mixture, sesame oil, and white pepper. Add chicken and stir to coat, then stir in 1 tablespoon salad oil and let marinate for 15 minutes.

In another bowl, combine flour, the ¼ cup corn-starch, and baking powder. Add water and 1 table-spoon salad oil; blend until smooth. Let batter stand for 10 minutes.

Set a wok in a ring stand. Pour salad oil into wok to a depth of 1½ inches and heat to 350°F on a deep-frying thermometer. Dip each piece of chicken in bat-ter, then lower into oil; add as many pieces as will fit without crowding. Cook, turning occasionally, until crust is golden brown and meat is no longer pink in center; cut to test (about 2 minutes for breast pieces, about 4 minutes for thigh pieces). Adjust heat as needed to maintain oil temperature at 350°F.

Lift out cooked chicken with a slotted spoon and drain on paper towels. Keep warm until all pieces have been cooked. Offer Plum Sauce or Lemon Sauce to spoon over chicken. Makes 3 or 4 servings.

Plum Sauce. In a bowl, stir together ¾ cup **water,** 1½ teaspoons **cornstarch,** 2 teaspoons **sugar,** 1 teaspoon **soy sauce,** and ¼ cup **canned plum sauce.**

Heat 1 tablespoon **salad oil** in a small pan over medium-high heat. Add 2 tablespoons thinly sliced **pickled red ginger** and stir-fry for 30 seconds. Pour in plum sauce mixture and cook, stirring, until sauce boils and thickens slightly (about 2 minutes). Let cool to room temperature before serving. Makes 1 cup sauce.

Lemon Sauce. Cut 1 large thin-skinned **lemon** into thin slices; discard end pieces and any seeds. Heat 1 tablespoon **salad oil** in a small pan over medium-high heat. Add lemon slices and stir-fry for 30 seconds. Add 1 cup **regular-strength chicken broth,** and 3 tablespoons *each* **sugar** and **lemon juice.** Bring to a boil, then reduce heat and simmer for 2 minutes. Blend 1 tablespoon **cornstarch** with 1 tablespoon **water.** Pour into sauce and cook, stirring, until sauce boils and thickens slightly. Season to taste with **salt.**

Reheat sauce and pour over chicken just before serving.

Per serving: 427 calories, 20 g protein, 50 g carbohydrates, 17 g total fat, 41 mg cholesterol, 703 mg sodium

Chili Chicken Chunks

Preparation time: About 20 minutes for chicken, 5 to 10 minutes for each dip

Cooking time: About 30 minutes

Crusty, bite-size chunks of chicken take on a Western character when liberally seasoned with chili powder and herbs. Offer your choice of dips—guacamole, horseradish, or creamy mustard—alongside the chicken.

Dips (choices and recipes follow)
3 whole chicken breasts (about 1 lb. *each*), split; 3 pounds chicken thighs (10 to 12); or half of each
¾ cup all-purpose flour
¼ cup yellow cornmeal
2 teaspoons chili powder
½ teaspoon *each* paprika and salt
¼ teaspoon *each* ground cumin and dry oregano leaves
⅛ teaspoon pepper
¾ cup beer
Salad oil

Prepare dips of your choice; set aside.

Skin and bone chicken; then rinse, pat dry, and cut into 1½-inch chunks. Set aside. In a bowl, mix flour, cornmeal, chili powder, paprika, salt, cumin, oregano, and pepper. Add beer and stir until batter is smooth.

Add chicken pieces to batter; if making a combination batch, keep light and dark meat separate and add an equal amount of batter to each. Stir chicken to coat evenly.

Set a wok in a ring stand. Pour oil into wok to a depth of 1½ inches and heat to 350°F on a deep-frying thermometer. Lift chicken from batter, 1 piece at a time, and add to oil; add as many pieces as will fit without crowding. Cook, turning occasionally, until chicken is richly browned on outside and no longer pink in center; cut to test (about 2 minutes for breast pieces, 3 minutes for thigh pieces). Adjust heat as needed to maintain oil temperature at 350°F. Lift out cooked chicken with a slotted spoon, drain on paper towels, and keep warm until all chicken has been cooked. If made ahead, let cool, then cover and refrigerate until next day. To reheat, arrange on paper towels in a rimmed 10- by 15-inch baking pan; bake in a 350° oven until hot (about 15 minutes).

Mound chicken in a napkin-lined basket. To eat, pick up pieces and dunk into dips. Makes 8 to 10 appetizer servings, 4 or 5 entrée servings.

Dips. You'll need 1½ to 2 cups. Use 1 dip or, for variety, make up several half-recipes. (All 3 dips can be made ahead and refrigerated for up to 1 day; stir well before serving.) If you like, include purchased sauces, such as a barbecue sauce or seafood cocktail sauce.

■ *Guacamole dip.* Pit, peel, and mash 2 medium-size ripe **avocados.** Blend avocados with ¼ cup **sour cream** or plain yogurt, 2 tablespoons **lime or lemon juice,** 2 tablespoons chopped **fresh cilantro** (coriander), ½ teaspoon **ground cumin,** and 2 to 4 tablespoons **canned diced green chiles.** Season to taste with **salt** and **liquid hot pepper seasoning.** Makes about 2 cups.

■ *Dijon dip.* Blend 1 cup **mayonnaise** or sour cream with 8 to 10 tablespoons **Dijon mustard,** 2 teaspoons **lemon juice,** and ¼ teaspoon **pepper.** Makes about 1½ cups.

■ *Horseradish dip.* Blend 1 cup **mayonnaise** or sour cream with 8 to 10 tablespoons **prepared horseradish** and 4 teaspoons **lemon juice.** Makes about 1½ cups.

Per entrée serving chicken: 394 calories, 44 g protein, 22 g carbohydrates, 14 g total fat, 102 mg cholesterol, 348 mg sodium

Per tablespoon Guacamole dip: 22 calories, .33 g protein, 1 g carbohydrate, 2 g total fat, .10 mg cholesterol, 8 mg sodium

Per tablespoon Dijon dip: 73 calories, .10 g protein, 1 g carbohydrate, 8 g total fat, 5 mg cholesterol, 219 mg sodium

Per tablespoon Horseradish dip: 68 calories, .17 g protein, .83 g carbohydrate, 7 g total fat, 5 mg cholesterol, 58 mg sodium

Fish & Shellfish

(Pictured on facing page)

Seafood & Vegetable Tempura

Preparation time: About 45 minutes

Cooking time: About 30 minutes

For the lightest, crispest tempura coating, make the batter thin, cold, and lumpy; the lumps contribute to the lacy, delicate appearance. The fragile coating softens quickly, though, so serve the frittered seafood and vegetables immediately after frying.

> **Seafood (suggestions follow)**
> **Vegetables (suggestions follow)**
> **Tempura Dipping Sauce (recipe follows)**
> **Salad oil**
> **Tempura Batter (recipe follows)**

Prepare seafood and vegetables and arrange on platters. Prepare Tempura Dipping Sauce and pour it into 4 small individual bowls.

Set a wok in a ring stand. Pour oil into wok to a depth of 2 inches and heat to 375°F on a deep-frying thermometer. While oil heats, prepare Tempura Batter.

Using chopsticks or tongs, dip prepared seafood and vegetables, a piece at a time, into batter. Let excess batter drip off, then gently lower into hot oil (cook several pieces at a time; do not crowd wok). Cook, turning occasionally, until crisp and light golden (2 to 3 minutes); adjust heat as needed to maintain oil temperature at 375°F. Remove and drain briefly on a wire rack. Serve at once, with sauce for dipping. As you fry, frequently skim and discard any bits of batter from oil. Makes 4 servings.

Seafood. You'll need about 1 pound **large raw shrimp** or 1 pound firm-fleshed **fish** (or use ½ lb. of each). Shell shrimp, leaving tails attached. Devein, rinse, and pat dry.

For fish, use salmon, swordfish, or cod steaks or fillets. Remove and discard bones and skin; cut fish into 1½- by 3-inch strips about ¼ inch thick.

Vegetables. Choose at least 3 from the following: 2 medium-size **carrots,** cut into 2½- to 3-inch lengths, then into ¼-inch-thick lengthwise slices; ⅓-pound wedge of a large **eggplant,** cut crosswise into ¼-inch-thick slices (to make eggplant fans as shown in photograph on facing page, cut wedges 1 inch thick by 3 inches long, then slice wedges lengthwise into

¼-inch slices, leaving one end intact); 12 large **mushrooms;** 1 medium-size **sweet potato,** peeled and cut into ¼-inch-thick rounds; 1 medium-size **zucchini,** cut in ¼-inch-thick diagonal slices.

Tempura Dipping Sauce. In a small pan, combine 1 bottle (8 oz.) **clam juice** with ¼ cup *each* **soy sauce** and **dry sherry.** Bring to a boil over medium-high heat; then remove from heat and let cool to room temperature. In separate small bowls, place 3 tablespoons *each* finely shredded **fresh ginger** and **daikon.** Let diners add ginger and daikon to individual bowls of sauce according to taste. Makes about 1½ cups.

Tempura Batter. In a small bowl, lightly beat together 1 cup plus 2 tablespoons **ice-cold water,** 1 **egg,** and ¼ teaspoon *each* **baking soda** and **salt.** Add 1 cup unsifted **cake flour;** mix just until blended (batter will be lumpy). Sprinkle another ⅓ cup unsifted **cake flour** over top of batter. With a fork, stir batter 1 or 2 strokes (do not blend thoroughly; most of the last addition of flour should be floating on top). Half-fill a larger bowl with **ice;** set bowl of batter in it to keep batter cold while you cook.

Per serving seafood tempura: 239 calories, 21 g protein, 17 g carbohydrates, 9 g total fat, 174 mg cholesterol, 240 mg sodium

Per serving vegetable tempura: 255 calories, 5 g protein, 34 g carbohydrates, 12 g total fat, 34 mg cholesterol, 126 mg sodium

Per tablespoon dipping sauce: 4 calories, .27 g protein, .60 g carbohydrate, 0 g total fat, 0 mg cholesterol, 193 mg sodium

Phoenix-tail Shrimp

Preparation time: About 30 minutes

Cooking time: About 20 minutes

A puffy, crunchy batter coats the shrimp in this simply prepared dish. Serve it as a main course or an appetizer, with your choice of dips.

> **Sweet & Sour Kumquat Sauce or Salt-Pepper Mix (recipes follow)**
> 1 pound medium-size or large raw shrimp
> 1 cup all-purpose flour
> 2½ teaspoons baking powder
> ¼ teaspoon salt
>   Dash of white pepper
> 1 cup water
>   Salad oil

Prepare Sweet & Sour Kumquat Sauce or Salt-Pepper Mix (or both); set aside.

Shell shrimp, but leave tail sections on for handles. Devein, rinse, and pat dry. In a bowl, com-

Continued on page 120

So irresistibly good is Seafood & Vegetable Tempura
(recipe on facing page) that each lacy morsel will disappear almost as soon
as you can lift it from the wok. Serve the frittered bites
before they start to cool and soften.

bine flour, baking powder, salt, and white pepper. Add water and stir until batter is smooth.

Set a wok in a ring stand. Pour oil into wok to a depth of 1½ inches and heat to 375°F on a deep-frying thermometer. Hold each shrimp by tail and dip into batter so batter covers shrimp but not tail; then lower into hot oil. Add as many shrimp at a time as will fit without crowding; cook, turning occasionally, until crisp and golden (2 to 3 minutes). Adjust heat as necessary to maintain oil temperature at 375°F.

Remove cooked shrimp from oil with a slotted spoon, drain on paper towels, and keep warm until all shrimp have been cooked. Serve with Sweet & Sour Kumquat Sauce or Salt-Pepper Mix. Makes 4 servings.

Sweet & Sour Kumquat Sauce. In a pan, combine ¾ cup *each* **sugar** and **white wine vinegar.** Bring to a boil, stirring until sugar is dissolved; then remove from heat and let cool. Drain 1 can (about 1 lb.) **apricot halves,** reserving syrup. In a blender, whirl apricots, sugar-vinegar mixture, and 1 small can (8 oz.) **applesauce** until smooth.

Drain 1 jar (14 oz.) **kumquats;** cut kumquats in half lengthwise and remove seeds. Add kumquats and 1 jar (2 oz.) sliced **pimentos** (drained) to blender; whirl until kumquats are coarsely chopped. For a subtler flavor, stir in ½ cup of the reserved apricot syrup. If made ahead, cover and refrigerate for up to 1 month. Makes 3½ cups.

Salt-Pepper Mix. Place ¼ cup **salt** and 1 tablespoon **Szechwan peppercorns** in a wide frying pan. Cook over medium-low heat, shaking pan occasionally, until salt begins to brown and peppercorns become fragrant (about 10 minutes). Let cool. Coarsely crush with a mortar and pestle or with a rolling pin. (Do not whirl in a blender.) Store in a covered container at room temperature. Makes ¼ cup.

Per serving: 303 calories, 22 g protein, 25 g carbohydrates, 12 g total fat, 140 mg cholesterol, 538 mg sodium

Per tablespoon Sweet & Sour Kumquat Sauce: 29 calories, .06 g protein, 8 g carbohydrates, .03 g total fat, 0 mg cholesterol, 9 mg sodium

Trout on a Spinach Bed

Preparation time: About 15 minutes, plus 30 minutes to soak mushrooms

Cooking time: About 20 minutes

Trout, pork, and spinach make an unusual but savory combination in this dish for two. The fried trout is presented on a bed of cooked spinach, then topped with a pork and mushroom sauce.

6 medium-size dried Oriental mushrooms
    Cooking Sauce (recipe follows)
    About 1 pound spinach
2 cleaned trout (about ½ lb. *each*)
    Salt
    Cornstarch
    Salad oil
2 cloves garlic, minced or pressed
½ pound lean boneless pork (such as shoulder or butt), trimmed of excess fat and cut into ⅛- by 1- by 2-inch strips
1 teaspoon grated fresh ginger
2 green onions (including tops), thinly sliced

Soak mushrooms in warm water to cover for 30 minutes, then drain. Cut off and discard stems; squeeze caps dry and cut into thin strips. Set aside.

While mushrooms are soaking, prepare Cooking Sauce and set aside. Also remove and discard tough stems and any yellow or wilted leaves from spinach; rinse remaining leaves thoroughly. Set aside.

Rinse trout and pat dry. Sprinkle each fish lightly with salt and coat with cornstarch; shake off excess.

Place a wok in a ring stand. Pour oil into wok to a depth of about 1 inch and heat to 400°F on a deep-frying thermometer. Add fish and cook, turning as needed, until crisp and browned on both sides (about 5 minutes); adjust heat as needed to maintain oil temperature at 400°F. Lift out, drain on paper towels, and keep warm.

Carefully pour off oil from wok and wipe any remaining bits of browned fish from wok. Place wok over high heat. When wok is hot, add 1 tablespoon oil. When oil is hot, add spinach and half the garlic. Stir-fry just until spinach is wilted (about 30 seconds). Turn into a shallow serving dish.

Pour 2 tablespoons more oil into wok. When oil is hot, add remaining garlic, pork, and ginger. Stir-fry until pork is browned (about 4 minutes); then add mushrooms. Stir Cooking Sauce and add; stir until sauce boils and thickens (about 1 minute).

Arrange fish on spinach. Pour pork sauce over fish and sprinkle with onions. Makes 2 servings.

Cooking Sauce. Stir together 1 tablespoon *each* **cornstarch, soy sauce,** and **dry sherry;** ¼ teaspoon **salt;** ⅛ teaspoon **pepper;** and ¾ cup **regular-strength chicken broth.**

Per serving: 560 calories, 52 g protein, 25 g carbohydrates, 29 g total fat, 142 mg cholesterol, 1,431 mg sodium

Noodles

Thai Crunchy Noodles

Preparation time: About 30 minutes, plus 30 minutes to soak tamarind

Cooking time: 25 to 30 minutes

In this exotic Thai specialty, brittle rice noodles are deep-fried, then dressed with a sweet-sour sauce of pork, shrimp, and chicken. Though authentic in flavor, our recipe isn't as sweet as the classic—almost candied—version served in Thailand.

- ⅓ **cup tamarind liquid (directions follow) or lemon juice**
  Salad oil
- 4 **ounces dried thin rice noodles (rice sticks)**
- ½ **cup sugar**
- ¼ **cup bean sauce (also called yellow bean sauce)**
- 2 **tablespoons tomato paste**
- 2 **tablespoons fish sauce (*nam pla*) or soy sauce**
- 1 **small onion, finely chopped**
- 4 **cloves garlic, minced or pressed**
- ½ **pound lean boneless pork (such as shoulder or butt), trimmed of excess fat and cut into ⅛- by ½- by 2-inch strips**
- 1 **whole chicken breast (about 1 lb.), skinned, boned, and cut into ⅛- by ½- by 2-inch strips**
- ½ **pound medium-size raw shrimp, shelled and deveined**
  Garnishes (suggestions follow)

Prepare tamarind liquid and set aside.

Set a wok in a ring stand. Pour oil into wok to a depth of 1 inch and heat to 375°F on a deep-frying thermometer. Drop in about a sixth of the noodles. As they puff and expand, push them down into oil; when crackling stops, turn entire mass over. Cook until all are puffy (10 to 15 seconds); remove and drain on paper towels. Skim and discard any bits of noodles from oil before cooking next batch; adjust heat as necessary to maintain oil temperature at 375°F. Keep cooked noodles warm in a 200° oven. (At this point, you may let cool, package airtight, and hold at room temperature for up to 1 day. To reheat, scatter noodles in a rimmed 10- by 15-inch baking pan and place in a 200° oven until hot—about 10 minutes.)

In a bowl, stir together tamarind liquid, sugar, bean sauce, tomato paste, and fish sauce; set aside.

Carefully pour off all but 2 tablespoons of the oil from wok, then place over high heat. When oil is hot, add onion and garlic; stir-fry for 1 minute. Add pork and stir-fry for 3 more minutes. Add chicken and shrimp and stir-fry until shrimp turn pink (about 3 minutes). Stir in sauce mixture; stir until sauce boils, thickens, and turns glossy (about 3 minutes). Remove from heat and let cool for 3 minutes. Using 2 forks, fold in noodles, about a fourth at a time, until all are lightly coated with sauce. Mound noodles on a platter; surround with garnishes. Serve immediately. Makes 4 servings.

Tamarind liquid. In a bowl, combine ⅓ cup **hot water** and 2½ tablespoons **packaged tamarind pulp** or a 4- to 5-inch-long whole tamarind pod (shell and coarse strings removed). Let stand for 30 minutes. Knead pulp from seeds; discard seeds.

Garnishes. Arrange around finished dish (or place on a separate serving plate): ⅓ pound **bean sprouts,** coarsely chopped; 3 **green onions** (including tops), cut into thin strips; and 1 **lime,** cut into wedges.

Per serving: 554 calories, 44 g protein, 60 g carbohydrates, 15 g total fat, 160 mg cholesterol, 1026 mg sodium

Thai Crunchy Noodles in Peanut Sauce

Deep-fry 4 ounces **dried thin rice noodles** (rice sticks) as directed for **Thai Crunchy Noodles.** Omit tamarind liquid, sugar, bean sauce, tomato paste, fish sauce, onion, garlic, and garnishes. Instead, prepare this peanut sauce: in a food processor or blender, combine 2 tablespoons **creamy peanut butter;** 2 tablespoons **salad oil;** ½ cup **canned or thawed frozen coconut milk;** 1 clove **garlic,** minced or pressed; 1 teaspoon grated **fresh ginger** or ¼ teaspoon ground ginger; 1 teaspoon **curry powder;** and ¼ teaspoon **ground red pepper** (cayenne).

Stir-fry pork, chicken, and shrimp in 2 tablespoons salad oil as directed for **Thai Crunchy Noodles.** Add peanut sauce and 2 **green onions** (including tops), thinly sliced; cook until sauce is thickened (about 10 minutes). Remove from heat and fold in noodles as directed for **Thai Crunchy Noodles.** Garnish with 2 **green onions** (including tops), thinly sliced.

**The striking flavor of fragile Crisp-fried Leaves
(recipe on facing page) enhances simple foods, from plain baked potatoes
to the Brie and quail eggs shown here. Choose spinach,
watercress, mint, or other greens.**

Fried Fresh Leaves

Deep-fried leaves? A bit outlandish, perhaps, but surprisingly delicious. Dropped into hot oil, leaves of spinach, mustard, watercress, cilantro, mint, and parsley very quickly turn brittle, translucent, and intensely green. Fragile and shattery-crisp, they're a striking complement to simply cooked seafood, eggs, meat, or composed salads; they also make an intriguing garnish for baked potatoes or hot melted cheese appetizers like the one featured below.

Wash and dry leaves thoroughly before frying. Even carefully dried leaves tend to spatter as they hit the hot oil, though, so be sure to wear an apron and stand back from the wok as you work.

Stored as directed, fried leaves stay crisp for several days. Add them to dishes just before serving; as soon as they touch a liquid or moist food, they go limp.

Crisp-fried Leaves

Remove and discard thick stems from 2 ounces **spinach,** mustard greens (small leaves work best), watercress, fresh cilantro (coriander), parsley (flat-leaf or curly), or mint. Wash leaves thoroughly, drain well, and pat dry. If you like, cut spinach leaves and mustard greens across the grain into ¼-inch-wide strips.

Wrap leaves loosely in towels and enclose in a plastic bag. Refrigerate for at least 1 hour or until next day to dry thoroughly.

Set a wok in a ring stand. Pour **salad oil** into wok to a depth of about 2 inches and heat to 370°F on a deep-frying thermometer. Fry greens a handful at a time (stand back, because oil may spatter). Turn leaves with a slotted spoon until they take on a brighter green color and are at least partly translucent (5 to 20 seconds); leaves may not turn completely translucent in oil, but will become more translucent as they stand. If leaves turn a darker green and begin to scorch, they're overcooked.

Lift leaves from oil with a slotted spoon; drain on paper towels. Serve hot or at room temperature. If made ahead, store airtight at room temperature in a paper towel–lined container for up to 3 days. Makes about 2 cups.

Per ¼ cup: 31 calories, .14 g protein, .17 g carbohydrate, 3 g total fat, 0 mg cholesterol, 4 mg sodium

(Pictured on facing page)
Quail Eggs in Crisp-fried Nest

About 2 cups whole or shredded Crisp-fried Leaves (recipe at left)
12 to 18 quail eggs
1 tablespoon sesame seeds
Salt

Prepare Crisp-fried Leaves; set aside.

Fill a 1- to 2-quart pan with about 2 inches of water; add eggs. Bring water to a boil; then reduce heat and simmer, uncovered, for 5 minutes. Drain and cover with cold water. Let stand until cool. Carefully shell eggs. (At this point, you may cover and refrigerate until next day.)

Toast sesame seeds in a small frying pan over medium heat until golden (about 2 minutes), shaking pan often. Set aside.

Pat eggs dry with a towel. Place fried leaves in a basket or bowl and nest eggs in leaves. Sprinkle sesame seeds and salt to taste over eggs and greens. Eat with fingers, picking up some of the greens with each egg. Makes 4 to 6 appetizer servings.

Per serving: 93 calories, 4 g protein, .69 g carbohydrate, 8 g total fat, 228 mg cholesterol, 6 mg sodium

(Pictured on facing page)
Melted Cheese with Crisp-fried Leaves

Place 1 small wheel (8 oz.) **Brie or Camembert cheese** in a 6- to 7-inch shallow pan or heatproof dish. Bake, uncovered, in a 350° oven just until cheese begins to melt (12 to 15 minutes).

Set hot cheese on a tray. Place alongside in separate baskets or bowls about 2 cups **Crisp-fried Leaves** (recipe at left; use watercress, mint, cilantro, or parsley) and 1 **baguette** (8 oz.), thinly sliced and toasted.

To eat, spread hot cheese on a toasted baguette slice and sprinkle with fried leaves. Makes 12 appetizer servings.

Per serving: 138 calories, 6 g protein, 11 g carbohydrates, 8 g total fat, 19 mg cholesterol, 230 mg sodium

Salads

Crispy Shrimp Salad

Preparation time: About 30 minutes

Marinating time: 30 minutes

Cooking time: About 5 minutes

Crisp deep-fried shrimp top a light cabbage and carrot salad in this Vietnamese-inspired entrée.

- 1 **medium-size onion, thinly sliced**
- 3 **tablespoons** *each* **sugar and distilled white vinegar**
- ¼ **teaspoon white pepper**
- ¾ **pound medium-size raw shrimp, shelled and deveined**
- ¼ **cup lime juice**
- 2 **tablespoons soy sauce**
- 2 **tablespoons fish sauce (***nam pla***)**
- 1 **clove garlic, minced or pressed**
  Salad oil
- 4 **cups finely shredded green cabbage**
- 2 **cups shredded carrots**
- ¼ **cup cornstarch**
- ⅓ **cup thinly slivered fresh mint leaves**
- 3 **tablespoons unsalted peanuts, chopped**

In a bowl, mix onion, sugar, vinegar, and white pepper. Cover; refrigerate for 30 minutes.

In another bowl, combine shrimp, 2 tablespoons of the lime juice, and soy; toss well and set aside at room temperature until ready to use.

Stir remaining 2 tablespoons lime juice, fish sauce, garlic, and ¼ cup oil into marinated onion; toss onion mixture with cabbage and carrots.

Set a wok in a ring stand. Pour oil into wok to a depth of 1 inch and heat to 350°F on a deep-frying thermometer. Working quickly, lift shrimp, 1 at a time, from marinade and dip into cornstarch to coat; shake off excess, then add shrimp to oil (you can cook 5 to 7 at a time). Cook until golden brown (about 30 seconds); adjust heat as needed to maintain oil temperature at 350°F. Remove cooked shrimp with a slotted spoon, drain on paper towels, and keep warm until all have been cooked.

Spread cabbage-onion mixture on a platter and top with hot shrimp. Sprinkle with mint and peanuts; serve at once. Makes 4 to 6 servings.

Per serving: 176 calories, 12 g protein, 21 g carbohydrates, 6 g total fat, 70 mg cholesterol, 778 mg sodium

Spinach Salad with Warm Feta & Crisp Chiles

Preparation time: About 15 minutes

Cooking time: About 7 minutes

Wonderful flavors come to life in this unusual combination of tender spinach, tangy feta, and spicy fried chiles.

- 1 **pound spinach**
  Lime Dressing (recipe follows)
- 3 **large dried red New Mexico or California chiles**
- 1 **medium-size red onion, thinly sliced**
- 2 **large ripe avocados**
  Salad oil
- 1 **egg**
- 1 **tablespoon water**
- 1 **cup fine dry bread crumbs**
- 8 **ounces feta cheese, drained and cut into 1-inch cubes**

Remove tough spinach stems and any yellow or wilted leaves. Rinse remaining spinach well; drain. Wrap in paper towels, enclose in plastic bags, and refrigerate until chilled. Prepare Lime Dressing; set aside. Cut chiles crosswise with scissors into thin strips; discard stems and seeds. Set aside.

Pinch off and discard stems from chilled spinach leaves; tear or cut leaves into small pieces and toss in a serving bowl with onion. Pit and peel avocados; dice and add to spinach mixture.

Set a wok in a ring stand. Pour oil into wok to a depth of 2 inches and heat over medium heat to 300°F on a deep-frying thermometer. Meanwhile, beat together egg and water in a shallow dish; spread bread crumbs in another shallow dish.

Add chiles all at once to oil and cook until just crisp (about 10 seconds). Remove with a slotted spoon and drain on paper towels. Increase heat; when oil reaches 375°F, quickly dip feta pieces in egg, then coat with bread crumbs. Add cheese cubes to oil, a portion at a time, and cook until crisp and brown on the outside and just melted on the inside (about 30 seconds); adjust heat as needed to maintain oil temperature at 375°F. As cheese cubes are cooked, remove from oil with a slotted spoon and drain.

Toss spinach mixture with Lime Dressing and chiles. Spoon onto individual plates and top with cheese cubes. Serve at once. Makes 4 to 6 servings.

Lime Dressing. Whisk together ¼ cup **lime juice,** ½ teaspoon **Dijon mustard,** and ⅓ cup **salad oil** until smooth. Season to taste with **pepper,** if desired.

Per serving: 501 calories, 11 g protein, 24 g carbohydrates, 42 g total fat, 80 mg cholesterol, 582 mg sodium

Vegetables

Eggplant with Sesame Sauce

Preparation time: About 10 minutes

Cooking time: About 20 minutes

Japanese eggplant aren't exclusively from Japan—
but the Japanese may have the best method of cooking them. Quick frying in oil produces soft and
creamy eggplant that absorbs almost no fat.

- 8 **Japanese eggplants,** *each* **about 6 inches
  long and 2 inches in diameter
  (about 2 lbs.** *total***)**
- 1 **tablespoon sesame seeds
  Salad oil**
- ¼ **cup** *each* **regular-strength chicken broth
  and soy sauce**
- ½ **teaspoon grated fresh ginger**

Trim and discard ends from eggplant. In each one,
make four ⅓-inch-deep lengthwise slashes, extending to within ½ inch of ends and spaced evenly
around eggplant. Place a wok over medium heat;
when wok is hot, add sesame seeds and stir until
golden (about 2 minutes). Pour out of wok.

Set wok in a ring stand. Pour oil into wok to a
depth of 1½ inches and heat to 350°F on a deep-
frying thermometer. Slip several eggplant at a time
into oil. Cook, turning occasionally, until soft when
pressed (about 4 minutes); adjust heat as needed to
maintain oil temperature at 350°F. Lift out cooked
eggplant, drain on paper towels, and keep warm
until all eggplant have been cooked.

Mix broth, soy, ginger, and sesame seeds. Spoon
over eggplant. Makes 4 servings.

*Per serving: 206 calories, 5 g protein, 16 g carbohydrates, 15 g total fat,
0 mg cholesterol, 1,102 mg sodium*

Eggplant with Sherry Sauce

Cut and cook eggplant as directed for **Eggplant with
Sesame Sauce;** keep warm in a 200° oven.

In a small pan, mix 1 tablespoon **cornstarch** with
2 tablespoons **soy sauce.** Gradually stir in 1 cup **regular-strength chicken broth** and ¼ cup **dry sherry.**
Cook over medium heat, stirring, until sauce boils
and thickens. Spoon sauce over eggplant and
sprinkle with 2 tablespoons *each* minced **green
onion** (including top) and grated **daikon.**

Corn Fritters

Preparation time: 50 to 55 minutes

Cooking time: 45 minutes

Use your food processor or blender to prepare these
Indonesian corn and shrimp fritters.

- 5 **or 6 large ears corn, husked**
- ¼ **to ½ pound raw shrimp, shelled,
  deveined, and finely chopped**
- 1 **egg**
- 1 **green onion (including top), finely
  chopped**
- ½ **medium-size onion, finely chopped**
- 1 **clove garlic, minced or pressed**
- ¼ **cup finely chopped celery leaves or fresh
  cilantro (coriander)**
- ⅛ **teaspoon pepper**
- 1 **tablespoon ground coriander**
- 1 **teaspoon sugar
  About 1 teaspoon salt**
- ½ **to ¾ cup all-purpose flour
  Salad oil**

Cut corn off cob, then scrape cob with knife to
remove pulp and "milk"; you should have 4 cups
corn in all. In a food processor or blender, whirl corn,
half at a time, until mixture is creamy but has some
pieces of coarsely chopped corn; scrape down sides
of processor bowl often.

Pour puréed corn into a bowl and add shrimp,
egg, green onion, onion, garlic, celery leaves, pepper, coriander, sugar, salt, and ½ cup of the flour. Set
aside for about 10 minutes.

Set a wok in a ring stand. Pour oil into wok to a
depth of 2 inches and heat to 350°F on a deep-frying
thermometer. Scoop up a rounded tablespoon of batter and carefully drop into oil; if this test fritter falls
apart, stir more flour into batter, 1 tablespoon at a
time, until a test fritter will hold together.

When batter has the correct consistency, add 4 or
5 fritters to oil, using a rounded tablespoon of batter
for each. As fritters come to surface, turn as needed
until evenly browned (about 5 minutes). Adjust heat
as needed to maintain oil temperature at 350°F; skim
and discard browned bits of batter frequently.

Lift out cooked fritters, drain on paper towels,
and keep warm until all fritters have been cooked.
Serve warm or at room temperature. Makes about
3½ dozen fritters (6 to 10 appetizer or vegetable
servings).

*Per serving: 179 calories, 7 g protein, 20 g carbohydrates, 8 g total fat,
55 mg cholesterol, 264 mg sodium*

Bread & Cheese

Navajo Fry Bread

Preparation time: About 20 minutes

Cooking time: About 20 minutes

These chewy breads—also called Papago popovers—are great for tostada bases. Or try them as a snack, sprinkled with sugar or drizzled with honey.

> **About 2 cups all-purpose flour**
> ½ **cup instant nonfat dry milk**
> 1 **tablespoon baking powder**
> ½ **teaspoon salt**
> 2 **tablespoons lard or solid vegetable shortening**
> ¾ **cup water**
> **Salad oil**

In a bowl, stir together 2 cups of the flour, dry milk, baking powder, and salt. With your fingers, crumble in lard until mixture is like cornmeal. Add water; stir with a fork just until dough clings together. Turn out onto a floured board and knead until smooth and satiny (about 5 minutes).

Divide dough into 6 portions; shape each into a ball. On a floured board, press out 1 ball to a 6- to 7-inch round; cover loosely. Repeat with remaining dough.

Set a wok in a ring stand. Pour oil into wok to a depth of 1 inch and heat to 350°F on a deep-frying thermometer. To fry each bread, place it on a wide spatula; lower into oil. Cook, turning often, until golden brown on both sides (1½ to 2 minutes); adjust heat as needed to maintain oil temperature at 350°F. Drain breads on paper towels and serve hot. Makes 6 fry breads.

Per bread: 252 calories, 6 g protein, 35 g carbohydrates, 9 g total fat, 5 mg cholesterol, 427 mg sodium

Spicy Fry Bread

Follow directions for **Navajo Fry Bread** adding 1 teaspoon **chili powder,** 1 teaspoon **paprika,** ½ teaspoon **ground cumin,** ¼ teaspoon **ground coriander,** and ⅛ teaspoon **ground red pepper (cayenne)** to flour mixture.

Mozzarella in Carrozza (Italian Cheese Sandwiches)

Preparation time: About 15 minutes

Cooking time: About 20 minutes

"Mozzarella in a carriage" is a tasty dish from southern Italy; we've given it a new lightness by deep-frying it without the traditional egg coating and topping it with a zesty tomato sauce. Serve the hot fried cheese sandwiches with steamed zucchini for a satisfying meatless supper.

> **Quick Tomato Sauce (recipe follows)**
> 4 **slices mozzarella cheese,** *each* ¼ **inch thick (about 4 oz.** *total***)**
> 8 **slices French or Italian bread,** *each* ½ **inch thick, crusts removed**
> ½ **cup milk**
> ⅓ **cup all-purpose flour**
> **Salad oil**

Prepare Quick Tomato Sauce, cover, and keep warm.

Trim cheese slices to make them just slightly smaller than bread slices. Assemble sandwiches, using 2 bread slices and 1 cheese slice for each. Gently pinch together edges of bread to seal. Place milk in a shallow dish; place flour in another shallow dish.

Set a wok in a ring stand. Pour oil into wok to a depth of 2 inches and heat to 375°F on a deep-frying thermometer. Cook sandwiches 1 at a time: dip each first in milk, then in flour; then place in wok and cook, turning once, until golden brown and crisp on both sides (about 2 minutes). Adjust heat as needed to maintain oil temperature at 375°F. Remove from oil with a slotted spoon and drain on paper towels.

Quickly reheat tomato sauce. Transfer mozzarella "carriages" to a warm platter; spoon sauce over and around them. Serve immediately. Makes 4 servings.

Quick Tomato Sauce. Heat 2 tablespoons **salad oil** in a medium-size frying pan over medium heat. Add 1 small **onion,** chopped, and 1 clove **garlic,** minced or pressed; cook, stirring, just until onion is soft. Add 1 can (about 1 lb.) **tomatoes** (break up with a spoon) and their liquid; stir in ½ teaspoon **dry marjoram or oregano leaves.** Bring sauce to a boil, stirring frequently; then reduce heat and simmer, uncovered, until slightly thickened (about 5 minutes). Season to taste with **salt** and **pepper,** if desired.

Per serving: 607 calories, 15 g protein, 54 g carbohydrates, 37 g total fat, 24 mg cholesterol, 712 mg sodium

A showy dessert, Caramel Fried Apples (recipe on page 128)
arrive hot at the table, then get a quick dip in ice water to cool and harden
their sweet coating. Banana slices are every bit as delicious as apples
in this Chinese treat.

Desserts

(Pictured on page 127)
Caramel Fried Apples

Preparation time: About 10 minutes

Cooking time: About 30 minutes

Caramelizing the sugar for this show-stopper dessert calls for split-second timing; it goes so quickly that you don't have time to use a candy thermometer. You may want to practice this step once before making the whole dessert.

       ½ **cup all-purpose flour**
       2 **tablespoons cornstarch**
       ¾ **teaspoon baking powder**
       ½ **cup water**
       2 **Golden Delicious apples or 2 bananas**
          Salad oil
          Ice cubes
       ⅔ **cup sugar**
       ⅓ **cup warm water**
       2 **teaspoons sesame seeds**

In a bowl, mix flour, cornstarch, and baking powder. Add the ½ cup water and stir until smooth. Peel and core apples; cut each into 8 wedges. (If you use bananas, peel, then cut diagonally into ½-inch slices.) Place fruit in batter and turn to coat evenly.

   Set a wok in a ring stand. Pour oil into wok to a depth of about 1½ inches and heat to 350°F on a deep-frying thermometer. Lift fruit, a piece at a time, from batter. Let excess batter drip off; then lower fruit into oil (cook several pieces at a time; do not crowd wok). Cook until coating is golden brown (about 2 minutes); adjust heat as needed to maintain oil temperature at 350°F. Remove with a slotted spoon and drain on paper towels.

   When all fruit has been cooked, generously oil a shallow pan or flat serving dish. Fill a serving bowl to the brim with ice cubes; add water to cover.

   To make the caramel coating, place sugar, the ⅓ cup warm water, and 1 tablespoon oil in a 10-inch frying pan; stir to blend. Place pan over high heat. When mixture begins to bubble (about 1 minute), shake pan continuously to prevent burning. Continue cooking and shaking pan until syrup *just* turns a pale straw color (about 9 minutes). Immediately remove from heat, add sesame seeds, and swirl to mix. (Syrup will continue to cook after you remove it from heat and will turn to a golden color in a few seconds.) Drop a few pieces of fruit into syrup and swirl to coat evenly. Using 2 spoons, immediately remove each piece of fruit; arrange on oiled pan (pieces should not touch). Repeat with remaining fruit. At the table, dip fruit in ice to harden coating and cool fruit. Makes 6 servings.

Per serving: 204 calories, 1 g protein, 39 g carbohydrates, 5 g total fat, 0 mg cholesterol, 54 mg sodium

Ricotta Puffs

Preparation time: About 10 minutes

Cooking time: About 30 minutes

In flavor and appearance, these tempting puffs can pass for doughnuts—but they're plumped up with protein rather than calories.

       8 **ounces (1 cup) ricotta cheese**
       3 **eggs**
       ¼ **cup granulated sugar**
       1 **cup all-purpose flour**
       4 **teaspoons baking powder**
       ¼ **teaspoon salt**
          Salad oil
          Powdered sugar

In a large bowl, beat ricotta cheese, eggs, and granulated sugar until blended and smooth. In another bowl, stir together flour, baking powder, and salt; add to ricotta mixture, beating until batter is smooth.

   Set a wok in a ring stand. Pour oil into wok to a depth of about 1½ inches; heat to 360°F on a deep-frying thermometer. For each puff, drop a rounded teaspoon of batter into oil (cook several puffs at a time; do not crowd wok). Cook, turning occasionally, until golden brown (about 1½ minutes); adjust heat as needed to maintain oil temperature at 360°F. Lift out cooked puffs with a slotted spoon; drain well on paper towels.

   If made ahead, let cool, then wrap airtight and refrigerate. To reheat, arrange puffs in a single layer on a rimmed baking sheet; place in a 350° oven until heated through (about 10 minutes).

   Dust with powdered sugar and serve hot. Makes about 3½ dozen puffs.

Per puff: 48 calories, .74 g protein, 5 g carbohydrates, 3 g total fat, 20 mg cholesterol, 59 mg sodium

Steaming

A delicate and healthful technique, steaming in a wok helps to retain vitamins and minerals. It also requires less fat, if any. So, it's clearly the choice of fitness-aware cooks. But steaming offers much more than good nutrition alone. It allows flavors to mingle more thoroughly than other methods. And it produces moist, tender results that you can serve directly from the steaming basket. Avoid peeking under the lid during steaming, because this lets valuable moisture and heat escape, which slows the cooking. Also, hot steam can burn, so be careful whenever you do lift the lid.

Steaming Lemon Chicken with Fermented Black Beans (Recipe on facing page)

1 Cut rinsed and dried chicken into 1- to 1½-inch lengths, pressing down firmly on cleaver to cut through bones.

2 In a heatproof dish that will fit inside a steamer basket or wok, arrange black bean-coated chicken pieces snugly; top with lemon slices.

3 Lay a wax-paper round on dish to catch drips from lid of wok (use outside rim of dish as a template for cutting wax paper).

4 Steam chicken in basket or on a rack directly over, but not touching, water. Cut to test for doneness; meat near bone should not be pink.

5 Steaming gives succulent, flavorful results. Serve chicken with steamed rice and, for an elegant presentation, garnish with sliced green onions, lemon, and parsley.

How to steam in a wok

You can steam anything in a wok—from seafood to poultry, desserts to breads—and master the technique in no time.

To convert your wok to a steamer, you'll need a ring stand (unless you have a flat-bottomed wok), a lid, and a metal rack. Steaming racks made just for the wok are readily available (see photo on page 7), but a regular round metal cake rack works well, too. Also available are stacking bamboo steaming baskets with lids. If you invest in two or more of these baskets, you'll be able to cook more than one food at a time; and because the basket lids absorb moisture, you needn't be concerned about condensed steam dripping into the food during cooking.

To steam, place the wok in a ring stand over the heat source. Pour in 1½ to 2 inches of hot water; set the rack in place. Check the water level; food arranged on the rack should be directly above the water, but not touching it. Cover the wok and bring the water to a boil. Then place the food on the rack or set it on a shallow plate or in a steaming basket atop the rack. To ensure that the steam can circulate freely, be careful not to cover all the holes in the rack. If you're not using a steaming basket, it's a good idea to drape some foods (such as custards) with wax paper, so drops of water won't fall from the inside of the wok lid into the dish.

Cover the wok, adjust the heat to keep the water at a boil, and steam for the time specified in your recipe or in the chart for steaming vegetables (see page 132). In general, you can allow about the same amount of time for steaming foods as you would for boiling them. Throughout the cooking time, check the water level periodically and add more water as needed to keep the wok from boiling dry; when you lift the wok lid, remember to keep an eye out for moisture dripping from the lid into the food.

Remove cooked food from the steaming rack carefully, using a single large spatula or two spatulas placed at right angles to each other.

(Pictured on facing page)

Lemon Chicken with Fermented Black Beans

Preparation time: About 15 minutes

Cooking time: About 30 minutes

The photos on the facing page show you just how easy it is to steam this flavorful entrée in your wok. Tender chicken pieces, cut into short lengths for faster cooking, are seasoned with black beans, garlic, and tangy lemon.

- 2 teaspoons sugar
- ¼ cup cornstarch
- 2 teaspoons sesame oil
- 3 tablespoons soy sauce
- 2 tablespoons dry sherry
- ¼ cup fermented salted black beans, rinsed, drained, and patted dry
- 1 clove garlic
  About 2½ pounds chicken thighs and legs
- 2 lemons
- 4 green onion tops, thinly sliced (optional)
  Thin lemon slices (optional)
  Fresh cilantro (coriander) sprigs (optional)

In a large bowl, smoothly blend sugar, cornstarch, oil, soy, and sherry. In a small bowl, mash black beans with garlic; add to cornstarch paste.

Rinse chicken and pat dry. With a heavy cleaver or knife, cut each piece through bones into 1- to 1½-inch lengths. Add chicken to cornstarch mixture; stir to coat well. (At this point, you may cover and refrigerate for up to 4 hours. Stir well before continuing.)

Arrange chicken evenly in a 10- to 11-inch-wide rimmed heatproof serving dish that will fit inside your wok. Cut 1 of the lemons in half; squeeze juice over chicken. Trim ends from remaining lemon; then slice lemon and cut each slice in half. Arrange half-slices over chicken.

Set dish on a rack in wok over 1½ to 2 inches of boiling water. Cover and steam until meat near bone is no longer pink; cut to test (about 30 minutes). Garnish with onion, lemon slices, and cilantro, if desired. Makes 4 servings.

Per serving: 420 calories, 40 g protein, 12 g carbohydrates, 23 g total fat, 130 mg cholesterol, 1805 mg sodium

Western-Style Lemon Chicken

Follow directions for **Lemon Chicken with Fermented Black Beans,** but omit sesame oil and black beans. Press garlic and mix into cornstarch paste. Garnish the finished dish with 1 small firm-ripe **avocado,** pitted, peeled, and sliced.

Steaming Fresh Vegetables

Steaming is one of the best techniques you can choose for cooking vegetables. Colors stay bright, flavors sweet and fresh; and because the vegetables cook in swirling steam rather than boiling water, there's no loss of vitamins and minerals into cooking liquid.

To steam vegetables, place a steaming rack in your wok (you can also use a collapsible metal steaming basket). Pour in water to a depth of 1 to 1½ inches, making sure the water doesn't touch the bottom of the rack. Bring water to a boil over high heat; then place the vegetable on the rack. Cover the wok, reduce heat to medium, and begin timing. The water should boil throughout the cooking time; adjust the heat as needed and add boiling water to the wok as necessary to maintain the level at 1 to 1½ inches.

Total cooking time will depend on the freshness and maturity of the vegetables—and on personal taste. Test after the minimum cooking time; if necessary, continue to cook, testing frequently, until vegetables are done to your liking. Most cooked vegetables should be just tender when pierced; whole potatoes should be tender throughout. Leafy vegetables should appear wilted and have bright color.

Vegetable	Amount to buy for 4 servings	Steaming time (in minutes)	Test for doneness
Artichokes. Whole	4 medium to large	30–45	Stem end tender when pierced
Asparagus.			
Spears	1½–2 pounds	8–12	Tender when pierced
Slices (½ to 1 inch)	1½–2 pounds	5–7	Tender when pierced
Beans, green, Italian, wax.			
Whole	1 pound	5–10	Tender-crisp to bite
Pieces (1 to 2 inch)	1 pound	4–7	Tender-crisp to bite
Broccoli.			
Spears	1–1½ pounds	15–20	Stalks tender when pierced
Pieces (1 inch)	1–1½ pounds	8–15	Tender when pierced
Cabbage. Wedges	1–1½ pounds	9–14	Tender when pierced
Carrots.			
Whole, baby	1 pound	8–12	Tender when pierced
Slices (¼ inch)	1 pound	5–10	Tender when pierced
Cauliflower.			
Flowerets	1½ pounds	10–18	Stem end tender when pierced
Slices (¼ inch)	1½ pounds	7–12	Tender-crisp to bite
Celery. 1-inch slices	1½ pounds	8–10	Tender when pierced
Celery hearts.	1½ pounds	10–14	Tender when pierced
Okra. Whole	1 pound	15–20	Tender when pierced
Onions. Small white boiling (whole, 1- to 1½-inch diameter)	1 pound	20–25	Tender when pierced
Parsnips. Whole	1 pound	15–25	Tender when pierced
Potatoes, red or white. Thin-skinned ½-inch slices	4 medium to large	8–10	Tender when pierced
Potatoes, sweet (or yams). Whole, 3-inch diameter	4 medium to large	30–40	Tender throughout when pierced
Snow peas.	1 pound	3–5	Tender-crisp to bite
Spinach. Whole leaves	1½ pounds	3–5	Wilted appearance, bright color
Squash, summer. ¼-inch slices	1–1½ pounds	4–7	Tender when pierced
Squash, winter. ½-inch slices	1½–2 pounds	9–12	Tender when pierced
Sunchokes. ¼- to ½-inch slices	1–1½ pounds	12–15	Tender when pierced
Swiss chard. Stems, leaves	1¼–2 pounds	Stems 3 minutes; add leaves and steam for 2–4 more minutes	Tender when pierced

Appetizers

Pork-stuffed Clams

Preparation time: About 30 minutes

Cooking time: About 20 minutes

Small clam shells filled with a savory pork and clam mixture are an attractive appetizer. Present them three or four to a plate, with small forks for scooping out the filling.

We suggest steaming the clams as a first step, but you can also simmer them in a cup of water for about 5 minutes, then drain off the cooking liquid to use in seafood soups or stews.

- 2 **pounds small live hard-shell clams, scrubbed**
- ½ **pound lean boneless pork (such as shoulder or butt), trimmed of excess fat and finely chopped or ground**
- ¼ **cup finely chopped water chestnuts**
- 1 **green onion (including top), minced**
- 1 **tablespoon *each* soy sauce, dry sherry, and cornstarch**
- ½ **teaspoon *each* salt and minced fresh ginger**
- 1 **teaspoon sugar**
  Dash of white pepper

Place clams in a heatproof serving bowl (at least 1 inch deep) that will fit in your wok. Place bowl on a rack in wok over 1½ to 2 inches of boiling water. Cover and steam until clam shells open (about 10 minutes); discard any unopened clams.

Remove clams from shells; finely chop meat. Separate each shell into 2 halves; turn upside down to drain. In a bowl, mix chopped clams with pork, water chestnuts, onion, soy, sherry, cornstarch, salt, ginger, sugar, and white pepper.

Mound about 4 teaspoons of the clam mixture in each half-shell. Arrange shells, filled side up, on 2 heatproof plates that will fit inside your wok. (At this point, you may cover and refrigerate for up to 8 hours; bring to room temperature before steaming.)

To steam each plate, set on a rack in wok over 1½ to 2 inches of boiling water. Cover and steam until meat is no longer pink in center; cut to test (about 20 minutes). Makes about 20 appetizers.

Per appetizer: 29 calories, 3 g protein, 1 g carbohydrate, 1 g total fat, 10 mg cholesterol, 118 mg sodium

Quick Mini-tamales

Preparation time: About 45 minutes

Cooking time: About 45 minutes

Tamales are surprisingly quick to prepare when you make your wrappers from squares of foil instead of the traditional corn husks. These little tamales feature a filling of minced turkey, ripe olives, and salsa enclosed in masa dough.

- 2 **cups dehydrated masa flour (corn tortilla flour)**
- 1¼ **cups regular-strength chicken broth**
  Salt
- ½ **cup salad oil**
- 2 **cups finely diced cooked turkey or chicken**
- ½ **cup pitted ripe olives, coarsely chopped**
- 1 **medium-size onion, finely chopped**
- ½ **cup purchased green chile salsa**

Cut thirty 6-inch-square pieces of foil. Set aside.

In a bowl, stir together masa flour, broth, ½ teaspoon salt, and oil to make a thick paste. Spread about 1½ tablespoons of the paste into a 3-inch square in the center of each piece of foil.

In another bowl, mix turkey, olives, onion, and salsa. Season to taste with salt. Place about 1½ tablespoons of the filling down center of each masa square. Fold foil edges together so masa edges meet, then seal all sides.

Arrange tamales on a rack in a wok over 1½ to 2 inches of boiling water, stacking tamales to permit air circulation. Cover and steam until masa is firm to touch; unfold a tamale to test (about 45 minutes). Serve hot. Makes 2½ dozen small tamales.

Per tamale: 83 calories, 4 g protein, 6 g carbohydrates, 5 g total fat, 7 mg cholesterol, 90 mg sodium

Pearl Balls

Preparation time: About 25 minutes, plus 2 hours to soak rice and 30 minutes to soak mushrooms

Cooking time: About 45 minutes

These plump little meatballs get a special coating of soaked, uncooked sticky rice; during steaming, the grains become translucent, almost pearl-like. Long-grain rice won't work in this recipe, so don't be tempted to use it; take the time to look for sticky rice (sometimes labeled sweet, glutinous, or *mochi* rice) at an Asian market.

⅔ **cup sticky rice (also called sweet or glutinous rice)**

4 **medium-size dried Oriental mushrooms**

1 **pound lean boneless pork (such as shoulder or butt), trimmed of excess fat and finely chopped or ground**

¼ **cup finely chopped water chestnuts**

1 **green onion (including top), finely chopped**

1 **egg**

1 **teaspoon** *each* **salt, cornstarch, and dry sherry**

½ **teaspoon** *each* **sugar and grated fresh ginger**

½ **teaspoon crushed Szechwan peppercorns or ¼ teaspoon white pepper**

1 **tablespoon soy sauce**

Soak rice in cold water to cover for 2 hours, then drain and spread on a plate. Also soak mushrooms in warm water to cover for 30 minutes, then drain. Cut off and discard stems; squeeze caps dry and finely chop.

In a bowl, combine mushrooms, pork, water chestnuts, and onion. In another bowl, beat egg with salt, cornstarch, sherry, sugar, ginger, peppercorns, and soy. Add to pork mixture; mix lightly.

With wet hands, roll 2-tablespoon portions of meat mixture into walnut-size balls. Roll each ball in drained rice to coat completely. Arrange balls (be sure they don't touch each other) on 2 heatproof plates that will fit inside your wok. (At this point, you may cover and refrigerate for up to 8 hours.)

To steam each plate, drape with a piece of wax paper, then set on a rack in a wok over 1½ to 2 inches of boiling water. Cover and steam until meat is no longer pink in center; cut to test (about 45 minutes). Makes 8 servings.

Per serving: 176 calories, 13 g protein, 16 g carbohydrates, 6 g total fat, 73 mg cholesterol, 453 mg sodium

---

(Pictured on facing page)

Shrimp-stuffed Mushrooms

Preparation time: 20 minutes, plus 30 minutes to soak dried mushrooms

Cooking time: About 10 minutes

Succulent mushroom caps make flavorful containers for a light shrimp filling dotted with crunchy water chestnuts. If you like, substitute rich-tasting dried mushrooms for the fresh ones; in either case, you'll need even-sized, well-shaped mushrooms.

16 **fresh button mushrooms,** *each* **about 2 inches in diameter, or medium-size Oriental mushrooms**

½ **teaspoon** *each* **salt and sugar**

1 **tablespoon soy sauce**

1 **cup regular-strength chicken broth Shrimp Filling (recipe follows)**

1 **jar (2 oz.) sliced pimentos, drained (optional) Parsley leaves**

Remove stems from fresh mushrooms; place caps in a pan with salt, sugar, soy, and broth. Simmer in broth mixture for 10 minutes. (If using dried mushrooms, soak in warm water to cover for 30 minutes, then drain. Cut off and discard stems. Squeeze caps dry, then simmer in broth mixture for 30 minutes.)

While mushrooms are simmering, prepare Shrimp Filling; set aside.

Remove mushrooms from broth, drain, and let cool slightly.

Mound about 2 teaspoons of the filling in each mushroom. Arrange mushrooms, filled side up, on 1 or 2 serving plates that will fit inside your wok. (At this point, you may cover and refrigerate for up to 8 hours; bring to room temperature before steaming.)

To steam each plate, place on a rack in wok over 1½ to 2 inches of boiling water. Cover and steam until filling is cooked through (about 10 minutes). If you cook mushrooms on 2 plates, serve the first portion while the second is cooking. Garnish with pimentos and parsley, if desired. Makes 16 appetizers.

Shrimp Filling. In a bowl, beat 1 **egg white** until foamy. Blend 2 teaspoons *each* **dry sherry** and **cornstarch,** then stir into egg white along with ½ teaspoon *each* **salt** and grated **fresh ginger.** Add ¼ cup finely chopped **water chestnuts** and ½ pound **raw shrimp,** shelled, deveined, and finely chopped; mix well.

Per appetizer: 31 calories, 3 g protein, 4 g carbohydrates, .35 g total fat, 17 mg cholesterol, 284 mg sodium

Flaunting a garnish of bright red pimento, Shrimp-stuffed Mushrooms (recipe
on facing page) beckon to hungry guests at a party.
Brimming over with a savory filling, the tender mushroom caps
make tempting nibbles.

Beef, Veal & Pork

Beef-stuffed Cabbage Leaves in Tomato Sauce

Preparation time: About 40 minutes

Cooking time: About 35 minutes

Stuffed cabbage leaves are traditionally baked in sauce, but this version of the familiar dish is a bit different. You steam the beef- and rice-filled leaves, then top them with a simple tomato sauce (easily made while the leaves are cooking).

  1 **large head green cabbage (about 2 lbs.)**
  ¾ **pound lean ground beef**
  1 **medium-size onion, chopped**
  1 **cup cooked rice**
  2 **tablespoons butter or margarine, melted**
  ½ **cup fine dry bread crumbs**
  ¾ **teaspoon salt**
  ¼ **teaspoon** *each* **pepper and dry rubbed sage**
     Tomato Sauce (recipe follows)

Cut out and discard core from cabbage. Place cabbage, cored end down, on a rack in a wok over 1½ inches of boiling water. Cover and steam until leaves are bright green and limp throughout (about 8 minutes). Remove cabbage with tongs; let cool slightly, then peel off leaves. You will need about 15 leaves. Set aside 3 of the largest leaves for lining the wok rack; use remaining 12 leaves for stuffing.

In a bowl, combine beef, onion, rice, butter, bread crumbs, salt, pepper, and sage.

To fill leaves, mound some of the meat mixture near base of each leaf—3 to 4 tablespoons for larger leaves, 2 to 3 tablespoons for smaller leaves. With base of leaf toward you, fold leaf up over meat and roll toward tip. Hold roll with seam underneath and fold outer edges of leaf under, making a pillow-shaped roll. (At this point, you may cover and refrigerate until next day.)

Line rack in wok with the 3 reserved leaves, leaving some of rack exposed. Carefully place cabbage rolls on top of leaves. Cover and steam over 1½ to 2 inches of boiling water until filling is no longer pink

in center; cut to test (about 35 minutes; 45 minutes if refrigerated). Meanwhile, prepare Tomato Sauce.

Serve cabbage rolls with hot sauce. Makes about 12 rolls (4 servings).

Tomato Sauce. Melt ¼ cup **butter** or margarine in a small pan. Add ½ teaspoon **chili powder** and 2 tablespoons **all-purpose flour.** Stir to make a smooth paste; then bring to a boil over high heat, stirring. Remove from heat and gradually stir in 2 cups **tomato juice.** Return to heat and stir until sauce boils and thickens. Season to taste with **salt.**

Per serving: 566 calories, 21 g protein, 41 g carbohydrates, 36 g total fat, 111 mg cholesterol, 1,486 mg sodium

Gingered Veal Loaf

Preparation time: About 30 minutes

Cooking time: About 50 minutes

Standing time: 30 minutes

If you're like many of us, you probably consider meat loaf a boring entrée or school cafeteria fare. When you try this party-worthy recipe, though, you'll be glad you gave meat loaf another chance.

  2 **tablespoons butter, margarine, or salad oil**
  1 **medium-size onion, finely chopped**
  2 **stalks celery, finely chopped**
  1 **clove garlic, minced or pressed**
  2 **pounds ground veal**
  1 **egg**
  1 **cup fine dry bread crumbs**
  ½ **cup milk**
  1 **tablespoon minced fresh ginger**
     Salt and pepper
  6 **to 8 large mustard green leaves,** *each* **about 8 inches long**
  8 **to 12 cups boiling water**
     Rosemary Tomato Sauce (recipe follows)

Place a wok over medium-high heat. When wok is hot, add butter or oil. When butter is melted (or oil is hot), add onion, celery, and garlic. Stir-fry until onion is soft; then let cool.

In a large bowl, combine onion mixture, veal, egg, bread crumbs, milk, and ginger. Mix well with your hands or a heavy spoon. Season to taste with salt and pepper. Clean and dry wok.

In a 5- to 6-quart pan, immerse mustard greens in 8 to 12 cups boiling water; lift out as soon as wilted. Trim off and discard tough part of stems.

Open leaves flat and use to line bottom and sides of a loaf pan (about 4½ by 8½ inches), letting leaves overlap on pan bottom and sides and extend over pan rim. Firmly and evenly pat veal mixture into pan; fold leaves extending beyond pan rim over meat.

Cover pan tightly with foil. Set pan on a rack in wok over 1½ to 2 inches of boiling water. Cover and steam until loaf feels firm in center when pressed through foil (about 50 minutes). Let stand for at least 30 minutes before serving. Meanwhile, prepare Rosemary Tomato Sauce.

If made ahead, cover and refrigerate in pan for up to 2 days; serve at room temperature. Or, to reheat, cover loaf in pan tightly with foil; steam as directed until hot through (about 50 minutes).

To unmold, remove foil; invert loaf onto a serving dish, cut into about ½-inch-thick slices, and accompany with Rosemary Tomato Sauce. Makes 6 to 8 servings.

Rosemary Tomato Sauce. In a 5- to 6-quart pan, combine 2 tablespoons **olive oil** or salad oil, 1 tablespoon chopped **garlic,** ½ teaspoon **dry rosemary,** and ¼ teaspoon **crushed dried hot red chiles.** Cook over medium-high heat, stirring often, until garlic is golden.

Add 2 cans (about 1 lb. *each*) **tomatoes** and their liquid. Bring to a boil over high heat; boil, uncovered, breaking up tomatoes with a spoon, until reduced to 2 cups. Whirl in a food processor or blender until puréed. If made ahead, cover and refrigerate for up to 2 days. Serve hot or at room temperature. Makes 2 cups.

Per serving loaf: 303 calories, 26 g protein, 13 g carbohydrates, 16 g total fat, 125 mg cholesterol, 231 mg sodium

Per tablespoon sauce: 14 calories, .27 g protein, 1 g carbohydrate, .90 g total fat, 0 mg cholesterol, 46 mg sodium

Vietnamese Pork Loaf

Preparation time: About 25 minutes, plus 30 minutes to soak mushrooms and bean threads

Cooking time: About 50 minutes

Standing time: 45 minutes

Reheating won't dry out this pork loaf—it's guaranteed to stay moist. A far cry from the typical meat loaf, it's dotted with green onions, water chestnuts, and minced bean threads and crowned with whole mushroom caps. Serve it with a simple sauce of soy, rice vinegar, and ginger.

16 dried Oriental mushrooms, *each* about 2 inches in diameter
 1 ounce dried bean threads
 4 eggs
 1 pound lean ground pork
 ¾ cup minced green onions (including tops)
 1 clove garlic, minced or pressed
 ¼ cup minced water chestnuts
 1 tablespoon fish sauce (*nam pla*) or soy sauce
   Soy-Ginger Sauce (recipe follows)
   About 24 small butter or romaine lettuce leaves (optional)

Soak mushrooms in warm water to cover for 30 minutes; in a separate bowl, soak bean threads in warm water to cover for 30 minutes.

Drain mushrooms. Cut off and discard stems; rinse caps and drain. Lay 10 of the caps, dark side down, evenly over bottom of a loaf pan (about 4½ by 8½ inches). Finely chop remaining mushrooms.

Drain bean threads and coarsely chop. In a bowl, combine chopped mushrooms, bean threads, eggs, pork, onions, garlic, water chestnuts, and fish sauce; mix well with your hands or a heavy spoon. Carefully fill loaf pan with meat mixture, being sure not to disturb mushroom caps. Remove bubbles by rapping pan sharply on counter several times.

Cover pan tightly with foil. Set pan on a rack in a wok over 1½ to 2 inches of boiling water. Cover and steam until loaf feels firm in center when pressed through foil (about 50 minutes). Let loaf stand for at least 45 minutes before serving. Meanwhile, prepare Soy-Ginger Sauce.

If made ahead, cover and refrigerate in pan for up to 2 days; serve at room temperature. Or, to reheat, cover loaf in pan tightly with foil; steam as directed above until hot through (about 50 minutes).

To unmold, remove foil and run a knife blade around pan sides. Invert loaf onto a platter, cut into ½-inch-thick slices, and serve warm or at room temperature with sauce. Or, if desired, cut each slice in halves or quarters and place on a lettuce leaf to eat with sauce. Makes 5 or 6 servings.

Soy-Ginger Sauce. Stir together ¼ cup *each* **soy sauce** and **rice wine vinegar,** 2 tablespoons minced **fresh ginger,** 1 to 2 tablespoons **sesame oil,** and 1 teaspoon minced **garlic.** Season to taste with **liquid hot pepper seasoning.**

Per serving: 284 calories, 21 g protein, 16 g carbohydrates, 15 g total fat, 234 mg cholesterol, 961 mg sodium

Though they start with the same cut of meat, these Black Bean Spareribs (recipe
on facing page) bear little resemblance to their Texan counterpart.
But they're just as wonderful to eat, either on their own or
combined with other courses.

Pork & Yams with Rice Crumbs

Preparation time: About 25 minutes

Marinating time: 4 hours

Cooking time: About 40 minutes

Rice powder is a traditional ingredient in this recipe, but because it's hard to find, we've substituted toasted cream of rice cereal. Combined with sherry, soy sauce, and seasonings, the cereal makes a fluffy coating for pork cubes and yams.

- 3 tablespoons cream of rice cereal
- 1½ tablespoons *each* dry sherry, soy sauce, and salad oil
- 1 tablespoon sweet bean sauce or hoisin sauce
- 1 teaspoon *each* minced fresh ginger and minced garlic
- 1 teaspoon hot bean sauce or ¼ teaspoon liquid hot pepper seasoning
- ¼ teaspoon sesame oil
  Dash of white pepper
- 1 pound lean boneless pork (such as shoulder or butt), trimmed of excess fat and cut into ½-inch cubes
- 2 medium-size yams (about 1 lb. *total*)
- ¼ teaspoon salt
- 1 tablespoon dry sherry
- 2 green onions (including tops), thinly sliced

In a small frying pan, toast cereal over medium heat until lightly browned (about 5 minutes), shaking pan occasionally. Let cool.

In a bowl, combine the 1½ tablespoons sherry, soy, salad oil, sweet bean sauce, ginger, garlic, hot bean sauce, sesame oil, white pepper, and 2 tablespoons of the toasted cereal. Add pork and stir to coat. Cover and refrigerate for at least 4 hours or until next day.

Peel yams and cut into ½-inch-thick slices. Blend remaining 1 tablespoon toasted cereal with salt and the 1 tablespoon sherry; mix with yams.

Arrange pork cubes in a heatproof 1-quart casserole that will fit inside your wok. Distribute yam mixture on top. Place casserole on a rack in wok over 1½ to 2 inches of boiling water. Cover and steam until pork and yams are tender when pierced (about 40 minutes). Remove casserole from wok and let stand for a few minutes, then invert onto a serving plate. Scatter onions over top. Makes 4 or 5 servings.

Per serving: 318 calories, 20 g protein, 30 g carbohydrates, 13 g total fat, 62 mg cholesterol, 597 mg sodium

Beef with Rice Crumbs

Follow directions for **Pork & Yams with Rice Crumbs,** but substitute 1 pound **flank steak,** cut into 1-inch squares, for pork. Omit yams with their coating of sherry, salt, and cream of rice. Steam meat until tender when pierced (about 40 minutes); then invert onto a plate lined with **lettuce leaves** before sprinkling with onions.

(Pictured on facing page)

Black Bean Spareribs

Preparation time: About 15 minutes

Marinating time: 15 minutes

Cooking time: About 1 hour

A good choice to include in a Chinese meal of several courses, these spareribs require no last-minute attention. You'll need to have the ribs cut for you at the meat market; they're first sawed through the bones into 1½-inch strips, then cut apart between the bones.

- 2 tablespoons fermented salted black beans, rinsed, drained, and finely chopped
- 2 cloves garlic, minced or pressed
- 1 teaspoon chopped fresh ginger
- 1 tablespoon *each* cornstarch, dry sherry, and soy sauce
- ½ teaspoon *each* salt and sugar
- 1½ pounds spareribs, cut 1½ inches long, then cut apart between bones
- 2 tablespoons salad oil
  Thinly sliced green onion tops

In a bowl, stir together black beans, garlic, ginger, cornstarch, sherry, soy, salt, and sugar. Add ribs and turn until well coated; let marinate for 15 minutes.

Place a wok over high heat; when wok is hot, add oil. When oil is hot, add meat and cook, turning once, until browned on both sides (about 4 minutes). Transfer to an 8- or 9-inch round heatproof bowl.

Rinse wok. Place bowl on a rack in wok over 1½ to 2 inches of boiling water. Cover and steam until meat is tender when pierced (about 1 hour). Skim fat from sauce; sprinkle meat with onions. Makes 2 or 3 servings.

Per serving: 329 calories, 17 g protein, 6 g carbohydrates, 26 g total fat, 66 mg cholesterol, 1,050 mg sodium

Chicken & Turkey

Chicken with Ginger Sauce

Preparation time: About 15 minutes

Cooking time: About 1½ hours

Lightly seasoned with ginger, a steamed whole chicken is a succulent entrée. Serve hot, with a sauce made from the cooking juices; or chill and slice to use in salads and sandwiches.

> 2 **tablespoons dry sherry**
> 1 **tablespoon soy sauce**
> 1½ **teaspoons minced fresh ginger**
> 1 **large clove garlic, minced or pressed**
> 1 **frying chicken (3 to 3½ lbs.)**
> 1 **tablespoon** *each* **cornstarch and water, stirred together**
> ¼ **cup thinly sliced green onions (including tops)**
> **Salt and pepper**

In a small bowl, combine sherry, soy, ginger, and garlic. Set aside.

Remove chicken neck and giblets and reserve for other uses. Pull off and discard lumps of fat. Rinse chicken inside and out; pat dry. Place chicken, breast down, on a sheet of heavy-duty foil large enough to enclose it. Bring foil up around all sides of chicken, then pour sherry mixture over chicken. Enclose bird in foil, folding foil over on top so package can be opened easily.

Place foil-wrapped chicken, seam side up, on a rack in a wok over 1½ to 2 inches of boiling water. Cover and steam until meat near thighbone is no longer pink; cut to test (1 to 1¼ hours). Open foil and transfer chicken to a platter, draining juices back into foil container; keep chicken warm.

Skim and discard fat from juices, then measure; you need 1¼ cups. (If you have more, boil to reduce; if you have less, add water.) In a 1- to 2-quart pan, mix juices and cornstarch-water mixture. Stir over medium heat until sauce boils and thickens. Stir in onions; season to taste with salt and pepper. Spoon some of sauce over chicken; pass remaining sauce at the table. Makes about 4 servings.

Per serving: 435 calories, 48 g protein, 4 g carbohydrates, 24 g total fat, 154 mg cholesterol, 402 mg sodium

Chicken Pot-au-Feu

Preparation time: About 15 minutes

Cooking time: About 1¼ hours

An herb-seasoned chicken and vegetable stew is an appealing light entrée for two. You can steam it in an ordinary mixing bowl, but if possible, use a Chinese Yunnan pot—a lidded clay pot with a cone-shaped spout in the center. (The spout lets some condensed steam fall back into the pot, making a sweeter, more flavorful broth.)

> ¼ **cup** *each* **dry white wine and regular-strength chicken broth**
> 2 **large leeks (about 1 lb.** *total***)**
> 2 **whole chicken legs, thighs attached (about 1 lb.** *total***), rinsed and patted dry**
> 4 **small thin-skinned potatoes,** *each* **1½ to 2 inches in diameter**
> 2 **large carrots, cut into 3-inch lengths**
> 2 **cloves garlic, crushed**
> 1 **dry bay leaf**
> ½ **teaspoon dry thyme leaves**
> **Dijon mustard**
> **Prepared horseradish**

In an 8- or 9-inch Yunnan pot or a 2-quart bowl that will fit in your wok, stir together wine and broth. Trim and discard ends and tops from leeks, leaving about 3 inches of green leaves. Discard tough outer leaves. Split leeks lengthwise; rinse well, then cut crosswise into 3-inch lengths. Arrange leeks, chicken, potatoes, carrots, garlic, and bay leaf in Yunnan pot or in bowl; sprinkle with thyme.

Place lid on Yunnan pot (if you're using a bowl, leave it uncovered). Carefully set pot or bowl on a rack in wok; pour water into wok until level reaches halfway up sides of pot (if you're using a bowl, pour in water to just beneath rack).

Cover wok and bring water to a boil over high heat. Then reduce heat and steam until meat near thighbone is no longer pink; cut to test (about 1 hour).

Lift out chicken and vegetables; accompany with mustard and horseradish. Skim and discard fat from broth; serve broth in cups. Makes 2 servings.

Per serving: 466 calories, 35 g protein, 47 g carbohydrates, 16 g total fat, 103 mg cholesterol, 1,123 mg sodium

Turkey Breast with Herb Mayonnaise

Preparation time: About 15 minutes

Cooking time: 1 to 2 hours, depending on size of turkey breast

Chilling time: 1½ to 4 hours for turkey, 30 minutes for mayonnaise

When you need a simple, easy-to-cook meal for a crowd, consider this juicy steamed turkey breast. You just top the meat with parsley and onion, wrap it in foil, and steam it for an hour or two. Serve the chilled, sliced meat with a fresh-tasting sauce of minced green herbs mixed with mayonnaise.

> 1 **whole or half turkey breast (3 to 6 lbs.)**
> 6 **parsley sprigs**
> 1 **small onion, sliced**
> **Green Herb Mayonnaise (recipe follows)**

Rinse turkey and pat dry. Then place turkey on a sheet of heavy-duty foil large enough to enclose it. Insert a meat thermometer into thickest part of breast (not touching bone). Top breast with parsley and onion; enclose in foil, shaping foil around thermometer on top.

Place foil-wrapped turkey on a rack in a wok over 1½ to 2 inches of boiling water. Cover and steam until thermometer registers 165°F (or until meat near bone is no longer pink; cut to test). For a 3- to 4-pound breast, allow 1 to 1½ hours; for 4½ to 6 pounds, allow 1½ to 2 hours.

Remove turkey from wok. Open foil; discard parsley and onion and save juices for other uses. When turkey is cool enough to handle, remove and discard skin and bones. Cover meat and refrigerate until cold (1½ to 4 hours) or for up to 2 days. Meanwhile, prepare Green Herb Mayonnaise.

To serve, slice breast across the grain and serve with mayonnaise. Makes 12 to 24 servings (4 servings per pound).

Green Herb Mayonnaise. In a food processor, combine 1 cup lightly packed **watercress** (coarse stems removed), 1 cup lightly packed **parsley sprigs,** ⅓ cup sliced **green onions** (including tops), 1 clove **garlic** (chopped), and ¼ teaspoon **dry rosemary.** Whirl until greens are finely chopped. Blend in ½ cup **mayonnaise;** cover and refrigerate for at least 30 minutes or up to 2 days. Makes enough for a 4-pound turkey breast; if breast is over 4 pounds, double this sauce recipe. Makes about ¾ cup.

Per serving turkey: 148 calories, 22 g protein, .27 g carbohydrate, 6 g total fat, 57 mg cholesterol, 49 mg sodium

Per tablespoon mayonnaise: 69 calories, .32 g protein, .85 g carbohydrate, 7 g total fat, 5 mg cholesterol, 55 mg sodium

Fish & Shellfish

Fish & Clams in Black Bean Sauce

Preparation time: 10 to 15 minutes

Cooking time: About 15 minutes

Calorie-conscious diners will delight in this succulent combination of fish and clams in a pungent black bean sauce. If you're trying to cut down on sodium as well as calories, use low-sodium soy sauce.

> 1 **rockfish or cod fillet (about 1 lb.), about 1 inch thick**
> 1½ **tablespoons fermented salted black beans, rinsed, drained, and patted dry**
> 2 **cloves garlic**
> 1 **tablespoon *each* soy sauce and dry sherry**
> 2 **green onions (including tops)**
> 3 **thin, quarter-size slices fresh ginger**
> 12 **small live hard-shell clams, scrubbed**
> 2 **tablespoons salad oil**

Rinse fish and pat dry. Place in a heatproof dish (at least 1 inch deep) that will fit inside your wok.

Mince or mash black beans and garlic; add soy and sherry. Drizzle mixture over fish. Cut 1 of the onions into thirds; place cut onion and ginger on top of fish. Cut remaining onion into 2-inch lengths; cut lengths into thin shreds and set aside. Arrange clams around fish.

Place dish on a rack in wok over 1½ to 2 inches of boiling water. Cover and steam until fish flakes when prodded in thickest part (about 10 minutes). If clams open before fish is done, remove them and continue to cook fish for a few more minutes; then return clams to dish.

Lift dish from wok. Discard ginger and onion pieces from top of fish. Sprinkle onion slivers over fish. Heat oil in a small pan until it ripples when pan is tilted; pour over fish (oil will sizzle). Makes 2 or 3 servings.

Per serving: 166 calories, 13 g protein, 26 g carbohydrates, 2 g total fat, 35 mg cholesterol, 940 mg sodium

Tea-smoked Duck

A favorite Szechwan technique for preparing duck involves smoking the bird over tea leaves, then steaming it, then deep-frying it to brown the skin. We offer a streamlined version of the recipe; the steaming step is omitted, and the bird is roasted, not fried. The results are still superb, though: crisp skin, juicy meat, and a fruity, subtly smoky flavor.

Steamed Buns (recipe follows) or brown-and-serve rolls

1 **duck (about 4 lbs.), thawed if frozen**

1 **teaspoon salt**

1 **tablespoon Szechwan peppercorns**

2 **tablespoons dry sherry**

¼ cup *each* **rice, firmly packed brown sugar, and black tea leaves**

2 **tablespoons coarsely chopped orange peel or 2 tablespoons dried tangerine peel**

6 **thin, quarter-size slices fresh ginger, crushed**

5 **green onions (including tops)**
Hoisin sauce
Fresh cilantro (coriander) sprigs

Prepare Steamed Buns; set aside. Remove duck neck and giblets; reserve for other uses. Rinse duck inside and out and pat dry. Trim off and discard excess neck skin; discard lumps of fat. With a fork, pierce skin all over duck.

In a small frying pan over medium-low heat, cook salt and peppercorns, shaking pan often, until salt begins to brown and peppercorns become fragrant (about 10 minutes). Let cool, then coarsely crush with a mortar and pestle or a rolling pin. Combine mixture with sherry; rub over duck, inside and out.

To smoke duck, you'll need a wok at least 14 inches in diameter (*do not* use an electric wok with a nonstick finish). Line wok with heavy-duty foil. Add rice, sugar, tea leaves, and orange peel; stir together. Position a round 9-inch cake rack or steamer rack in bottom of wok, at least 1 inch above tea mixture. Set duck on rack; place wok over high heat.

When mixture begins to smoke, cover wok tightly and smoke for 5 minutes. Reduce heat to medium and continue to smoke, without uncovering wok, for 15 minutes. Turn off heat and leave covered until smoke subsides (15 more minutes). Remove duck; discard tea mixture. Place ginger and 2 of the onions inside body cavity; fasten opening shut with a small skewer. Place duck, breast down, on a rack in a 12- by 15-inch roasting pan. Roast, uncovered, in a 350° oven for 1½ hours. Drain and discard fat from pan and turn bird over; continue to roast until thigh feels soft when pressed (45 to 60 more minutes). Drain and discard all fat from pan. Increase oven temperature to 450°; return duck to oven and roast just until skin is crisp (about 5 more minutes).

Meanwhile, reheat buns as directed, steaming for about 5 minutes (10 minutes if frozen). Or place rolls slightly apart in a pan; cover and steam until hot (5 to 10 minutes).

Slice duck meat from bones; cut remaining 3 onions into thin slivers. Place duck slices in a warm bun; top with onions, hoisin, and cilantro, then close and eat out of hand. Makes about 3 servings.

Steamed Buns. In a large bowl, dissolve 1 package **active dry yeast** in 1 cup **warm water** (about 110°F); blend in ⅓ cup **sugar,** 2 tablespoons **salad oil,** and 1 teaspoon **salt.** Let stand in a warm place until bubbly (about 15 minutes). Add 3¼ cups **all-purpose flour;** mix until dough holds together. Scrape out onto a floured board; knead until smooth and elastic (8 to 10 minutes). Place in a greased bowl, turn over to grease top, cover, and let rise in a warm place until doubled (about 1¼ hours).

Turn dough out onto a lightly floured board and knead for 1 minute. Shape into a rectangle, then cut into 12 equal pieces. Roll each piece into a ball; place each ball on a 3-inch square of foil. Cover and let rise in a warm place until puffy and light (about 30 minutes).

Arrange buns (on foil squares) on a rack in a wok over 1½ to 2 inches of boiling water. Cover and steam until tops are glazed and smooth (12 to 15 minutes). Serve warm; or let cool, wrap airtight, and freeze for up to 1 month. To reheat, steam frozen buns until hot (about 10 minutes). Makes 1 dozen buns.

Cilantro, green onions, and hoisin sauce surround crisp
and spicy Tea-smoked Duck (recipe on facing page). Slice the meat,
then tuck it inside fluffy steamed buns or brown-and-serve rolls for
a rich-tasting and delightful meal.

Steam-poached Fish Fillets

Preparation time: About 5 minutes

Cooking time: About 20 minutes

Like our Chicken with Ginger Sauce (page 140), these seasoned fish fillets steam in a snug foil packet. Accompany the fish with an herbed tomato-onion sauce (you can make the sauce while the fish cooks).

> 1½ **pounds halibut, snapper, or cod fillets or steaks**
>
> 6 **parsley sprigs**
>
> 3 **thin slices onion**
>
> ½ **dry bay leaf or 3 thin, quarter-size slices fresh ginger**
>
> **Portuguese Tomato Sauce (recipe follows)**

Place fish fillets on a piece of foil large enough to enclose them, arranging pieces in a compact, evenly thick layer. Top fish with parsley, onion, and bay leaf.

Wrap foil around fish, sealing edges securely. Place on a rack in a wok over 1½ to 2 inches of boiling water. Cover and steam until fish flakes when prodded in thickest part (about 10 minutes for each inch of thickness). Meanwhile, prepare Portuguese Tomato Sauce.

Remove fish from wok. Open foil carefully, lift out fish, and arrange on a warm plate (discard seasonings and juices). Spoon sauce over and around fish. Makes 4 servings.

Portuguese Tomato Sauce. Melt 1 tablespoon **butter** or margarine in a wide nonstick frying pan over medium heat. Add 1 medium-size **onion,** thinly sliced; cook, stirring, until barely soft (3 to 5 minutes).

Add 1 large clove **garlic,** minced or pressed; 1 can (about 14 oz.) **pear-shaped tomatoes** (break up with a spoon) and their liquid; and ½ teaspoon *each* **dry basil** and **dry thyme leaves.** Cook, uncovered, stirring often, until reduced to about 2 cups (about 5 minutes).

Per serving: 248 calories, 37 g protein, 8 g carbohydrates, 7 g total fat, 62 mg cholesterol, 308 mg sodium

Basil & Green Chile Fish Pâté

Preparation time: About 35 minutes

Cooking time: 8 to 22 minutes, depending on size of container

Standing time: At least 10 minutes

Thai fish pâtés have a delicate texture that's reminiscent of French pâtés, but the similarity ends there. These pâtés, lacking the mildness of their French cousins, feature bold, take-notice seasonings. This one starts with a highly spiced green chile paste that you blend with coconut milk and fish; the mixture can be steamed in small or large containers, as you prefer. Garnished with pink shrimp, the finished pâté is a lovely and out-of-the-ordinary first course or light entrée.

> **Steeped Shrimp (recipe follows)**
>
> **Hot & Sour Sauce (recipe follows)**
>
> **Green Chile Paste (recipe follows)**
>
> ⅓ **pound boned and skinned rockfish or cod fillets, cut into 1-inch pieces**
>
> 1 **tablespoon fish sauce (*nam pla*) or soy sauce**
>
> ½ **cup canned or thawed frozen coconut milk**
>
> 1 **egg**
>
> 2 **tablespoons minced fresh basil**
>
> 2 **tablespoons thinly sliced green onion (including top)**
>
> 1 **piece banana leaf (about 12 inches square) or 3 large cabbage leaves (if steaming pâté in a bamboo basket)**
>
> **Fresh cilantro (coriander) sprigs and small dried hot red chiles (optional)**

Prepare Steeped Shrimp and Hot & Sour Sauce; set aside.

Prepare Green Chile Paste; scrape from blender into a food processor and add fish, fish sauce, coconut milk, and egg. Whirl until smoothly puréed. (Or, using a food chopper fitted with a medium blade, grind fish into a bowl; mix in Green Chile Paste, fish sauce, coconut milk, and egg.) Scoop purée into a bowl; stir in basil and onion.

Prepare to steam in 1 of the following containers.

Bamboo steaming basket. Select a 5- to 6-inch bamboo steaming basket (about 2 inches deep, with natural finish). Rinse banana leaf and pat dry; fold leaf in thirds, shiny side in. Center leaf on basket. Push leaf down into basket and gently open, pleating along sides to line basket as smoothly as possible. Let leaf extend above rim. (If using cabbage leaves, overlap stem ends of leaves to cover bottom of basket.)

Scrape fish purée onto leaf or leaves and spread smooth. Fold leaf over purée to cover. Top basket with lid or foil. (At this point, you may refrigerate until next day.)

Scallop shells or small ramekins. Use 6 scallop shells for baking (about 5½ inches wide) or 6 shallow ½-cup ramekins. Put a sixth of the pâté in each dish. In shells, smoothly spread purée into a 3½- to 4-inch-wide circle; in ramekins, smooth surface of purée.

Cut six 6-inch-square pieces of foil and oil 1 side of each. Cover containers snugly with foil, oiled side down. (At this point, you may refrigerate until next day.)

To steam, set bamboo basket or shells on a rack in a wok over 1½ to 2 inches of boiling water. (Cook shells or ramekins in sequence, or use 2 woks.)

Cover and steam until fish mixture feels slightly firm in center when touched; fold back leaves or foil to test (17 to 22 minutes for a large container, 8 to 12 minutes for small containers).

Remove pâté from wok; uncover and let stand for at least 10 minutes. If any liquid accumulates as pâté stands, gently tip container and pour it off.

Serve pâté warm or cool. Garnish large container with cilantro and chiles, if desired; scoop pâté onto salad plates and accompany with Steeped Shrimp. Garnish small containers with cilantro, chiles, and shrimp. Serve pâté with Hot & Sour Sauce to spoon on individual portions. Makes 6 servings.

Steeped Shrimp. Shell and devein 6 **medium-size raw shrimp.** In a 1- to 2-quart pan, combine 1½ cups **water,** 1 **green onion** (including top), and 2 thin, quarter-size slices **fresh ginger.** Bring to a boil over high heat; then add shrimp, cover, and remove from heat. Let stand until shrimp turn pink (2 to 3 minutes). Lift shrimp from liquid; split lengthwise. Use hot or cool.

Hot & Sour Sauce. Stir together 2 tablespoons *each* **seasoned rice wine vinegar** and **lime juice** and ⅛ teaspoon **crushed dried hot red chiles.**

Green Chile Paste. In a blender, place 1 **fresh jalapeño or serrano chile,** seeded and chopped; 1 clove **garlic,** minced or pressed; 2 tablespoons **salad oil;** 1 tablespoon chopped **shallot** or red onion; 1 tablespoon **fresh cilantro (coriander) leaves;** 1 teaspoon minced **fresh ginger;** ½ teaspoon grated **lime peel;** and ¼ teaspoon *each* **ground cumin, ground coriander, anchovy paste,** and **pepper.** Whirl until smoothly puréed, stopping motor frequently and scraping mixture down into blades.

Per serving: 130 calories, 7 g protein, 3 g carbohydrates, 10 g total fat, 61 mg cholesterol, 219 mg sodium

Gingered Steamed Fish

Preparation time: About 10 minutes

Cooking time: 10 to 20 minutes, depending on size of fish

Gentle steam heat cooks whole fish or fillets perfectly. You can vary this dish by encircling the fish with clams before steaming—just as in Fish & Clams in Black Bean Sauce (page 141).

- 1 or 2 whole mild-flavored, white-fleshed fish, such as rockfish, red snapper, or kingfish, cleaned and scaled (1½ to 2½ lbs. *total*); or 1½ pounds fillets, such as rockfish, turbot, sole, or sea bass
- 2 teaspoons salt
- 3 thin, quarter-size slices fresh ginger
- 4 green onions (including tops)
- 2 to 3 tablespoons salad oil
- 5 sprigs fresh cilantro (coriander)
- 2 tablespoons matchstick pieces fresh ginger
- 2 tablespoons soy sauce

With a sharp knife, make three ½-inch-deep diagonal slashes across each side of fish. Rub fish inside and out with salt. (If you use fillets, decrease salt to 1 teaspoon; rub over all sides of fillets.) Place fish on a heatproof dish or platter that will fit inside your wok. Place ginger slices on fish.

Cut 2 of the onions into 1½-inch pieces and place on fish. (At this point, you may cover and refrigerate for up to 4 hours; bring to room temperature before steaming.) Cut remaining 2 onions into 1½-inch lengths, then slice lengthwise into thin shreds; set aside.

Place dish on a rack in wok over 1½ to 2 inches of boiling water. Cover and steam until fish flakes when prodded in thickest part (8 to 10 minutes for small fish or fillets, 10 to 12 minutes for a 1½-lb. fish, 16 to 18 minutes for a 2½-lb. fish).

While fish is cooking, heat oil in a small pan over medium-low heat until it ripples when pan is tilted (use larger amount of oil for large fish).

Remove dish with fish from wok; discard ginger slices and onion pieces. Tip dish slightly to drain off cooking liquid. Sprinkle onion shreds, cilantro, matchstick pieces of ginger, and soy over fish. Pour hot oil over fish just before serving. For easier serving, slide a second dish under hot cooking dish before bringing fish to the table. Makes 4 servings.

Per serving: 264 calories, 33 g protein, 2 g carbohydrates, 13 g total fat, 60 mg cholesterol, 1,169 mg sodium

Salmon's delicate flavor and texture call for a gentle
cooking method. For Chilled Salmon with Lomi Lomi Relish (recipe on
facing page), the fillet is steamed in a bamboo basket, then lifted out by
the edges of the cheesecloth that cradles it.

(Pictured on facing page)

Chilled Salmon with Lomi Lomi Relish

Preparation time: About 15 minutes

Cooking time: 6 to 10 minutes

Chilling time: 30 minutes to 1 hour

Classic *lomi lomi* is a combination of chopped salted salmon, tomatoes, and onions. In this variation, though, the salmon is steamed and chilled separately, then served with an all-vegetable lomi lomi relish.

> **Lomi Lomi Relish (recipe follows)**
> **About 2 pounds salmon or turbot fillets,** *each ¾ to 1 inch thick*
> 1 **or 2 dry bay leaves**
> **Whole black peppercorns**
> 4 **lemon slices**
> **Butter lettuce leaves**
> **Lemon wedges**

Prepare Lomi Lomi Relish; cover and refrigerate.

Place fish on a double layer of cheesecloth that is slightly bigger all around than fish. Place bay leaves, peppercorns, and lemon slices on fish. Then place fish on a rack in a wok over 1½ to 2 inches of boiling water, folding cheesecloth up around edges. Cover and steam until fish flakes when prodded in thickest part (6 to 10 minutes). Grasp cheesecloth and lift out fish; let cool. Discard seasonings, then cover and refrigerate fish until cold (30 minutes to 1 hour).

Arrange lettuce on 4 individual plates and top with serving-size pieces of fish. Serve with relish and lemon wedges. Makes 4 to 6 servings.

Lomi Lomi Relish. In a bowl, combine 2 medium-size **tomatoes,** chopped; 1 large **green bell pepper,** seeded and chopped; ½ cup thinly sliced **green onions** (including tops); 1 small **onion,** chopped; 2 to 3 tablespoons **canned diced green chiles;** 2 tablespoons **lemon juice;** and 1 teaspoon **salt.** Makes about 2 cups.

Per serving salmon: 330 calories, 34 g protein, .42 g carbohydrate, 20 g total fat, 59 mg cholesterol, 113 mg sodium

Per ¼ cup relish: 13 calories, .55 g protein, 3 g carbohydrates, .12 g total fat, 0 mg cholesterol, 298 mg sodium

Soft-shelled Crabs

Preparation time: 30 to 45 minutes, depending on sauce used

Cooking time: About 10 minutes

A soft-shelled crab's shell isn't just soft, it's edible—and the combination of crackly parchment-like shell and sweet, moist meat is unusually delicious. Serve these steamed crabs hot or chilled, with your choice of sauces.

> **Ginger Sauce or Cayenne Sauce (recipes follow)**
> 6 **fresh or thawed frozen soft-shelled crabs (about 2 oz.** *each*)

Prepare your choice of sauce and set aside. (If you intend to serve crabs chilled, wait to prepare Cayenne Sauce until shortly before serving.)

If using live crabs, first kill them by holding claws away from you and snipping off shell ¼ inch behind eyes. Then clean, if desired: lift up flexible back shell on each side of crab; pull off and discard soft gills. Also pull off and discard triangular flap of shell on belly of crab.

Thoroughly rinse cleaned crabs and pat dry. Then lay crabs, backs up, in a single layer on a rack in a wok over 1½ to 2 inches of boiling water. Cover and steam until crabs are opaque in center of body; cut to test (about 8 minutes).

Serve crabs hot or chilled; accompany with sauce. Makes 6 appetizer servings, 2 or 3 entrée servings.

Ginger Sauce. Stir together ⅓ cup **rice wine vinegar,** 1 to 2 tablespoons sliced **green onion** (including top), 1½ tablespoons minced **fresh ginger,** and 1 teaspoon **sugar.** Serve to spoon onto crab, or dip crab into sauce. Makes about ¾ cup.

Cayenne Sauce. In a 6- to 8-inch frying pan, combine ¼ cup **dry white wine,** 3 tablespoons chopped **shallots,** 2 tablespoons **red wine vinegar,** and ¼ to ½ teaspoon **ground red pepper** (cayenne). Bring to a boil over high heat; boil, uncovered, until liquid is reduced to about 1 tablespoon. Scrape mixture into a blender; add 2 **egg yolks.** Whirl until blended; then, with motor running, slowly add ¾ cup (¼ lb. plus ¼ cup) hot melted **butter** or margarine. Serve hot or at room temperature; do not reheat. Makes 1¼ cups.

Per entrée serving: 98 calories, 20 g protein, .83 g carbohydrate, 1 g total fat, 67 mg cholesterol, 335 mg sodium

Per tablespoon Ginger Sauce: 3 calories, .02 g protein, .72 g carbohydrate, 0 g total fat, 0 mg cholesterol, .13 mg sodium

Per tablespoon Cayenne Sauce: 69 calories, .37 g protein, .34 g carbohydrate, 7 g total fat, 46 mg cholesterol, 71 mg sodium

Noodles & Rice

Filled Fresh Rice Noodles

Preparation time: About 20 minutes

Cooking time: About 30 minutes

In Chinese noodle factories, rice noodles are pressed out between rollers in long sheets, like lengths of fabric. You don't really need special equipment to make them, though; they're easy to duplicate using a batter made with cake flour in place of rice flour. You steam the batter, a portion at a time, in a 9-inch pie pan; once cooled, the round, flat noodles are topped with a variety of fillings and rolled up jelly roll style.

         Fillings (directions follow)
    1   **cup unsifted cake flour**
    1   **tablespoon cornstarch**
    ½   **teaspoon salt**
    1¼   **cups cold water**
    2   **tablespoons salad oil**
         Soy sauce
         Sesame oil or sesame seeds

Prepare fillings and set aside.

In a bowl, mix flour, cornstarch, and salt. Combine water and salad oil; pour into flour and blend until batter is smooth and free of lumps. Ladle ⅓ cup batter into a lightly greased 9-inch pie pan. Place pan on a rack in a wok over 1½ to 2 inches of boiling water; cover and steam for 5 minutes.

Remove pan from wok and set in a baking pan filled with water and ice cubes to hasten cooling.

When noodle is cool, loosen edges from pie pan with the tip of a knife; roll up noodle jelly roll style.

Wipe pan clean with a paper towel and grease lightly; spoon in and steam another ⅓ cup batter. Repeat until all batter has been used; for faster cooking, you can use 2 pie pans, so 1 noodle can be steaming while another cools. (At this point, you may cover cooked noodles and hold at room temperature in a cool place for up to 8 hours.)

To serve, unroll noodles and distribute fillings equally over each circle; then roll up again. Cut each roll into 1½-inch-long sections and arrange pieces on a platter. Drizzle rolls with a few drops of soy; then sprinkle with a few drops of sesame oil or a few sesame seeds. Makes 5 rolls (4 to 6 servings).

Fillings. Prepare the following: ½ cup **cooked ham**, in matchstick pieces; **Egg Shreds** made from 2 eggs (page 73); ¼ pound **bean sprouts**, cooked in boiling water for 10 seconds, drained, rinsed in cold water, and chilled; and 2 **green onions** (including tops), cut into 1½-inch lengths, then into thin lengthwise shreds.

Per roll: 211 calories, 8 g protein, 22 g carbohydrates, 10 g total fat, 118 mg cholesterol, 491 mg sodium

Sticky Rice

Preparation time: About 5 minutes, plus 2 hours to soak rice

Cooking time: About 20 minutes

Cooling time: About 3 minutes

Sticky rice is sometimes called sweet rice—and as its names suggest, it has a sticky texture and a slightly sweet flavor when cooked. It's great for chopstick users, since the grains cling together in clumps.

    3   **cups sticky rice (also called sweet or**
         glutinous rice)

Soak rice in cold water to cover for at least 2 hours or until next day. Drain, rinse, and drain again. Place rice on a steaming rack lined with a clean towel. (If rack has no sides, loosely tie rice in towel.) Set rack in a wok over 1½ to 2 inches of boiling water; cover and steam until rice is tender to bite (about 20 minutes). Dump rice onto a dampened shallow tray or pan. With a wet spoon, lift and turn rice for 2 to 3 minutes to cool it slightly. Cover until ready to serve; serve warm or at room temperature. Makes about 4 servings.

Per serving: 538 calories, 13 g protein, 113 g carbohydrates, 2 g total fat, 0 mg cholesterol, 5 mg sodium

Salads

Sunchoke Salad

Preparation time: About 30 minutes

Cooking time: About 10 minutes

Chilling time: About 4 hours

Knotty, brown-skinned sunchokes are more commonly known as Jerusalem artichokes, though they're entirely unrelated to the familiar globe artichoke. The name "sunchoke" actually gives a better indication of this vegetable's family relationships—it's the root of a sunflower relative. Sunchokes have a crisp texture and nutlike flavor; here, they stand in for potatoes in a creamy salad.

    1 pound sunchokes
       Acidulated water (3 tablespoons vinegar
       per 4 cups water)
    1 cup sliced celery
    ½ cup thinly sliced green onions (including
       tops)
    2 hard-cooked eggs, diced
    5 slices bacon, crisply cooked, drained,
       and crumbled
    ½ cup mayonnaise
    2 tablespoons sweet pickle relish
    1 teaspoon Dijon mustard
       Salt and pepper
       Chopped parsley

Scrub sunchokes well or peel with a vegetable peeler. Cut sunchokes crosswise into ¼-inch-thick slices; as you cut slices, drop them into acidulated water to prevent discoloration.

When all sunchokes have been sliced, drain; then arrange on a rack in a wok over 1½ to 2 inches of boiling water. Cover and steam until tender when pierced (5 to 10 minutes). Let cool.

In a large bowl, combine sunchokes, celery, onions, eggs, and bacon. Stir together mayonnaise, relish, and mustard; pour over sunchoke mixture and mix well. Season to taste with salt and pepper. Cover and refrigerate for about 4 hours. Garnish with parsley. Makes 4 to 6 servings.

Per serving: 350 calories, 7 g protein, 6 g carbohydrates, 30 g total fat, 154 mg cholesterol, 399 mg sodium

Layered Niçoise Salad

Preparation time: About 45 minutes

Cooking time: 30 minutes

This version of classic *salade Niçoise* is designed especially for make-ahead preparation. You layer sliced cooked potatoes, green beans, tuna, hard-cooked eggs, and lettuce in a bowl and chill for up to a day, then mix the salad just before serving.

    1 pound small thin-skinned potatoes, each
       about 1½ inches in diameter, unpeeled
       Anchovy Dressing (recipe follows)
    1 pound green beans (ends removed), cut
       into 1-inch pieces
    ¼ cup *each* mayonnaise and plain yogurt
    1 large can (12½ oz.) tuna packed in water,
       drained
    3 hard-cooked eggs, thinly sliced
    8 cups lightly packed bite-size pieces
       butter lettuce

Arrange potatoes on a rack in a wok over 1½ to 2 inches of boiling water. Cover and steam until tender when pierced (about 20 minutes). Meanwhile, prepare Anchovy Dressing.

Remove potatoes from wok and let stand just until cool enough to touch. Peel, if desired; then slice ¼ inch thick into a deep 4- to 5-quart bowl. Evenly pour dressing over potatoes; let cool.

Arrange beans on rack in wok over 1½ to 2 inches of boiling water; cover and steam until bright green and just tender to bite (10 to 12 minutes). Immediately immerse in cold water; when cool, drain and pat dry.

In a small bowl, blend mayonnaise and yogurt; add to potatoes and mix lightly to coat. Layer beans over potatoes. With a fork, break tuna into bite-size pieces and distribute in an even layer over beans. Layer eggs over tuna, then cover with lettuce. If made ahead, cover and refrigerate until next day.

Mix salad just before serving; serve immediately after mixing. Makes 6 servings.

Anchovy Dressing. Stir or whisk together ¼ cup **salad oil;** ½ cup *each* **lemon juice** and finely chopped **parsley;** 1 small **red onion,** finely chopped; 3 tablespoons **Dijon mustard;** 1 tablespoon drained **capers;** 4 canned **anchovy fillets,** minced; 1 large clove **garlic,** minced or pressed; ¼ teaspoon **dry dill weed;** and ⅛ teaspoon **pepper.**

Per serving: 353 calories, 26 g protein, 17 g carbohydrates, 21 g total fat, 174 mg cholesterol, 290 mg sodium

Vegetables

(Pictured on facing page)

Green Corn Tamales with Cheese & Chiles

Preparation time: About 1½ hours

Cooking time: About 1 hour

Like delicate corn pudding enclosed in fresh green corn husks, these *tamalitos* are a tasty accompaniment to barbecued meats. The mild, slightly sweet filling gets a little zip from Longhorn Cheddar cheese and green chiles.

    5 or 6 large ears corn in husks
      (about 5 lbs. *total*)
    ¼ cup lard, melted
    2 teaspoons sugar
      Salt
    ¾ cup shredded Longhorn Cheddar cheese
    ⅓ cup (half of a 4-oz. can) canned diced
      green chiles

With a sharp, heavy knife or cleaver, cut through husk, corn, and cob of each ear of corn, removing about ¼ inch of cob on both ends of each ear.

Peel off husks without tearing them; rinse if soiled. To keep moist, put in plastic bags and seal; set aside. Pull and discard silk from corn. Rinse corn.

With a knife or a corn scraper, cut kernels from cobs; you need 4 cups, lightly packed. Put corn through a food chopper fitted with a fine blade (or whirl in a food processor until finely ground). Mix ground corn with lard and sugar, then season to taste with salt. Stir cheese and chiles into corn.

To shape each tamale, center 1⅓ tablespoons of the cheese-corn filling near stem (firmer) end of a large single husk. Fold 1 side of husk over to completely cover filling, then fold other side over top. Fold up flexible end to seal in filling. Gently stack tamales, folded ends down, in a steamer; support them against other tamales so ends stay shut. Tamales should be loosely fitted into steamer so air can circulate.

Set steamer on a rack in a wok over 1½ to 2 inches of boiling water. Cover and steam until tamales in center of steamer are firm to touch, not runny; pull a tamale out and unwrap to test (about 1 hour).

Serve tamales, or keep warm over hot water for several hours. To freeze, let cool completely; place in a single layer on baking sheets and freeze until firm, then transfer to plastic bags and return to freezer for up to 6 months. To reheat, let thaw, then steam as directed above until hot through (about 15 minutes).

Makes about 3 dozen tamales (3 to 6 servings).

Per serving: 217 calories, 6 g protein, 20 g carbohydrates, 14 g total fat, 23 mg cholesterol, 149 mg sodium

(Pictured on page 2)

Marinated Broccoli & Mushrooms

Preparation time: About 20 minutes

Cooking time: About 3 minutes

Marinating time: 1 to 2 hours

Serve this fresh-tasting dish cold on a hot day. You start by steaming broccoli, then mix in celery, green onions, mushrooms, and a sweet-sour vinaigrette.

      About 1½ pounds broccoli
    ¾ pound mushrooms, thinly sliced
    1 cup *each* thinly sliced green onions
      (including tops) and thinly sliced celery
    ¼ cup sugar
    ⅓ cup cider vinegar
    1 teaspoon *each* paprika and celery seeds
    1 cup salad oil
      Salt and pepper

Cut off and discard tough ends of broccoli stalks. Cut flowerets into bite-size pieces; peel stalks, then cut into ¼-inch-thick slanting slices. Arrange broccoli on a rack in a wok over 1½ to 2 inches of boiling water; cover and steam until barely tender-crisp to bite (2 to 3 minutes). Immerse in cold water; when cool, drain well. In a large bowl, combine broccoli, mushrooms, onions, and celery.

Stir together sugar and vinegar until sugar is dissolved. Stir in paprika, celery seeds, and oil. Pour over vegetable mixture; stir to coat. Cover and refrigerate for 1 to 2 hours, stirring occasionally. Season to taste with salt and pepper. Makes 6 to 8 servings.

Per serving: 299 calories, 3 g protein, 13 g carbohydrates, 28 g total fat, 0 mg cholesterol, 30 mg sodium

A specialty of the Southwest, mild-mannered Green Corn Tamales
(recipe on facing page) are wrapped in green corn husks and gently steamed.
Enriched with a little chile and some cheese, these bite-size tamales
are a great partner for grilled meats.

Broccoli Oriental

Preparation time: About 10 minutes

Cooking time: 5 to 8 minutes

How to dress up plain steamed broccoli? A pat of butter and a squeeze of lemon are the usual embellishments, but here's another idea: a light dressing of rice wine vinegar, sugar, and soy.

- ¾ **to 1 pound broccoli**
- ½ **cup unseasoned rice wine vinegar or ¼ cup *each* cider vinegar and water**
- 1 **tablespoon sugar**
- ½ **teaspoon soy sauce**

Cut off broccoli flowerets; discard stalks or reserve for another use. Arrange flowerets on a rack in a wok over 1½ to 2 inches of boiling water. Cover and steam just until tender when pierced (5 to 8 minutes). Remove from wok; place in a bowl.

Stir together vinegar, sugar, and soy; pour over warm broccoli and mix well. Drain immediately and serve. Makes 4 servings.

Per serving: 41 calories, 3 g protein, 9 g carbohydrates, 27 g total fat, 0 mg cholesterol, 68 mg sodium

Carrot & Mushroom Loaf

Preparation time: About 1 hour

Cooking time: About 1¼ hours

Standing time: 30 minutes

This all-vegetable loaf is an eye-catching first course or light entrée. Before spooning in the herbed carrot-mushroom filling, you line the loaf pan with steamed sliced carrots; the overlapping "coins" both ease unmolding and make a decorative topping for the loaf.

- 9 **or 10 large carrots**
- ¼ **cup butter or margarine**
- 1 **medium-size onion, finely chopped**
- 2 **cloves garlic, minced or pressed**
- 1 **pound mushrooms, finely chopped**
- 5 **eggs**
- 1 **cup fine dry bread crumbs**
- ¼ **cup chopped parsley**
- ½ **teaspoon dry thyme leaves**
  Salt and pepper

Peel carrots. Cut enough of the thick part of about 3 carrots into ¼-inch-thick slices to make about 1 cup. Arrange carrot slices on a rack in a wok over 1½ to 2 inches of boiling water; cover and steam until tender when pierced (5 to 10 minutes). Meanwhile, finely shred remaining 6 or 7 carrots; you need 4½ cups. Set aside.

Neatly cover bottom of a 5- by 9-inch loaf pan with overlapping carrot slices. Set pan aside.

Place a wok over medium-high heat; when wok is hot, add butter. When butter is melted, add onion and garlic; stir-fry until onion is soft. Add shredded carrots and mushrooms; cook for 1 minute. Then cover and continue to cook until carrots are tender to bite (about 10 more minutes). Remove vegetables from wok; let cool uncovered. Clean and dry wok.

In a large bowl, combine eggs, bread crumbs, parsley, and thyme; beat to blend. Add vegetable mixture and mix with your hands or a heavy spoon until evenly blended; season to taste with salt and pepper. Carefully spoon mixture into carrot-lined pan, press down very firmly, and spread evenly. Rap pan on counter several times to remove air bubbles. Cover pan tightly with foil.

Set pan on a rack in wok over 1½ to 2 inches of boiling water. Cover and steam until loaf feels firm in center when pressed (about 1¼ hours); top of loaf will look and feel dry. Let loaf stand for at least 30 minutes before serving. If made ahead, cover and refrigerate in pan for up to 2 days; serve at room temperature. Or, to reheat, cover loaf in pan tightly with foil; steam as directed above until hot through (about 50 minutes).

To unmold, remove foil and run a knife blade around pan sides. Invert loaf onto a serving dish; slice about ½ inch thick. Makes 6 to 8 servings.

Per serving: 222 calories, 8 g protein, 26 g carbohydrates, 10 g total fat, 187 mg cholesterol, 241 mg sodium

Bread

Chinese Steamed Buns

Preparation time: About 1¼ hours, plus 1½ hours for dough to rise

Cooking time: About 15 minutes

For a vegetarian luncheon or hearty first course, you might serve these tender whole wheat buns. Tucked inside is a filling of soy-seasoned mushrooms and cashews.

> 1 package active dry yeast
> 1 cup warm water (about 110°F)
> 1 tablespoon sugar
> 2 tablespoons salad oil
> 1 teaspoon salt
>   About 2¾ cups whole wheat flour
>   Mushroom-Cashew Filling (recipe follows)

In a large bowl, dissolve yeast in warm water; blend in sugar, oil, and salt. Let stand until bubbly (about 15 minutes). Add flour and mix with a heavy spoon until dough holds together. Scrape dough out onto a lightly floured board and knead until smooth and elastic (8 to 10 minutes). Place dough in a greased bowl and turn over to grease top; cover and let rise in a warm place until doubled (about 1 hour).

Meanwhile, prepare Mushroom-Cashew Filling; set aside.

Turn dough out onto a lightly floured board and knead for 1 minute. Cut dough into 12 equal pieces. Roll each piece into a 4½-inch-diameter circle. Press outside edge of circle to make it slightly thinner than rest of circle. Place about 2 tablespoons of the filling in center of each circle. Pull edges of dough up around filling and twist to seal.

Place each bun, twisted side down, on a 2-inch square of foil; then place on a baking sheet. Cover and let rise in a warm place until puffy and light (about 30 minutes). Set buns—still on foil—in a single layer on a rack in a wok over 1½ to 2 inches of boiling water. Cover and steam until dough wrapper is firm to the touch and cooked through (about 15 minutes). Serve warm; or let cool, then wrap and refrigerate or freeze. To reheat, steam buns as directed above until hot through (5 to 10 minutes). Makes 1 dozen buns (about 6 first-course servings, 4 entrée servings).

Mushroom-Cashew Filling. Place a wok over high heat; when wok is hot, add 1 tablespoon **salad oil.**

When oil is hot, add ¼ pound **mushrooms,** chopped; 1 small **onion,** chopped; 1 clove **garlic,** minced or pressed; and 1 teaspoon minced **fresh ginger.** Stir-fry for 3 minutes.

Add ½ cup coarsely chopped **bamboo shoots,** ¾ cup coarsely chopped **cashews,** and 2 **green onions** (including tops), thinly sliced. Stir-fry for 2 more minutes. Stir together 3 tablespoons **soy sauce,** 1 tablespoon **dry sherry,** 1 teaspoon **sugar,** ¼ cup **water,** and 1 tablespoon **cornstarch;** pour into wok and stir until sauce boils and thickens. Stir in 1 teaspoon **sesame oil.** Remove from heat and let cool.

Per bun: 191 calories, 6 g protein, 26 g carbohydrates, 8 g total fat, 0 mg cholesterol, 444 mg sodium

Brown Bread

Preparation time: About 15 minutes

Cooking time: About 45 minutes

Cooling time: 10 minutes

Complement your favorite baked beans with a New England-inspired recipe for bread made with whole wheat flour, molasses, and buttermilk. Steaming keeps the cooking time down for this moist, dark bread.

> 2 tablespoons melted butter or margarine
> ⅓ cup firmly packed brown sugar
> 2 tablespoons light molasses
> 1 cup buttermilk
> 1 cup whole wheat flour
> ¼ cup *each* all-purpose flour and wheat germ
> 1 teaspoon baking soda
> ½ teaspoon salt
> ½ cup raisins or currants

In a large bowl, place butter, brown sugar, and molasses; beat until smooth, then stir in buttermilk. In a separate bowl, stir together whole wheat flour, all-purpose flour, wheat germ, baking soda, and salt until thoroughly blended. Add to buttermilk mixture and beat until combined. Stir in raisins. Spoon batter into a well-greased 1½-quart ring mold. Cover mold tightly with foil.

Set mold on rack in wok over 1½ to 2 inches boiling water. Cover wok and steam until a wooden pick inserted in center of bread comes out clean (about 45 minutes). Let bread cool for 10 minutes, then turn out of mold. Serve warm. To reheat, wrap in foil and steam as directed above until warm through (about 20 minutes). Makes 1 bread (8 to 10 slices).

Per slice: 124 calories, 4 g protein, 22 g carbohydrates, 3 g total fat, 7 mg cholesterol, 243 mg sodium

Converting your wok to a steamer is easy—
and that makes it simple to prepare old-fashioned steamed puddings
like this one. The recipe for our spicy Carrot Pudding is
on the facing page.

Desserts

(Pictured on facing page)

Carrot Pudding

Preparation time: About 15 minutes

Cooking time: 3 to 3¼ hours

Cooling time: 10 to 15 minutes

Shredded carrots contribute to the moist texture of this rich, spicy dessert. The pudding shown on the facing page was steamed for about 3 hours in a 5-inch-deep 6-cup mold partially submerged in boiling water; puddings made in shallower 6- to 8-cup molds can be steamed on a rack above 1½ to 2 inches of boiling water for about the same length of time.

- ½ cup (¼ lb.) butter or margarine, at room temperature
- ½ cup *each* sugar and dark molasses
- ¼ cup dark rum
- 1½ cups all-purpose flour
- 1 teaspoon *each* ground ginger and cinnamon
- ½ teaspoon *each* baking soda, ground nutmeg, ground cloves, and ground allspice
- 1½ cups shredded carrots (about 2 large or 3 medium-size)
- 1 cup raisins
- ¾ cup chopped walnuts
  Carrot curls and mint leaves (optional)
  Half-and-half or light cream

In large bowl of an electric mixer, beat butter, sugar, and molasses until smoothly blended; mix in rum. Stir together flour, ginger, cinnamon, baking soda, nutmeg, cloves, and allspice; beat into butter mixture. Add carrots, raisins, and walnuts; mix well.

Thoroughly butter a 6- to 8-cup tube mold or deep 6- to 8-cup metal bowl. Scrape batter into mold or bowl. Butter a piece of foil and place, buttered side down, over batter; crimp foil tightly against edges of mold (including center hole) or bowl. Set mold in wok on a low rack or canning jar ring. Pour in boiling water to reach halfway up mold. Cover and cook at a gentle boil until edges of pudding spring back when lightly pressed (3 to 3¼ hours; center may feel slightly sticky).

Remove pudding from wok and let cool for 10 to 15 minutes. Run a knife blade around edges of mold to loosen pudding, then invert onto a plate. Rap top

of mold to loosen. Garnish pudding with carrot curls and mint, if desired. Serve warm or at room temperature; add half-and-half to taste.

If made ahead, let cool, then wrap pudding airtight and refrigerate for up to 2 weeks; freeze for longer storage. To reheat, thaw if frozen, then seal in foil and steam as directed above for about 45 minutes. Makes 6 to 8 servings.

Per serving pudding: 417 calories, 5 g protein, 61 g carbohydrates, 17 g total fat, 31 mg cholesterol, 200 mg sodium

Apples with Cinnamon Dumplings

Preparation time: 10 to 15 minutes

Cooking time: About 40 minutes

Typical apple dumplings are whole apples enclosed in pastry, but this version of the old-fashioned dessert is more like a cobbler. The dumplings are much like drop biscuits; sweet, spicy, and vanilla-scented, they crown a cinnamony apple filling.

- 4 large tart apples, peeled, cored, and sliced (5 to 6 cups)
  Juice and grated peel of 1 lemon
- ⅔ cup sugar
- 1 tablespoon all-purpose flour
- ¼ teaspoon ground cinnamon
- ⅛ teaspoon ground nutmeg
  Dumpling Dough (recipe follows)
  Half-and-half or light cream

Mix apples, lemon juice, lemon peel, sugar, flour, cinnamon, and nutmeg in an 8- or 9-inch round baking dish. Place dish on a rack in a wok over 1½ to 2 inches of boiling water. Cover and steam until apples are tender when pierced (18 to 20 minutes). Meanwhile, prepare Dumpling Dough.

Using a large spoon, scoop out dough in 6 spoonfuls; drop on top of fruit in a circle around edge of dish. Cover wok and steam for 15 minutes. Remove from wok and let stand for 5 minutes. To serve, spoon dumplings onto dessert plates; top with apples and sauce. Offer half-and-half to pour on top. Makes 6 servings.

Dumpling Dough. Stir together 1 cup **all-purpose flour,** 2 teaspoons **baking powder,** ⅛ teaspoon **salt,** ¼ cup firmly packed **brown sugar,** ½ teaspoon **ground cinnamon,** and ¼ teaspoon **ground nutmeg.** Combine ⅓ cup **milk** and ½ teaspoon **vanilla;** add to dry mixture, stirring just until blended.

Per serving: 271 calories, 2 g protein, 60 g carbohydrates, 4 g total fat, 2 mg cholesterol, 243 mg sodium

Index

Combining the cuisine of one culture with the cooking techniques
of another, Italian Stir-fried Pasta (recipe on page 75) is a magnificent meal
whenever you serve it. Bread sticks and chilled white wine
nicely complement this light entrée.